OCEAN
TITANS

DANIEL
SEKULICH

OCEAN
TITANS

JOURNEYS IN SEARCH OF
THE SOUL OF A SHIP

THE LYONS PRESS
Guilford, Connecticut
An imprint of The Globe Pequot Press

To buy books in quantity for corporate use
or incentives, call **(800) 962–0973**
or e-mail **premiums@GlobePequot.com**.

First Lyons Press Edition © 2007

Originally published in 2006 by Penguin Group

Copyright © Daniel Sekulich, 2006

Maps copyright © Nevena Niaglova, 2006

All interior photos copyright © Daniel Sekulich, 2006

The Lyons Press is an imprint of The Globe Pequot Press.

10 9 8 7 6 5 4 3 2 1

Printed in the United States of America

ISBN: 978-1-59921-038-4

Library of Congress Cataloging-in-Publication Data is available on file.

For Gavin

Dear Katie, I am bound to the sea,
The clock strikes the hour to tell;
My shipmates lie waiting for me,
Now then, Katie, I must now bid you farewell.

So, it's good-bye, fond one, adieu,
My thoughts on you, darling, remain;
When I'm sleeping in my watch down below,
I'll wander back to Katie in my dreams.

We are out on the troublesome tide,
Rocked by the billows we are tossed;
And our barque o'er the ocean do glide,
While the man at the wheel keeps the watch.

So, it's good-bye, fond one, adieu,
My thoughts on you, darling, remain;
When I'm sleeping in my watch down below,
I'll wander back to Katie in my dreams.

—TRADITIONAL NEWFOUNDLAND SAILOR'S BALLAD

Map of the Americas

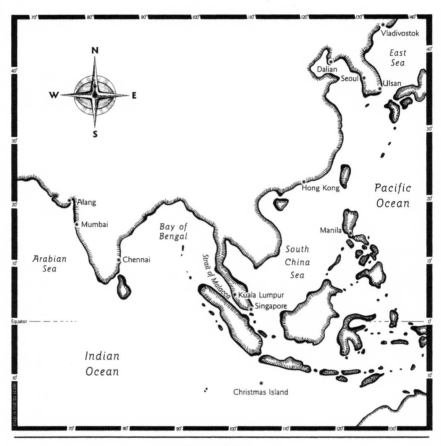

Map of Asia

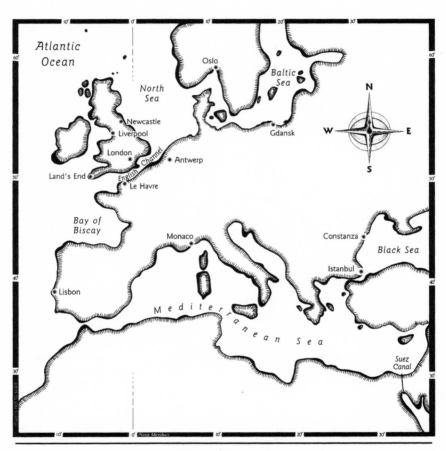

Atlantic
Ocean

North
Sea

Oslo

Baltic
Sea

Gdansk

Newcastle
Liverpool
London
English Channel
Antwerp
Land's End
Le Havre

N
W   E
S

Bay of
Biscay

Monaco

Constanza

Black Sea

Istanbul

Lisbon

Mediterranean Sea

Suez
Canal

map is not to scale

Prime Meridian

Map of Europe

CONTENTS

OCEAN
TITANS

PROLOGUE: Ghosts

The voice of the sea speaks to the soul.

—KATE CHOPIN, *THE AWAKENING*

There is a stiff breeze coming in off the bay, tugging at me as I stand on the deck of a ship. The wind carries with it the aroma of salty brine and the essence of freedom and isolation, hallmarks familiar to anyone who's spent any time near the sea. Yet the ship I'm on is not coursing through the waves or navigating any waterway; she is motionless, lifeless and without sea-going purpose. She harbours only ghosts.

The vessel is the SS *Sag River,* an immense tanker currently beached on the sandy shores of the Bay of Khambhat at a place called Alang. This ten-kilometre stretch of northwestern India is the site of the biggest shipbreaking operation on the planet, where ocean-going vessels come to be deconstructed and turned into scrap metal. If you want to see a cross-section of the world's shipping fleets and ponder the existence of these leviathans and those whose lives revolved around them, Alang is the place to be. Up and down the beach are scattered other tankers, container ships, bulk carriers, passenger liners, car carriers, cattle carriers, cable layers and pretty much anything else you can imagine.

The oceans, seas, lakes and rivers of the Earth are teeming with over forty-six thousand merchant vessels not unlike the hulks that are beached around me here in Alang, and as many as two million people make their livelihood from seafaring. Merchant shipping is a multi-billion-dollar, multinational endeavour that carries over 90 percent of global trade: crude oil, cooking oil, beer, wine, vodka, wheat, fresh fruit, vegetables, livestock, medicine, computers, televisions, cell phones, camcorders, running shoes, blue jeans, tuxedos, perfume, iron ore, coal, gold, lumber, newsprint, furniture, automobiles and even expensive French water. It is the tie that truly binds us together, more so than religion or sporting events or the internet.

In the last thirty years, commercial shipping has seen dramatic and sweeping changes. Technology, international regulations, global economics, environmental laws, ship owners, officers and crews—everything is different. But perhaps the biggest change is the fate of the ships themselves. Throughout the 1970s, the commercial shipping industry was in the midst of a boom period and expanded in response to the growth of global economies, with more and larger vessels being launched weekly at yards throughout the world.

However nothing lives forever and ocean-going vessels are no exception. Their lifespan will rarely exceed forty years; often it is even further shortened by the extreme physical stress of marching headlong into the pounding seas day after day, year after year. Eventually the metal fatigues, the engines break down, the costs of maintenance exceed profitability, and these aging vessels must leave the sea and return to the land whence they were born.

What fascinates me is that each vessel being scrapped here in Alang—indeed, every ship that has ever sailed—was once the home to a tightly knit group of people both metaphorically and literally. The frames of these vessels once contained individuals who ate, slept, worked, argued, cried, prayed and sometimes died within their steel embrace. They were shipwrights, architects, owners, engineers, able-bodied seamen, ordinary sailors, bosuns, mates, captains, cooks, motormen, electricians, stewards and passengers. They spent days, months or years constrained by wood and steel, engulfed by a vast sea that was variously placid or demonic. I believe humans have souls; is it possible that ships have them as well? And if you believe that energy can be neither created nor destroyed, merely transferred from one source to another, then perhaps it's possible that some of the energy of those whose lives revolved around these ships has seeped into the vessels.

To glimpse the ghosts who once inhabited these ocean titans, all you have to do is follow that offshore breeze as it swirls around, over and into the ship, gliding through empty corridors and darkened cabins. The winds moan and murmur as they explore the vessel, at times pausing until the air becomes heavy with the smell of sweat, steel and heat. Then they resume their airborne journey through the leviathan until the gusts grow bored and exit into the brilliant sunshine of northwestern India.

Aboard the *Sag River*, I caress the teak-covered railing on the portside wing of the wheelhouse as I wonder how many seafarers once stood here while staring out to sea. Inside the bridge the ship's wheel is warm to the touch, the plastic having absorbed the intense heat of the subtropics or the firm hands of many a helmsman. Close by is the engine telegraph, still in the Full Ahead position set when the great ship crashed her bow onto dry land. Bits of paper litter the deck in here, sometimes catching a whiff of the breeze and swirling into the corners. There's a compass deviation form, dutifully stamped and signed by the *Sag River*'s former master, while some other paperwork reveals she was built at the Sparrow's Point Shipyard near Baltimore back in 1972, for ARCO Marine. As long as the *Titanic,* the 70,000-tonne vessel apparently plied the West Coast between Alaska and the Lower Forty-Eight as she carried North Slope crude oil to the insatiable energy markets of America.

Down a linoleum-lined staircase, I arrive at B-Deck, where some of the crew's quarters are located. The wind whistles through open port-holes, a banshee-like wail of remorse. As I peer through various door-ways, the cabins seem desolate and sad, revealing only soiled mattresses and garbage strewn about the floors. Another flight of stairs leads to the galley, where the crews' meals were once prepared. Here I find cutlery and dishes lining the cupboards, and the smell of rotting food is rank and ubiquitous. Cockroaches, the only animate inhabitants to greet me on my exploration, skitter about the stainless steel surfaces. Through a nearby door marked "Engine Compartment" I call out a weak "Hello," though the only reply is the echo of my own voice. It's quieter in here and also much hotter, the wind having deigned to ignore these nether regions. The *Sag River's* power plant towers above and below, rising as high as a small office building, but not a sound emanates from its once-powerful engines. There's an open vent near the ceiling through which a shaft of light streams into the compartment, guiding me down a narrow ladder to a catwalk that stretches the width of the tanker. I cautiously make my way past vertical pipes and electrical tubing, clutching at the greasy railing that was once a lifeline to an engineer in a storm, until I arrive at a wide platform. Along one bulkhead are open storage lockers containing firefighting suits, the safety garments hanging like corpses from their hooks.

Down and to the right is the engineering station, where the distinct smell of fuel oil permeates, like that in the basement of an old home. The metal deck below is strewn with empty cans of Coca-Cola, packets of artificial sweetener, half-eaten bags of Orville Redenbacker microwave popcorn and crushed boxes of Marlboro cigarettes—the diet of someone striving to stay awake.

On the corkboard above the engineer's desk is pinned a note from one of the ghosts, a first assistant engineer, to someone named Paul, listing instructions for shutting down the ship's water evaporators and stating, "You should hear something on your watch whether or not we are going in tomorrow morning."

Below that is a large nautical chart protected by Plexiglas; I pull out my flashlight, brush aside the dust and see that the chart is the approach to Port Valdez, Alaska, through the Valdez Arm and the Narrows. A cryptic note has been taped to the map: "What an extra five inches feels like." I realize that this is a reference to the shallow waters and narrow shipping channels that make up the area near Prince William Sound where the tanker *Exxon Valdez* was famously grounded in 1989, spilling 250,000 barrels of oil into the pristine Alaskan waters. It makes me stop for a moment, for I realize the *Sag River* had been there, too, that her ghosts had traversed those shipping routes.

By now the heat in the engine room has left me thoroughly drenched in sweat, so I decide to leave the tanker's bowels and head back topside. A wrong turn somewhere leads to a different door from the one I'd entered, which sticks when I try to open it. Stepping back, I give it a mighty push before the door swings open to reveal a scene of utter devastation. I am standing in a vast open space the size of a basketball court, what was once the main deck level of the ship's accommodations, but every wall that partitioned the area has been removed, as has every piece of furniture, equipment, wiring and even the ceiling tiles. This renovation job gone awry has left nothing more than the outlines of the rooms and a few toilets scattered about like the stumps of clear-cut trees, each surrounded by a square of ceramic tiles.

Over in the corner is an old newspaper, now aged and yellow. It's the *Baltimore Sun,* dated Tuesday, February 1, 1972, which must have been left by a shipyard worker, since that's about the time the *Sag River* was built. Perhaps he read it over lunch before shoving it behind a wall partition, a time capsule from the tanker's birth. The paper is open to an article headlined "Westmoreland predicts big enemy offensive," detailing B-52 bomber missions against North Vietnamese troops near Khe Sanh. The article ends with a prediction from an unnamed American adviser stating that the South Vietnamese "are going to win."

Finally, I head outside to reach the main deck, where the sea breeze cools my body before drawing me to a pile of garbage: technical binders, old magazines and reams of paperwork billowing ever so slightly from the wind. Atop the heap lies a sheet of lined paper, beckoning me. The handwritten note is smudged and dirty, but as I pick it up I can see it is still legible.

Dearest Juliana,

    I don't think you're ready to get married; I'm not ready to give you away, and having met him, I know he's not ready for marriage…

I stop reading and sheepishly look around. Should I continue? Will I be caught red-handed with someone's private correspondence, this heart-felt missive about marriage and life written to a daughter, a sister, maybe a lover? But the ghost is calling out to me, so I read on.

I see that you mean to leave your parents' home, travel across country, begin a physical, sexual relationship, set up housekeeping and live together as a couple…pretty much everything but the ceremony.

There is clumsiness to the letter, the crude penmanship reflecting someone who probably does not write very often, definitely a man. But the content of the document is an honest and forthright expression that bears no corrections, no amendments, no alterations. Whoever wrote it was firm in his resolve to deal with something openly, not to shy away from it. And yet here it sits, atop a pile of garbage reeking in the hot tropical sun.

    I flip the note over, but there is no signature, no name attached to it. Instead, the black ink fades away as though the thoughts of the writer trailed off into nothingness. I stare in fascination at this moment in someone's life, thinking of how the note had travelled across oceans, canals, seas and bays before being unceremoniously cast aside. Perhaps the author changed his mind at the last moment, thinking it better not to get involved. Or maybe he revised it. Either way, I picture him sitting here on the deck, staring at the sea while the ship lumbered along, his thoughts of Juliana troubling him.

    I know I'll never find out who the author is; tracking down every former crew member of the *Sag River* would take more time and money than is worth the effort and, who knows, the man could be dead by now.

It doesn't really matter, though. Unlike nautical charts, empty cigarette packets or yellowing newspapers, this letter is a more personal connection with a seafarer who once called the *Sag River* home. It's a glimpse into someone's life aboard a sea-going vessel, for while standing watches or loading crude oil in Alaska, this mariner was thinking of Juliana. It's a start, a signal that there are memories calling out to me, waiting to be discovered.

The lives of mariners like the writer to Juliana seem to have fallen off our collective radar, eclipsed by Hollywood movie stars, jumbo jets and missions to Mars. Few of us pay attention to the business of merchant shipping, unless an oil tanker spills its cargo of crude oil on the shore of some far-off beach or we glance at a story buried in the back pages of a newspaper about the sinking of a container ship. When a cargo vessel slips its moorings and steams over the horizon, it vanishes from the memory of most, just as these aging titans lie forlorn and forgotten here in India.

How forgotten is this world? Well, consider the situation in Iraq. According to the U.S. Department of Defense, 1852 American, British and other coalition troops were killed in that nation during the two-year period from March 2003 to April 2005, an average of 71 per month. In that same time frame, the United Nations' International Labour Organization, as well as several other shipping observers, estimate some 13,000 mariners died at sea. If you factor in those who make their livelihoods from fishing, the figure rises to 52,000 deaths on the Earth's waters. That's over 2,000 a month. Every year, more than 100 commercial vessels are lost at sea, roughly 2 each week. To be a professional mariner is to engage in the most dangerous profession on the planet, and one of the most invisible.

Looking for romance or symbolism in a business like modern-day commercial shipping may seem a naïve pursuit, unlike that of the chroniclers of tales of old with imagery of sailing ships fighting their way around Cape Horn or battling the North Atlantic's fierce winter storms. But the memories of those days linger, if only because the reality of modern-day mariners is still quite similar to the experiences of their predecessors. Seafaring is—and always has been—a hard, lonely, dangerous endeavour. There really never was a "golden age of sailing," for the ships and crews who plied the oceans in the eighteenth and nineteenth centuries lived perilously, with little pay for the dangers they endured.

Nevertheless, the sea and those who sail upon it have always been surrounded by a certain aura, highlighted by the omnipresent threats that can still seize a vessel and wrestle her to her doom in the depths below. Scan any bookstore shelves and you will find a lengthy list of titles about that golden age of sailing or the memoirs of individuals who have single-handedly circumnavigated the globe in a small boat, but fewer works about the daily lives of those whose profession is seafaring.

I believe there is an innate bond between those who leave dry land for the perils of the sea today and those who went before them. This unspoken thread splices the experiences of American, European, African and Asian mariners with those of the great Polynesian, Viking, Hanseatic and Phoenician cultures. This is the heart and soul of seafaring.

I also believe we all have a primordial connection with the sea, one that goes back to the infancy of our planet and a time when there was no such thing as terra firma, merely a molten ocean from which all life would eventually emanate. Even as we crawled from our watery birthplace, though, we still remained close to Poseidon's embrace: Most of the planet's population continues to live on or near water—oceans, seas, lakes and rivers—and this is where you will invariably find the world's greatest cities.

The slow and pedantic pace of ocean-going vessels seems at odds with today's world, in which speed is everything. The lengthy periods of isolation one needs to endure crossing the seas mean that even passenger cruises are now designed so that travellers need not miss dry land and duty-free shopping for more than a few days. The idea of spending months—or years—at sea makes merchant sailors a distinctly unique breed of individuals and so, too, their ships.

To paraphrase a cliché, ships can mean many things to many people. And though I will likely never know the full story of any single ship's life, I hope I can piece together enough parts from various sources to give me a broader picture of mariners, ships and the sea. The breaking yards here offer one the chance to glimpse some of that in the moments before a vessel is torn asunder and obliterated from existence, especially in the few short days these marine entities lie in state awaiting the arrival of the undertakers.

As I look at the shipbreaking yards that engulf me here in India, I marvel at the modern technology and ponder those who built and sailed the leviathans, torchbearers of a tradition that goes back at least five thousand years in recorded history. Perhaps by seeking out the designers, shipyard workers, owners, officers, ordinary sailors and anyone else I can find whose life revolves around commercial vessels, I can figure out if a ship has a soul.

At this moment I decide to focus my quest on "working ships," since humans ventured out to explore, trade and harvest the seas well before they decided to make war or pamper vacationers there. For the time being, I'll leave the study of battleships and passenger liners to others.

And so I turn away from the Hades vista that surrounds me, intent on beginning my quest into the world of ships and mariners who are eternally bound to the sea. I want to find out who these ghosts really are.

1

DREAMERS

There is nothing like a dream to create the future.

—VICTOR HUGO, *LES MISÉRABLES*

I n the beginning, a ship is a concept, nothing more. And, I might add, a somewhat adventurous concept for a species like ours that has evolved to live on dry land. We take it for granted today that anyone can step aboard a vessel—any vessel, whether it be a container ship, passenger liner, ferryboat or canoe—and put out upon the waters of the planet with a relative assurance of returning safely to shore. Yet the faith sea-going humans place in these craft is the result of many millennia of trial and error, with an inordinate amount of the latter having influenced marine design.

To create an ocean-going vessel entails the marshalling of great resources, capital and manpower. It requires vision, imagination, an understanding of the sea and its vicissitudes, an appreciation for the depredations that will be endured and an innate awareness of the technical challenges this feat of construction creates. The evolution of ships ranks as one of humankind's greatest achievements, one that has allowed us to explore every corner of the globe, to successfully achieve heavier-than-air flight and even to explore space. But above all, it begins with an individual and an idea.

Below a commuter jet outbound from Miami, the turquoise waters of the Straits of Florida glisten invitingly from my window seat. Most of the other passengers appear to be dreaming of a weekend filled with fun in the sun at the resorts and casinos of the Bahamas, but I am en route to Nassau to meet a very different sort of dreamer. Antony Prince is the head of G.T.R. Campbell Marine Consultants (better known as GTRC), an international firm specializing in ship design and project management, and I want to find out from him just how one goes about envisioning and designing a commercial vessel. An elusive man constantly on the move, Antony Prince has been marooned at his home and head office in the Bahamas for the last couple of weeks, providing me with a short opportunity to learn from a veteran of the business. While the jet banks over the northern tip of Andros Island, I idly scan my research notes before flipping open a small book written over a hundred years ago, one devoted to the detailed understanding of a vessel's strengths and weaknesses, and to a dream.

ON A MIDWINTER DAY in 1892, a seasoned merchant captain sat in Boston contemplating a journey that many had imagined but none had achieved. Joshua Slocum had been born in Nova Scotia but spent most of his life in New England; coming from a sailing family, he once said that "the wonderful sea charmed me from the first" and so embarked on a career that would take him from a small village overlooking the Bay of Fundy to Brazil, Argentina, Australia, Japan, Hong Kong, Alaska, San Francisco and many other exotic ports of call. The sea was truly in his blood and he worked his way up to master mariner and part owner of several vessels.

To Joshua Slocum, shipbuilding was just one notch below seafaring in terms of appeal. He was intimately aware of the fragility of a ship, having seen one of his favourite vessels wrecked on the coast south of Rio de Janeiro. That ship, the *Aquidneck,* he reflected upon as "a little bark which of all man's handiwork seemed to me the nearest to perfection of beauty." Stranded with his wife and two young children in Brazil, Slocum came up with the design for a small, thirty-five-foot dory rigged with a sail and, using some local help, built the vessel with an eye to getting his family home to the United States. He succeeded, and that feat—taking an open sailboat through five thousand miles of open water to landfall in South Carolina—was a testament to his courage, abilities, perseverance and knowledge of ships. It would set the stage for a later, far more audacious voyage, in which everything he had come to understand about the sea would be embedded in the very timbers of another small boat and allow him to pursue a nautical dream.

By the end of the nineteenth century, Joshua Slocum was unable to find work as a captain of sail ships owing to a decline in their use as steam-powered ships took over the seas. In his own words, he felt he "had been cast up from old ocean." Unable to relax ashore, Slocum sat in his New England home and decided to make the best of his unemployment by returning to the sea, this time without a crew. He would sail around the world single-handedly, or die trying.

The idea of sailing solo across the globe's oceans and seas in the 1890s was ludicrous, to say the least. There were no GPS systems, no radios, few reliable charts, only the most limited of rescue agencies and, of course, the simple fact that one man would have to do the work normally done by a team of experienced mariners. As well, in this case that one man was in his early fifties; not a young pup by any measure. Yet Slocum was adamant that he *could* do this, even though no one had achieved the dream to date. To this end, he purchased a dilapidated thirty-six-foot sloop called *Spray* from a whaling captain acquaintance in Fairhaven, Massachusetts, and then spent the next two years meticulously rebuilding her for the upcoming excursion. This was a pleasant and peaceful time for Slocum, who wrote lovingly of the work entailed in fitting little *Spray* out prior to leaving.

> My ax felled a stout oak-tree near by for a keel ... I rigged a steam-box and a pot for a boiler. The timbers for ribs, being straight saplings, were dressed and steamed till supple, and then bent over a log, where they were secured till set. Something tangible appeared every day to show for my labor ... It was a great day in the *Spray* shipyard when her new stem was set up and fastened to the new keel. Whaling-captains came from far to survey it. With one voice they pronounced it "A1," and in their opinion "fit to smash ice."

When Slocum completed refitting the tiny sloop, "the rudder was then shipped and painted, and on the following day the *Spray* was launched. As she rode on her ancient, rust-eaten anchor, she sat on the water like a swan."

He had taken an ugly duckling of a ship, one the locals thought ought to be broken up, and painstakingly created a thing of beauty. *Spray* would indeed serve him well, taking him south through the Atlantic, around Cape Horn and across the wide Pacific to Australia, through the Indian Ocean to South Africa and northward across the Atlantic once more, until he made landfall in America at 1 A.M. on June 27, 1898. It was the first time anyone had circumnavigated the globe alone, a journey of more than forty-six thousand miles in which the master mariner endured fog, squalls, snowstorms, gales, pirates and weeks spent with no land in sight. It was a trip made possible only by Slocum's nautical skills and the sturdy construction of the *Spray*. In the book I cradle aboard the jet airliner, Slocum's *Sailing Alone Around the World*, he summed up the journey simply by writing, "No one can know the pleasure of sailing free over the great oceans save those who have had the experience."

I THINK ABOUT how Slocum combined his seafaring skills with an innate understanding of the inner workings of a vessel as I drag my luggage through the airport in Nassau. The flight had ended dramatically, complete with heavy turbulence, a forced landing and awaiting fire trucks, owing to some engine trouble. Somewhat shaken, I head downtown to my hotel while noting storm clouds beginning to swirl overhead. I'm due to meet Antony Prince for a get-acquainted dinner this evening. We've not yet met face to face but have been chatting on the telephone and via email for over three months, so I already know a lot about him and his business. This is an auspicious time for me to be delving into the industry, for there is a worldwide shipbuilding boom going on right now like none before.

The creation of an ocean-going vessel is unlike any other endeavour undertaken in society. There are similarities to the construction of a skyscraper or the manufacture of automobiles, but the key difference is that none of these creations are expected to bear the stresses and indulgences of merchant shipping. An office complex in San Francisco might be designed to withstand an earthquake, but everyone hopes it will never be tested. However, a commercial ship will be built knowing that it will—absolutely—endure hurricanes, gales, extremes of heat and cold, heavy seas, unceasing corrosion and all the other brutalities that Poseidon can throw at it. A merchant vessel must be built for war, a constant, deadly battle with the elements.

But before the keel is laid and the construction can begin, someone must initiate the concept of these floating monsters. And one of these individuals is Antony Prince.

In the lobby of the hotel I wait for his arrival, which doesn't take long, for Prince is a punctual man. As the clock strikes seven, he strides across the marbled foyer with his family in tow, introducing me to his wife and son. Prince is a tidy man who seems to be in his mid-fifties, with a youthful, cherubic face and a trim moustache beneath wire-frame glasses. He speaks calmly, with a lilting, singsong accent that betrays his birth in southern India.

But his relaxed manner of speech belies the fact that Antony Prince is also one of the most energetic individuals I've met, constantly on the go and seeming never to tire of his hectic life. In the last two months he's sent me emails from Montreal, New York, Miami, Houston, London, Nassau, India and China, also from airports, shipyards, restaurants, cafés, shipping offices and design firms. My background file on him lists well over a half-dozen telephone numbers he uses. It's not often that he's together with his family (his daughter lives in New York, having recently graduated from medical school, and his son lives in Montreal), so he's combining a little work and pleasure here as he hustles us into his car and sets out for dinner.

While we wind our way through the narrow streets of downtown Nassau, the darkened skies explode with streaks of lightning. Prince calmly navigates his way through the downpour and then pulls up outside a restaurant just east of the downtown. Upstairs, the place is full of mostly locals and Prince leads us to a table on the veranda, overlooking the Yacht Haven Marina with its high-end pleasure craft. The sprawling Atlantis Resort on Paradise Island looms in the distance, a monument to dreams of riches built where pirates once counted their booty. This symbol of gambling nirvana is an apt background for my meeting, since the process of designing a ship is fraught with risks, especially financial risks. To secure the U.S.$30 million necessary to begin work on a new vessel, I'm told, entails international financing and legions of bankers and lawyers. A container ship will set you back between about $50 to $70 million, a large oil tanker about $100 million, and a liquid natural gas vessel (LNG) will cost you at least a cool $180 million.

As the waitress arrives, Prince takes charge and saves me from wondering what's best on the menu. He orders some fresh hog-toothed snapper and local beer, and then informs me that his schedule has changed yet again and he'll be flying to the mainland tomorrow afternoon to meet a client. "I am always on the move. Always. Some people think it's crazy and many would prefer something easier, especially as you get older. But if you have a good team," he glances at his wife and son, "it's manageable."

Since we'll only have a few hours together, Prince wastes little time in beginning my education into the world of ship design and construction.

"So, you want to know about how a ship is created, yes? Well, I will not say it is an easy thing to do, not at all. It is one of the most challenging things we can do, you know. It takes thousands of people, years of work, millions of dollars; it is a highly precise business, more than most people realize. It can be frustrating, nerve-racking and tense. Some people cannot take the pressure; some people go broke." Then he sits back and smiles. "But I will also tell you this: It is one of the most rewarding things I can think of."

Prince should know, as he's been in the shipbuilding business for three decades and involved in the creation of hundreds of vessels at shipyards around the globe, including tankers, bulk carriers, multipurpose vessels and even ferries. He's gone from a young man in southern India to a globetrotting business executive overseeing hundreds of millions of dollars in new ship construction. In the last decade alone, his firm has guided more than fifty commercial ships through the birthing process. And what makes this all the more interesting is that Antony Prince, like Joshua Slocum before him, is not a naval architect, nor did he begin his career intending to get into the shipbuilding business.

"You know, I was a mariner before I got into all this. I was an engineer—I became a chief engineer, in fact—but my father wanted me to become a doctor, which is very common in India, but I didn't want to do that. I always liked to tinker with things and I liked to solve problems, so I wanted to become a mechanic. We had a big argument about this, my father and me, but in the end he relented and I went to university in Kerala [a state in southwestern India] and got my degree in mechanical engineering. He suggested I consider taking those skills and going to sea, so I signed on with Shipping Corporation of India and spent seven years at sea. And once I started on the sea, well … there was no turning back."

Prince's desire to seek out problems and solve them led him to rise quickly within the engineering hierarchy, but he found that the "sea bug"—that desire to be a mariner—was waning. What he began to find more fascinating were the vessels themselves; he became more and more engrossed in the minutiae of ships, their strengths and weaknesses and, eventually, how they were constructed. He wanted to know more about ships from the ground up, so he received permission to be assigned to a yard to follow the building process. In 1972 he joined G.T.R. Campbell International, where he caught the eye of its legendary founder, George Campbell.

Antony Prince tells me more about this little-known figure whose impact on seafaring has been immense. He first reveals that *Lloyd's List*, the venerable shipping journal that has been published regularly for over 270 years, called George Campbell "probably the most successful and least known ship designer in the world."

"He was of the old school," Prince tells me, "a hard-working, no-nonsense man who left England for Canada during the war and then, when it ended, went to Japan where he almost single-handedly built up their ship construction industry. He had the ability to realize potential and to nurture it. Without George Campbell, I doubt Japan would be the great shipbuilding nation that it is. And I doubt I would be here talking to you."

What Campbell did was to simplify the building process, using the lessons learned during the years when the Allies had been forced to quickly—and economically—create new cargo ships to supply the war effort. He came up with a number of designs—most famously the Freedom, Fortune and Friendship series—that could be mass-produced, like automobiles or airplanes. This may not seem that revolutionary today, but prior to the Second World War most shipbuilding was done on a one-off, or bespoke, basis. There might have been three or four similar ships, sister vessels, but that was about it. Shipbuilding was a labour-intensive endeavour supplying a tight market, and the individuality of the vessels helped foster a sense of character for each of them.

But George Campbell was not a man prone to romantic notions about ships. By all accounts he was a difficult man to work with, a taskmaster who was as hard on himself as on those he employed. Antony Prince explains, "Mr. Campbell had to be tough to achieve what he wanted to do in Japan. That country was still recovering from the war and for one man to arrive there with the idea of rebuilding their industry and turning out a new series of vessels for the world market required an individual of great resolve. And that man was George Campbell."

When Campbell first arrived in Japan in 1949, the world was on the cusp of a new form of globalism. The changeover of various economies from war production to a more benign materialism was well underway; and in concert with the rise of the Cold War, in which democracy faced off against communism and socialism, the tentacles of nations were extending to new markets. Initially, in the West, these markets could be supplied by the fleets of cargo ships built throughout the war years, such as the famous Liberty ships. American yards had turned out 2700 of these utilitarian vessels at the astonishing rate of one every few weeks. (The record was five days, from keel-laying to hull launching.)

In 1949, though, there was a slump in worldwide shipping not unlike that which Joshua Slocum had encountered six decades earlier. But someone with a keen eye—like George Campbell—could see that things would soon change and that the small ships plying the oceans would soon be insufficient for international trade. If he could streamline the construction process, creating an efficient means of building the necessary components using inexpensive labour on a mass scale, then he might be able to achieve his vision. In concert with Greek owners eager to make their mark in commercial shipping and Japanese yards eager to get going again, Campbell set out to capitalize on these assets and prepare for the future.

"Above all else, this was an immense risk on the part of Mr. Campbell," Antony Prince continues. "Shipbuilding has always been a boom or bust business; it's either feast or famine. Because, you see, ships can only be built if there is a demand for them. And when the demand comes, it is usually quite large. But after you fulfill the orders, there may be decades that pass before the vessels need to be replaced. It is not like the automotive market, where people buy a new car maybe every six years or so. A ship can operate for twenty-five, thirty years. The risk that Mr. Campbell took was that there was no immediate demand for new ship construction in 1950. But he foresaw a demand coming soon and wanted to be up and running when it occurred."

Prince's time working with George Campbell saw the former chief engineer gain extensive firsthand experience in the shipyards of Japan while simultaneously learning from one of the best naval architects in the business. By 1989, though, there was another worldwide slump in the shipbuilding industry, so Campbell relocated back to Canada and began to think of retiring. Before his death in 1994, the aging dynamo allowed Prince to take over the company name and hoped his protegé would put into place all the lessons he'd learned. Just as his mentor had done four decades earlier, Prince realized that shipping would rebound from recession and that there would eventually be a demand for new vessels.

As Prince keeps glancing at his wristwatch, I realize our dinner conversation must end. Back on the streets of Nassau I see couples walking hand in hand, teenagers in the souvenir shops and middle-aged American men proudly smoking illicit Cuban cigars as they wait for their wives to finish perusing the jewellery stores. A half-dozen gleaming white cruise ships are nestled in the harbour near my hotel. Prince gestures at the floating palaces and remarks, "There must be a bad storm on its way if all those ships have come into port. You might want to check with your airline or CNN to see what's happening."

AFTER BEING DROPPED OFF at my hotel and confirming our get-together for first thing tomorrow morning, I make a beeline for the concierge's desk and discover that there are not one, but two storms lurking out there somewhere. One storm is veering north from Jamaica, aiming for Havana and then the west coast of Florida, while the second is fidgeting about in the Gulf of Mexico, so everyone's expecting a few days of bad weather. Oh, and tomorrow's Friday the thirteenth. The concierge tries to reassure me that the Bahamas should be fine, but nevertheless suggests I check in with him tomorrow to reconfirm my flights back to Canada.

I wander over to the hotel's ground-floor bar, which is nearly deserted, to have a nightcap and make some notes. The television above the bartender has ominous updates on the storms, with warnings to those on the Gulf Coast of Florida to flee inland. Another customer, an older man who sits nearby and orders a rum and Coke, soon joins me at the bar. He takes out a pack of Canadian cigarettes and lights one up, so I ask if he's a countryman of mine. In heavily accented English he tells me that, no, he's Romanian; he just got to liking this particular brand of cigarettes from his travels. For some reason a dim light goes off in my head and I ask the man, "Are you, by any chance, a mariner?" His face lights up and he tells me he is; in fact, he is an engineer on a ship, a small vessel that travels between the Bahamas and Florida. I introduce myself and tell him what I'm doing here, and he grasps my hand with a vise-like grip.

"I am Ion—just call me Ion—and am happy to meet you. I am chief engineer but ship is in port overnight, maybe for one day more, because of delay in cargo arriving in here. Storm is reason."

Ion tells me that he hails from Constanza, a Romanian port on the Black Sea north of the Bulgarian border, and is in his mid-fifties, though he looks much older. He has strong forearms, a raspy voice and tired eyes that have seen a lot in the thirty-seven years he's been a mariner. His career has taken him from Danube River barges to Black Sea freighters and he has been working the waters around the Bahamas for the last four years. "Is very small coastal trader I work on, about 500 tonnes, crew of three, and we carry cargo from here to Florida and back again. Back and forth, back and forth, day after day. Very boring."

Ion's reasoning for working on this small ship far from home is money. American dollars go a long way back in Romania, he tells me, allowing him to support an extended family. Of course he only sees them once every eight months, but he doesn't seem to mind the separation. "My children are adults now. And for me and my wife, I think this is good arrangement. She is good woman, but …" he takes a sip of his drink and lights another cigarette. In the uncomfortable silence that follows, I decide to change the subject and ask the chief his thoughts on ship design.

"This is interesting," he begins. "A ship is not always perfect, no? I see many that are difficult to operate. Some ships from Soviet Union and even from Romania under Ceausescu [the communist-era dictator Nicolae Ceausescu], they were very badly built. I think that sometime they should speak with the seaman, like me, about these things. But this is not normal, it does not occur. They build the ship, maybe is for new owner, and then we are hired. We come to ship and must live with the way it is. Maybe everything is *cacat*—shit—but they do not care. Just get the cargo from here to here quick."

Ion finishes the last of his drink and waves for the bartender, ordering another rum and Coke for himself and a fresh beer for me. I thank him for his generosity, we clink our glasses and he says, "Noroc!" Ion has now warmed up to me and he continues talking about ships without being prompted.

"Do you know, a ship is a special thing? It is full of smells—the oil, the petrol, the sweat of the sailor. It can be dirty. Dangerous. But it is freedom, too. Look at me, Romanian man, sit at bar in fancy hotel, I have my drink, I meet new friend—the coal miner in Jiu [in the Transylvanian Alps] he does not live like this. So, sometime I hate the ship, but sometime I am grateful for it."

Ion continues to talk as we finish our drinks, recounting visits to Montreal and memories of Canada in the 1970s. The freedom to travel to the West and see beyond the borders of the Socialist Republic of Romania was eye opening. He chuckles while telling me of an evening spent in Belfast with other crewmen, how they managed to elude the political officer on his ship for a night of pub-crawling. It's getting late, so I offer to buy him a last drink, but he graciously declines. Before I leave, I ask Ion if he'd ever like to work on the fancy new cruise ships that come into port here.

"Mmm … I do not think so. In first, I am not trained in these vessels. Once you begin with the ship, you must stay with this vessel. So I work on commercial ships, I stay on commercial ships. But the second is that I do not think the crew with the passenger ship have so much freedom as me. Maybe I am wrong, but I think they must have job more worse than me. Yes, ship is new and clean but I think it would be very boring." Then Ion shrugs and quietly adds, "I am too old, anyway. Old man will sail the old ship until he must retire. That is my life."

I thank the chief engineer for his candour and wish him well on whatever journeys will come. He grasps my hand in a hearty grip while a warm smile spreads across his creased features. I last glimpse Ion through the lobby windows, sitting alone in the bar with the last of his drink, staring at the television, surrounded by a smoky haze.

Ion's parting words linger with me, for they are likely true. The Romanian mariner came of age during the last great shipping boom and today's newer vessels are probably too sophisticated for an old sea dog like Ion. I'm not being condescending here toward his skills and experience, but rather reflecting what has been the trend in merchant shipping for hundreds of years. Whenever something new comes along in the design and construction of merchant ships, this has inevitably led to a schism between those able to embrace innovation and those unable or reluctant to do so.

Nevertheless, innovation has always won out over hesitation when it comes to ships. Throughout the darkest periods of the history of the world, naval architecture and marine exploration have been able to push the boundaries of technological advancement. Perhaps it was due to the fact that vessels never stayed in one place or maybe it was because they were able to flee over the horizon line, but the ravages of persecutions, inquisitions and war had less of an effect on mariners than on villagers stuck in poor communities or academics in universities.

Wealth was always the bottom line, and the need to maintain trade or expand into new markets was never far from the minds of religious tyrants or political despots. Indeed, if anything, noblemen and wealthy merchants wanted to speed up the process of transshipment and make a profit while the going was good and competitors might be in disarray. Taking advantage of a conflicted situation—a.k.a. war profiteering—is nothing new: The British East India Company, the Hudson's Bay Company, the Russian American Company, the Dutch East India Company, the Danish West Indies Company and many others were established by investors willing to risk their investments in "lawless" places. Their only prerequisite: Get the damn resources home as quickly as possible.

Shipbuilding, or at least hull construction, has been surprisingly similar wherever it has been done. From the beaches of Zanzibar to the fjords of Norway, from the Yellow River to the islands of Polynesia, and from the Mediterranean shores of the Levant to the Great Lakes of North America, the process was relatively straightforward. Most commonly, a keel would be laid first, the backbone of the vessel upon which its structural integrity would be built. Elm was the preferred choice of wood in Europe for hundreds of years, owing to its strength and its straightness. Then the framing would rise above the keel, curved sections that gave the hull its initial shape. Later the planking could be attached to this, providing the final measure of dynamics to give a vessel its seaworthiness.

There was a definite tactile sense to this sort of building as shipwrights cut, hewed, fitted, curved and jointed the various pieces of organic matter into a floating entity. The skills required to design a carrack, a complex type of sixteenth-century merchantman, should have been viewed as equal to those of such contemporary artists as Michelangelo; yet the names of the architects of these ships are lost forever, as are their very creations.

So, too, are the names of the great shipwrights from the Pacific Islands, who crafted vessels capable of sailing vast distances, possibly as far as South America. And these were not all small outrigger canoes. The Fijians built immense sail craft called *ndruas,* eighty feet long and capable of carrying over two hundred people at speeds of fifteen knots.

In Tahiti, as in many other communities, the process of building a sea-going vessel was a religious event as much as a technical achievement. Before construction of a new war canoe—graceful, hundred-foot-long vessels powered by teams of oarsmen—the shipwrights would gather in a sacred place on the island. Beneath the glow of the moon, they would bury their stone adzes in the ground, ceremoniously putting the tools to sleep. Then they would pray to Tane, the Tahitian god of the land, to empower the adzes with his strength. The next morning, the tools would be taken to the sea and dipped in the salt water to be awakened from their slumber.

With their newly charged tools in hand, the shipwrights would proceed to the tree to be felled for the canoe's hull. As trees were considered children of Tane, the men would ask their god's permission to cut a tree down. To these shipbuilders, the vessel was a living, breathing entity, possessed of spiritual power and to be considered a vital member of their community.

The design and building of floating vessels has always been a peculiar thing. It's the complete reverse of what happens on land, where labourers would build monuments to human ingenuity that would stand for eons. The pyramids still grace the sands of Egypt, the Coliseum defines Rome, Angor Wat remains graceful within its jungle realm, and the Great Wall of China is as steadfast today as when it was constructed. But the Pharaoh's Nile boats, Caesar's triremes and Admiral Zheng He's fleet are nowhere to be seen. Ships are merely fleeting images of our technical prowess, transient embodiments of society that can live on only as memories after their usefulness has passed.

When they are built, ships are also a strong reflection of the general state of world affairs. The sixteenth-century looting of the great Aztec and Incan empires by Spain necessitated the building of vast armadas to ship the hoards from New World to Old. And the fleets of immense clipper ships like the *Cutty Sark* came about during the nineteenth century, when Pax Britannica reigned and the Empire sought to bring home all the various raw materials it was extracting from its far-flung possessions (and, in return, to send the armies of soldiers, administrators and settlers abroad to consolidate its power).

Over the course of the past 150 years, the pace of technological change in seafaring has been immense, surpassing pretty much everything that occurred before. Easily the most important innovation was the introduction of mechanical power to replace the dependence on the winds. It certainly did not happen overnight, owing to the various problems with early propulsion systems, as well as the natural conservatism of the sailor. Having entrusted wooden-hulled, windborne vessels to safely transport them across the seas for thousands of years, sailors felt a natural hesitancy to throw their lot in with the smoke-belching steel beasts being sent down the ways at places like Tyneside in northeastern England. As always, economics overshadowed the concerns of sailors and they shipped out on whatever the owners gave them.

Britain did truly rule the waves in the nineteenth century, leading the way in nautical design, ship construction and fleet operation. The efficiency with which British yards were able to turn out new vessels had much to do with their access to raw materials. Oak, elm, hemp, cotton, flax, brass, copper and steel were all readily available either in the British Isles or within the Empire's realms. No other nation on Earth could compete with Britain, not even the quickly developing United States, for through isolated outposts, Britain controlled the world's markets as well as most of the prime shipping routes. The same year Princess Victoria was crowned queen, in 1838, the first transatlantic crossing was made by mechanical means, when the paddle steamer *Sirius* sailed from

Cork to New York with forty passengers aboard. Toward the end of her trip, though, the *Sirius* was desperately low on fuel and the crew was forced to throw cabin furniture and any other available wood into her furnaces to maintain steam.

Besides mechanical power, the shift to steel hulls from wood was the other main innovation of the nineteenth century. For a variety of reasons, this was inevitable. It took more than two thousand mature oak trees to build a large merchant vessel, and the supply of timber in Britain and Europe was somewhat limited, large tracts having already been denuded halfway into the century (though Britain was able to import marine timber from her colonies in Canada, Burma and elsewhere). Then there was the economic benefit of steel construction: An iron vessel could carry larger cargoes, since a wooden vessel required more internal cross-bracing (and, surprisingly, steel ships often weighed less than their timber-wrought sisters).

Sail ships did, for a time, have the advantage of speed and freedom to roam the seas unfettered by the demands for fuel. Square-riggers could leave Britain or France or Holland and sail around the Cape of Good Hope to Asia, whereas steam ships needed to constantly find coaling stations up and down the coasts of Africa and India to make the journey. Similarly, New England whalers could sail south around Cape Horn and into the Pacific for years at a time, needing only to replenish their supplies of food and fresh water. But as the development of marine engines proceeded through the industrializing nineteenth century, windborne sail vessels were quickly losing ground.

Another key factor in the demise of the sail ship era had nothing to do with the supply of timber or the efficiency of mechanical propulsion systems but with one man's vision to connect the Mediterranean and Red Seas by means of a canal. Ferdinand de Lesseps was a fifty-four-year-old obscure French bureaucrat with little interest in shipping per se, but with an abiding drive to fulfill the dreams of everyone from the ancient Pharaohs to Napoleon and to create an economical means of reaching the Far East. After entreaties to the Pasha of Egypt, Mohammed Said, de Lesseps's consortium began construction in 1859 of what would eventually be a 121-mile-long waterway through the Isthmus of Suez. When it opened a decade later, its impact on commercial shipping and shipbuilding was immediate.

The Suez Canal shortened the voyage from Europe to the Far East by 4000 miles; if you consider that a good clipper ship could sail about 250 miles a day, this was a considerable saving in time. Unfortunately, few sail ships could use the canal. The Red Sea is a difficult body of water for them to navigate, owing to indifferent winds, and the transit of the Suez Canal itself required steam tugs to tow the sail ships. The rush was on to build steam-powered steel ships that could make the trip to the East through Egypt. Older shipyards fell into disrepair without the ability to construct iron ships, while new ones sprang up; in Britain this led to a shift from the south to the north, to new yards in Newcastle, Barrow, Sunderland and on the river Clyde; on the Continent, German industry created vast new shipyards that were soon competing on a global scale.

The Suez Canal also allowed European nations to embark on another frenzy of imperialism: Germany set up an East African colony in what is now Tanzania; Britain took over control of India from the East India Company; and France settled on trying to tame Indochina. With the canal open for business, these and other nations could more easily manage their affairs in far-flung outposts and send their new fleets of merchant vessels out to gather the bounty reaped on the backs of the locals.

Though wooden vessels and steel-hulled sail ships would linger on the seas for a few decades more, they really were doomed, something that must have been painfully clear to Joshua Slocum as he pondered sailing around the world in *Spray*. The completion of the Panama Canal in 1914 only added to the demise of windborne vessels, as North American shipping finally dispensed with the long and dangerous journey around Cape Horn, one of the most truly horrific bodies of water on Earth.

By 1908, the world fleet of sea-going steam vessels numbered almost fifteen thousand, with the British Merchant Marine making up 42 percent of the world tonnage. The cycles of shipbuilding would continue: The losses incurred in the Great War would need to be replaced, as would those in the Second World War. Then there was the expansion of global economies throughout the 1960s, a period in which Great Britain alone employed two hundred thousand workers in her various yards. But it would be the Suez Canal that would again have a dramatic impact on the design and construction of ships when the Six Day War erupted between Israel and her Arab neighbours in 1967.

Heavily damaged in the fighting, the canal was closed to vessels, and suddenly shipping companies had to return to the long journey around southern Africa to maintain the supply of goods and—especially—crude oil from the Middle East. As most oil tankers were built for the Suez, their maximum size was 70,000 tonnes. (The weight of vessels is a most peculiar aspect of ship description; it can be expressed in deadweight tonnes, gross tonnage, displacement tonnage or net tonnage. In general, most vessels are referred to by their deadweight tonnage—dwt—the actual weight of cargo, crew, passengers, fuel, and supplies a ship can carry, and that's the usage here.) There were a few VLCCs—Very Large Crude Carriers—on the seas, 200,000-tonne tankers that took long, slow journeys from the Persian Gulf to markets. But these could not supply the worldwide demand for oil fast enough, and with the Suez Canal closed (it would not reopen until June 1975), shipyards began to turn out a new generation of vessels. These true behemoths were known as ULCCs—Ultra Large Crude Carriers—exceeding 300,000 tonnes and over 1000 feet in length, the size of the Empire State Building. With their large cargo capacities, they could bring the crude in quantity from Saudi Arabia, Iraq, Iran and elsewhere to the European and North American markets. Size suddenly mattered. And it was during this shipbuilding boom of the early 1970s that Antony Prince appeared.

THE NEXT MORNING I meet up with Prince once more, in the lobby of my hotel at nine sharp. Prince is in a jovial and relaxed mood as we walk next door to the complex that houses his office. GTRC is on the third floor of a fairly nondescript building, at the end of the hall and with only a small nameplate to advertise its presence. As he unlocks the door, Prince darts inside to disarm the alarm system before inviting me to enter. If I'd been expecting that the world headquarters of a major shipbuilding firm would be a bustle of activity, I'd be sorely disappointed.

GTRC occupies two rooms barely larger than a kindergarten class. There's a kitchenette in the corner, a minuscule meeting room beside it and an otherwise cluttered space with four workstations, each one topped with a computer and telephone. It could be the offices of a real estate company, a travel agency or any other small, white-collar consultant firm. Except for the models of freighters and photos of ships that are everywhere.

Antony Prince notes my surprise at the spartan office. "Ah, you were expecting something busier, yes? Well, today most of the actual design work is done overseas, near the shipyards themselves in Korea, Japan or India. From here we manage the projects, though I must travel to the design facilities and yards quite often. That's why I'm always on the road. There may only be a couple of us here—like my wife [Alice, who is his vice-president and chief financial officer] and myself—but there could be two or three hundred people doing the pre-production design work overseas. Everything must be mapped out: the structural engineering, mechanical, electrical, navigational, everything, right down to the closets and bunks. And that will take about a year to do, the pre-construction phase."

But where, I wonder, does it all begin? He waves me to a chair by his desk, the harbour visible through the windows behind it, and thinks for a minute. "I usually sketch out ideas when I have food, at dinner, on a napkin. I try to transfer a concept or thought or idea or something into a particular visual representation. Whether it's going to be a five-hold ship or a six-hold ship, a box hold or an open hold, all these ideas. Then computer-aided designers can take my idea and begin to work things out. Computers, though, can only do so much. Concepts come out of gut feeling. Not from software.

"There are many ways a design of a vessel takes place," he continues. "It could be generated by a design company or a shipyard, a ship owner or a cargo company. Anyone can be the originator of a ship project. A shipyard-originated project usually has the purpose of finding work for the yard. A ship owner or cargo company will generally be looking for a means to transport a certain cargo. We're in between the two of these. We use research, such as market research, to analyze trends and probable future requirements and then draw up a design based on that. Our designs are used as benchmarks."

What Prince and GTRC are doing is the continuation of George Campbell's work, the building of "standard ships." By looking at current trends in commercial shipping and using market research to peek into the future, Prince and his team seek to find a design that will satisfy the needs of a variety of different customers, rather like the way automobile manufacturers build cars on an assembly line. Considering that it takes twelve months to do the pre-construction work and another twelve months to build a prototype, it makes sense to continue building a number of similar ships once the yard is up and running. If, of course, there is a market for the completed vessels.

"There is a great demand today for new ships," Prince tells me. "This is unprecedented in the history of shipbuilding. New shipyards are opening, abandoned shipyards are reopening, repair facilities are turning to construction. It is the first time that every sector is doing well: tankers, containers, bulk carriers."

As he patiently explains to me, there are three main reasons for this shipbuilding boom. The first is the sheer age of most of the merchant fleets. Having been laid down during the years following the closing of the Suez Canal in 1967, many of these vessels are now thirty years old and no manner of refits can keep them seaworthy much longer. Just finding spare parts for old engines is difficult. Second, safety standards are today far more rigid than they were in the 1970s. Too many oil spills led the shipping industry and the United Nations' International

Maritime Organization (IMO) to come up with strict new guidelines for tanker construction. All tankers now being built must have double-hulls to provide an added level of protection for the environment (though a number of shipping insiders I've spoken to think that hulls are not the problem; it's the quality of the crews manning the ships they are more worried about).

The final reason for this surge in construction is the burgeoning economies of the world. China and India, with over two billion people, are importing raw materials at an astonishing rate, as well as exporting large quantities of commercial goods. Just a decade ago this was unheard of, and once you factor in the continued demand for oil by the developed nations of the West, you have a severe shortage of merchant ships plying the oceans of the planet.

Of the approximately 46,000 commercial vessels working today, it's expected that well over half will need to be replaced in the next ten years. In 2002 there were 1025 vessels contracted for construction at yards around the planet; in 2003 that figure jumped to 1871 ships. In the three busiest shipbuilding nations, Korea, Japan and China, the orders are backed up several years from now. If you want a new ship, you might have to wait until 2010 to see it.

One of the costs of churning out ships at such a rapid rate is that aesthetics lose out to utilitarian needs. Modern shipyards employ thousands of workers in a production process that is far more complex than in times gone by. Hulls are now built in sections to be lifted into building docks and welded together, beginning with the after end of the vessel. The superstructure will be built as a module and similarly hefted onto the hull; the bow section is the last to be attached and then the ship can be floated to a fitting-out area and another hull can begin to take shape in the dry dock.

Those nostalgic for the graceful lines of the wind ships have long decried the design of steel ships. Yet shipping has always followed the mantra of "form follows function," and those pleasant lines on the *Cutty*

Sark and other crack ships of the nineteenth century reflected the hydrodynamic qualities of their hulls. Mechanically powered vessels could be more brutish in design as their engines became more powerful.

"You see," states Prince, "cargo ships are not invested with a lot of aesthetics and beauty. It's more functional, to keep costs down." He waves his hands at the models of GTRC ships nearby, sitting in their glass cases. "Yes, I will admit that these ships are ugly, blunt and utilitarian. There is not an aesthetic beauty there. But the beauty in the design—to me—is in its inherent flexibility, its ease of operation and safety. These are things that are beautiful to me."

I point out a wooden model of a schooner mounted on the wall near the door and ask him if that's more beautiful than the cargo ships. "Absolutely, absolutely. But it is a completely different type of ship, from another time. It's there to remind me of the beginnings of ship design," he says while staring at the schooner and smiling.

To a certain degree, Prince has a relationship with ships not unlike that which exists between parent and child. He candidly admits to me that when he hears of the demise of vessels that he saw being built back in the 1970s, it tugs at his heartstrings. "You see, there is a little of me in each of them. I do not like to hear when they go to the breakers. But, of course, I know this is inevitable. But still ..." In the silence that follows, Prince stares at photographs on the walls of vessels no longer at sea.

"You know, you are looking for the 'soul' of a ship, yes? So I will tell you something: Yes, they do have a soul. I think so, absolutely. But it only applies to people who are closely associated with it. To all other people, it's just a piece of metal. This is why we give our ships names—Galaxy, Fortune, Fantasy—so that people who build them can relate to them. We don't call them 'hull number two thousand/bulk carrier.' People don't connect to that. I remember when the first Fantasy vessel was built, in China, and a shipyard worker with twenty-eight years' experience came up to me. He had tears in his eyes and said to me, 'This is the first time

I've related to a ship in twenty-eight years. Because you've been able to make me a part of this whole thing.' I felt proud about that, because we were able to make people part of the whole process. And something of that shipyard worker was embedded in that ship."

Too quickly, my time with Prince has come to an end. His cell phone has begun ringing with repeated urgency—his wife is warning him to get to the airport—so he politely ushers me out of the GTRC offices and down to the lobby of the office tower. The storm clouds have cleared and Nassau is now bathed in brilliant late-morning sun; peace has returned to this tropical paradise. Before we shake hands, Antony Prince describes one more personal event, also relating to that Fantasy vessel—the 29,000dwt (deadweight tonne) *Clipper Fantasy*. This was in 1996 and the *Clipper Fantasy* was the first ship to be built by Prince after George Campbell's death. The prototype bulk carrier was returning to the Dalian Shipyard in China after successfully completing her sea trials. As they reached the mouth of the harbour, Prince caught sight of an older ship lying at anchor and, as they got closer, he couldn't quite believe his eyes.

"It was a Fortune vessel, one of George Campbell's most famous designs. But it was not just any Fortune vessel, it was the *Athol,* one of the earliest of the series. 'Athol' was the name of George Campbell's father and this was also the first ship I served on for Mr. Campbell, back in 1972. And I had goose bumps on me. I couldn't believe it. Of all the ships to see—*Athol!* I said, 'George Campbell is waiting for me there.' His spirit lived on." With that, Prince smiles warmly to himself and heads off to continue Campbell's work.

What Antony Prince has revealed to me is that the bond between a ship designer and his offspring is lifelong. It is a combination of the connection an artist has with his work and the way an architect looks upon a building he has envisioned. Certainly it is true that these vessels are commercial enterprises created to deliver goods and make money, but they are also old friends to be fondly remembered and sometimes celebrated. They possess individual identities known only to people like

Prince, embodying nuances of character and memories that few others will ever understand.

For some who have envisioned and then created a vessel, the ability to see it as anything but beautiful dies hard. Perhaps this is another reason why mariners have always referred to ships as feminine, as "she," for they become like doting parents of daughters; their ships can be hard to give up to someone else, to some other man.

Joshua Slocum certainly knew that about his beloved sloop *Spray*, for he never sailed another vessel after her grand voyage circumnavigating the globe. In 1909, eleven years after that historic journey, the master mariner set off again for a short jaunt from New England to the Caribbean. He was sixty-five years old and his era, the era of the wooden-hulled sail ships, was over. The old sea dog from Nova Scotia's Annapolis Valley knew everything there was to know about barks, schooners and even full-rigged ships, those majestic three-masted vessels so emblematic of the nineteenth century. But the new generation of ocean carriers—those mechanically propelled, steel-encased successors—of those he knew little. So in his retirement he set sail from Martha's Vineyard on November 14, 1909, and at some point *Spray* should have skimmed across the sea near Nassau. Whether or not she did is unknown, though, for neither Joshua Slocum nor the *Spray* was ever seen again; the vessel, the designer and the dream simply vanished.

2

BUILDERS

Build me straight, O worthy Master!
Stanch and strong, a goodly vessel,
That shall laugh at all disaster,
And with wave and whirlwind wrestle!

—HENRY WADSWORTH LONGFELLOW,
"THE BUILDING OF THE SHIP"

As Antony Prince explained to me in the Bahamas, the shipping industry is currently in the midst of an unprecedented building boom. Almost every existing shipyard in the world is completely booked up for the next few years, old yards are being reopened and new ones planned. According to Clarkson Research Studies, one of the preeminent shipping observers, the business of ships and marine trade is worth over U.S.$100 billion and is one of the planet's fastest-growing heavy industries. The scramble is on to replace aging fleets and cash in on global trade, pushing the costs of new vessels up as demand outstrips supply. A few years ago a VLCC tanker cost about $63 million; by the end of 2004 that figure had risen to $87 million.

For most of the last thirty years, shipbuilding's nexus was Japan, thanks in part to the work of Prince's mentor, George Campbell. But by 2002 South Korea had surpassed its old archrival to take the lead, one that it seems certain to retain in the near future. Four decades ago the Republic of Korea ranked with the poorest nations in Africa; today this nation of forty-eight million has managed to build itself into an economic powerhouse, with the shipbuilding industry helping to lead the way. If you want to learn more about shipbuilding, there are few better places to visit.

While waiting to clear customs at Seoul's Incheon International Airport, I realize that I'm not the only foreigner with an interest in the shipping industry here. Standing in line in front of me are two slightly menacing-looking guys who keep staring my way. They're both much bigger than I am. One has a shaved head and sports a thin scar near his right eye, while the other guy—I mentally call him "The Boss"—has a tattoo on his wrist, visible beneath a coarse leather jacket. He notices me glancing at the purple ink on his skin, so I hastily turn my back to the men and try to act nonchalant, before a tap on my shoulder makes me jump. Just a little.

Mr. Shaven-head is standing before me with a quizzical look on his thuggish face. "Izvinite? Govorite po-russki?" He wants to know if I speak Russian; I'm certainly not fluent, but I know enough to answer, "N'et. Ya kanadanets." I'm Canadian. The guy turns to his friend and a quick conversation ensues before The Boss turns his attention to me, stepping close. Whatever threat I might have imagined from the man disappears as he looks at me with pleading eyes and asks in pidgin English, "Please to help … fill out document, da?" while extending a piece of paper toward me.

It turns out they're sailors arriving from Vladivostok who are having some trouble filling out the Korean entry/exit forms, so we huddle together and I somehow explain what's supposed to be written down. The two Russians are heading to the same place I am: Ulsan, South Korea, the site of several shipbuilding yards. By the time I've cleared customs and make my way to the check-in counter for my connecting flight to Ulsan, the number of foreigners milling around exceeds Koreans. A knot of East Indians is staring at the monitors that display flight times, a group of Filipinos huddle around the souvenir kiosk, and some blond Europeans—maybe Germans—are chain-smoking outside. The two Russians are drinking beer in the bar and wave at me, eagerly inviting me to join them, but my flight is already boarding so I decline the offer.

That so many seafarers are making their way to Ulsan surprises me, but with at least one new vessel being launched every week in this port, mariners are clearly in demand. Few people have heard of Ulsan, which is located on the southeast coast of Korea, an hour's flight from Seoul. But the name of the city's largest employer—Hyundai—will be more familiar. Ulsan is the home base for Hyundai's various divisions, including its automotive and shipbuilding operations, with the latter requiring a vast series of complexes spread over three different sites. Here are churned out supertankers, bulk carriers, container ships, general cargo vessels, naval warships and even offshore oil rigs; about the only thing they don't build is passenger ships. From meagre beginnings over thirty years ago, Hyundai's Ulsan yards have become the busiest in the world, helping to push South Korea into a leading role in the world's shipbuilding industry, while transforming Ulsan from a sleepy village into a metropolis of a million people that is colloquially known as "Hyundai City."

Ulsan's nickname is quickly apparent to any visitor arriving here. At the airport, you ride a Hyundai escalator to retrieve your luggage from a Hyundai carousel. You're driven into the city in a Hyundai car, built at the Hyundai automobile plant you pass en route to the Hyundai Hotel. A Hyundai elevator whisks you to your room that overlooks the Hyundai Department Store, the Hyundai Cultural Center and the Hyundai-built hospital. And blocks of nearby apartment towers for workers and their families are emblazoned with the Hyundai name, just in case you wondered who built them. This sort of corporate largesse is rarely seen in the West anymore, hearkening back to the days of "company towns" when employers controlled virtually all elements of workers' lives.

The omnipotent nature of Hyundai is further heightened by the fact that their industrial operations are clustered away from the city centre, on a small peninsula on the east side of the Taehwagang River. A series of green-covered hills form an additional barrier that hides the main ship-yards from the downtown core of Ulsan. Hugging the warm waters of the East Sea are three different shipyards. The largest is known as HHI, for Hyundai Heavy Industries, which builds supertankers, large container ships and liquid natural gas vessels. Close by is HHI's Offshore & Engineering Division, where oil rigs are constructed for deep-sea work. And right next door to that is the Hyundai Mipo Dockyard (HMD), where smaller tankers, container vessels, bulk carriers and the like are built.

Together, these yards employ over twenty-six thousand people who will spend up to a year putting together all the bits and pieces required to create an ocean-going titan. Within these sites you will find Hyundai maintains its own security guards, fire departments, medical clinics, restaurants, corner stores, bank machines, guest houses, management offices, design bureaus, fleets of limousines, translators, protocol officers, lawyers, gardeners, foundries, assembly sheds, fabrication huts, tugboats and just about everything else required to keep a small port city running. From my room in the Hyundai Hotel, I have a clear view of the HHI yard and can see at least a dozen vessels in various stages of construction. The unfinished superstructures of ships loom over the grey steel-work sheds, the ships' exteriors painted a dull yellow. Gantry cranes swing to and fro, and I hear what will be my constant audio companion while here: the din of tonnes of steel being hefted and dropped. From this perspective, it all seems like chaos, albeit organized chaos.

For a closer look at this industrial anarchy, I hook up with Lee Jin, an assistant manager from Hyundai Heavy Industries who has agreed to shepherd me around the shipyard. Lee is in his late twenties and is tall for a Korean; dressed in the ubiquitous Hyundai uniform—blue company windbreaker, dark blue pants, white shirt and tie—at his height he easily stands out in a crowd. As he guides me to a car waiting outside the hotel's front doors (a Hyundai car, of course, complete with a stony-faced driver), Lee is polite and reserved, traits common to many in Korea. I've no idea where he's taking me, but the car doesn't travel far. We merely cross the road from the hotel to the main gates (we could have walked the distance), where two uniformed guards come to attention and salute as we pass. I'm quite impressed by this performance, though I later realize they do this to all cars entering or exiting the shipyard.

At a three-storey stone building just inside the gates, Lee wordlessly ushers me out of the car, his arm extended to guide me along. We end up in a large wood-panelled presentation room, with two dozen plush chairs arranged in front of a giant video monitor, on which I'm shocked to see "Hyundai Heavy Industries Welcomes Mr. Daniel Sekulich, Journalist" splayed across the screen. Lee gets me seated in the front row and quickly says, "We have prepared a short video for you. Please watch and we can talk afterwards." There's a coffee table in front of me on which are placed two small flags: one of South Korea and the other the Hyundai corporate symbol. There are doilies on the arms of the chairs. I have a vision of those meetings between Richard Nixon and Chou En-Lai in Beijing decades ago, with world leaders sitting around stiffly and formally. I look at my Korean guide for assistance but he merely bows before retreating to the back of the room as the lights dim and a peppy promotional video begins, the type of thing shown to a potential customer or a foreign investor that extols the economic prowess of the firm and its history of shipbuilding.

That history is quite fascinating, but not the sanitized version presented in the promo video.

THE STORY OF HYUNDAI is the story of post-war Korea, and in this part of the world that means the 1950–1953 war that pitted the communist North against the South. The aftermath of this bitter "police action," as the United Nations referred to it, was a divided people, over 2.5 million dead, wounded or missing, and the destruction of virtually every major city and industrial centre. The only part of the entire peninsula to escape the carnage of war was a ten-thousand-square-kilometre pocket in the southeast known as the Pusan Perimeter, where United Nations' and South Korean forces managed to fend off the invaders from Kim Il Sung's People's Army. Ulsan just so happens to have been within the Perimeter, so this former fishing port emerged from the fighting unscathed.

In 1961, General Park Chung Hee led a *coup d'état* and became president of the Republic of Korea (South Korea). Among his ambitious goals was a master plan to build up the impoverished country's infrastructure and create a powerhouse nation, something that outsiders scoffed at. Park turned to a number of small companies that he felt had the potential to carry out his dream; chief among these was a firm called Hyundai, which means "modern" in Korean, led by the dynamic Chung Ju Yung. Along with several dozen other firms, Hyundai became part of a national system known as *chaebols,* family-owned enterprises that received lucrative government support and explicit directives as to what endeavours to pursue. (Some other famous Korean firms to develop from this system are Samsung, Daiwoo, Kia and LG.)

In the early 1970s, President Park's directive to Chung was the creation of a shipbuilding industry in Korea, something about which the Hyundai president had no background and nor did the nation as a whole. But having already founded a fledgling automobile plant in Ulsan, Chung embarked on a massive program to develop a yard that would rival the Japanese, the world leaders in shipbuilding at the time. Ulsan was the perfect place to create a shipyard: A number of harbours could be used, there was deep water in the East Sea to conduct sea trials, only a few fishermen's homes would need to be relocated, and the place was hundreds of kilometres from North Korea and its ever-present threat. Within just a few years, Chung had created HHI, which launched its first oil tankers in 1973. Two years later he opened a second shipyard, HMD. By the time Chung Ju Yung died in 2001, his workers had turned out thousands of vessels and helped transform Korea from a war-ravaged country into a modern nation equal to the West.

What's important to remember in this episode is that it took billions of dollars in investments and the personal livelihoods of tens of thousands to achieve the industrial prowess that surrounds me outside the Hyundai screening room. Chung might have had a vision, but it required the near-servile work of ordinary Koreans to achieve this. The *chaebols* placed the good of the nation (and their firms' prosperity) above the rights of the individual, an oddly socialist concept in a country that was, at that time, rabidly anti-communist. Throughout the 1970s, 1980s and 1990s, shipyard workers toiled incessantly here in Ulsan for at least six days a week, forgoing family life, vacations and any semblance of Western normality. To put it bluntly, these people worked their asses off to build the ships we demanded.

By the late 1980s, though, all this hard work led to frustrations among the workers, and labour strife began to rock Ulsan. In 1987, thirty thousand workers took to the streets to demand higher pay, eventually storming City Hall and setting vehicles ablaze. Union organizers were harassed, workers intimidated and riot police kept on standby. Thankfully, the last decade has seen a marked improvement in labour relations; just a few months before my visit here, Koreans saw their workweek reduced from six days to five. And with the incessant demand for new vessels, the last thing Hyundai needs is a strike or interruption in the delivery schedules.

WITH THE CORPORATE INTRODUCTION to Hyundai over, Lee Jin guides me back outside to tour the shipyard itself. I fear that I'm going to be given a somewhat perfunctory look at the operations, but Lee has other ideas. "Now that we have the formal part over, why don't we take a real look at things," he says in perfect English while getting behind the wheel of a company car. "Let's begin at the assembly sheds, OK?"

Listening to this young man describe how he ended up here in Ulsan is a crash course in the differences between Eastern and Western attitudes toward career, as well as the great costs entailed in creating ships. "I come from a small village, but was able to go to university—after my military service." Every Korean male must undergo a couple of years of service in the armed forces, South Korea being one of a handful of developed nations still to require this. Beyond the defence necessity, service helps to further forge a sense of cohesive unity that can be translated into the civilian workforce.

"You know," my guide explains, "there is a different way of work here in Korea, not like in America I think. It is a ... tradition, I guess, that if a worker does not complete his task at the end of the day, he will continue until it is completed. I believe it is more normal for a factory worker in the West to leave at end of the shift and finish the task perhaps the next day, yes?" And while this is a bit of a generalization, Lee is partially correct. Coming out of the ashes of war, Koreans spent decades building up their economy to the point it has currently achieved.

The zealous work ethic that consumes this nation is evident when I ask Lee Jin about his first memories of seeing this shipyard. He pulls our car over to the side of the roadway to allow a couple of transport trucks to pass and then answers. "I do not remember the shipyard itself. You see, when I applied to Hyundai I was one of perhaps a hundred applicants hoping to get this one job, which was in the office. Many, many people want to work here but there are few openings. So when I first came to Ulsan I was very nervous. I spent many days preparing for the interview and when I came here I did not notice the ships, the cranes, the steel—

none of it. I was completely focused on the interview. And I succeeded. It was only much later that I finally opened my eyes, but by then I think the fascination had worn off."

As we resume driving through the shipyard, my own fascination increases. One of the first things I notice is that the anarchy I'd thought would be here is less visible. In fact, I'm surprised at how quiet and calm the place feels. And how cramped things are—it seems like every inch of the shipyard site is taken up with sheds, warehouses, outdoor construction areas and other structures. "Yes, you are correct," Lee tells me. "It already takes up four kilometres along the shore, but there is no more room for expansion at this site. We are at peak production right now, with over two hundred vessels on backlog. Last year HHI delivered sixty-four ships and I believe we hope to produce a few more this year. But you can only work so fast."

Though worldwide demand for new ships is frantic, the yard does not work around the clock or even on weekends, except for some minor tasks and maintenance. Because the assembly is done in the nine immense outdoor dry docks, nighttime work could be dangerous. Even the weather can have an impact on production: If a typhoon strikes, the entire yard comes to a screeching halt with workers sent home until things improve.

At the far end of the shipyard, Lee stops beside a cream-coloured building stained with dirt and grit. This is where it all begins, he says, inside a two-hundred-metre-long shed where sections of high-grade steel are delivered by truck or by barge from steel mills north and south of Ulsan. The dull grey metal is stacked in piles waist-high, each piece about the size of several billiard tables. Running my hands along a sheet, I find the steel smooth and cold, and sniff a metallic smell that lingers in the building. The ends of each sheet have already been labelled with strips of bar-coding for each piece of the giant jigsaw that is a sea-going vessel.

Korean shipwrights have been working with steel for over four hundred years, well before Westerners. The legendary Admiral Yi Sun-sin designed what many consider to be the first ironclad warships, back in the late sixteenth century, thirty-metre vessels called *geobukseon* (or "turtle-shaped ships"). These wooden-hulled turtle ships had armour-plated tops studded with sharp spikes to repel boarders, and were fitted with dozens of small cannons and a dragon's head to spew flames and smoke. Yi used them effectively against Japanese invaders, allegedly never losing a ship in battle.

A shrill whine announces the arrival of an overhead gantry crane fitted with about thirty saucer-shaped magnets to pick up the metal and shift it to the middle part of the shed. Donning hard hats, Lee and I follow the crane as it deposits the steel on a series of rollers that feed the metal beneath an automated cutting machine. Properly called a numerically controlled flame cutter, the machine is a computerized robot that cuts and bevels automatically. As I watch, sparks begin to fly from the steel plate and the sheet begins its transformation into some pre-arranged shape.

We duck through a doorway into an adjacent part of the shed where a team of workers is beginning to weld the sections together. The shapes are still oblique, haphazard triangles, squares and open-faced boxes. A supervisor with a set of drawings hovers over two guys who are inspecting the V-shaped joints of a section; from my perspective they could be the ribs of a mechanical whale or a great white shark being built for a Hollywood action film.

Over to the right is a mechanical bending press that gently curves a metal plate into a perfect semi-circle, the steel groaning slightly as it gives way to the force of the machine. Once the press releases its grip on the plate, a shipwright approaches carrying a plywood mould to check the curvature, carefully eyeballing the shape. This reminds me that shipbuilding can never be completely automated, that creating a leviathan will always require the skilled eyes and hands of a human.

Creating ships has always been a labour-intensive endeavour, but it has become even more so today. This is largely due to the mass scale of production at yards like HHI, which can have twenty hulls in their dry docks while another dozen hulls are being fitted out alongside the quays.

They say it takes over five hundred thousand man-hours, or about ten months, to build a VLCC supertanker, and that's considered fast. (The *Queen Mary 2*, the largest passenger ship afloat, is about the same size as many of the vessels under construction at HHI, but she took nearly two years to be constructed, though much of that time was spent on fitting her out with accommodations and amenities for her passengers.) The various components that make up a vessel utilize enormous quantities of steel, brass, copper, aluminum and plastic, and shipyards consume energy at a staggering rate. To feed the electrical demands of Ulsan's shipyards (and other industries such as the car plant), there are two nearby nuclear power plants with eight combined reactors.

The scale of this shipyard is hard to discern from the ground, so Lee Jin takes me to a small hill that overlooks the site, where a guest house sits. This is where ship owners and dignitaries come to celebrate the launchings and other ceremonies, and it provides a bird's-eye view of HHI. Directly beneath me are four of the dry docks crammed with the developing forms of eight different vessels. Some of the hulls are almost finished, while others are barely discernible as ships. Presiding over the dry docks is one of the oversized cranes they call "Goliaths," capable of lifting 450 tonnes at a time (and this is the smallest of these cranes used by Hyundai). The crane gingerly hefts a section of hull that must weigh a couple of hundred tonnes and deposits it in the midship area of the developing vessel.

These immense sections are called blocks here at the shipyard, and the assembly of them, in a seemingly piecemeal fashion, is one of the ways the building process has been sped up. By fitting out each individual block in the assembly sheds, the dry docks become a place in which the sections are welded together and painted before the entire hull can be floated out to the harbour for finishing and another vessel's development can commence in these grave-like holes in the ground. This construction system has done away with the traditional means of crafting a ship, from the keel up.

For thousands of years, ship construction commenced with the laying of the keel, the spine that runs along the bottom of the hull and from which the vessel's structural ribs would emanate. The placing of the first piece of the keel, whether wood or steel, was always marked by ceremony, for it announced the creation of a new marine entity. This public announcement evoked a woman's declaration that she was pregnant, that a child was forming in her womb. And just as a child's birth was welcomed, so too would the launching of the vessel into the water that would be its home. Later still, the official naming of a ship provided the final chapter in the birthing process, allowing the entity to sail with a personality and character.

Nowadays shipyards like Hyundai have retained the keel-laying ceremony, even if there is no actual keel being emplaced in the dry docks. But symbolism dies hard in the maritime world, so gathering together shipyard workers and new owners remains integral to the construction of a vessel, as does the launching and naming. The number of ceremonies involved in shipbuilding—including the modern addition of celebrating the first piece of steel cut for a new hull—forces Hyundai to maintain a small cadre of people to organize and officiate at these events, and each week there are at least a half-dozen of these rituals taking place throughout the yard.

Today, however, I see nothing but regular shipyard work going on from my vantage point overlooking the site. A slight breeze is blowing from inland, carrying with it the faint smell of fresh paint and burning metal. I ask Lee if air pollution from the yard is a problem here and he shakes his head. "Actually, we have a worse situation with the pollution from China. Especially in summertime, when the wind blows from the northwest. It can make the city very smoggy." Walking down the hillside back to the yards, I hear an electronic song repeating over and over and realize it's Beethoven's "Für Elise." It's like some giant's cell phone going off with one of those annoying ring tones, but it turns out to be the warning alarm for a fabrication shelter that is mounted on rail tracks.

Lee explains, with a grin, "The sound is very distinct and carries well over the noise."

Suddenly my guide grabs my arm and suggests I move aside. A guy wearing a hard hat passes me on a bicycle and stares my way while ringing the bell on his handlebars. A second bell-ringing rider follows him, and then a section of ship comes sailing toward me. It's the bow section of a tanker, its blunt nose rearing ten metres above the ground, while the sweep of its curved sides resembles wings extended outward. Stepping aside, I watch in amazement as this piece of ship slowly trundles past me aboard a tennis court–sized flatbed transporter. These contraptions piggyback their charges around the shipyard, from shed to shed to dry dock, four bicyclists forming an honour guard around them. After the transporter disappears around a corner, Lee takes me to one of his favourite places: the propeller shop.

Stepping inside a long, narrow building, I am surrounded by shimmering golden works of sculpture. Littering the floor of the 150-metre-long shed are at least two dozen finely crafted propellers, the bronze alloy gleaming in the sun filtering through the building. They are as beautiful as anything displayed in the world's great museums, evoking the kinetic sculpture of Constantin Brancusi or Umberto Boccioni's futuristic masterpieces. Each propeller is about 5 metres in diameter, some with four blades, some with five or even six. They arrive here crudely foundered and the forms are placed within circular grinding machines that bevel the blades down, millimetre by millimetre.

Crouching down, I pick up some of the shavings on the otherwise immaculate floor. The corkscrew metal shards are like the springs inside a grandfather clock, brilliant yellow slivers that are delicate and thin, easily breaking apart in my fingers. This sort of naval brass is a concoction of copper and zinc, with aluminum, arsenic and tin added to increase its corrosion resistance while immersed in salt water. And while the shavings are fragile, the finished propellers are anything but; the sculpted forms are steadfast and convey great strength and power. Perhaps because they seem so much like works of art, I'm unsure if I can touch the brassy blades, but Lee Jin assures me that I won't be able to break them, so I gingerly reach out. Unlike the grey steel plates in other sheds, the propellers have a subtle warmth to them, radiating the gentle heat of the sun beaming down upon the blades.

Not far from the propeller shop are three marine engines lying out in the open, awaiting installation in a nearby container ship. These green-painted giants will provide the power to turn one of the propellers crafted nearby, but at present they appear lifeless and forlorn. The container ship in the dry dock also lies dormant, waiting to be awakened and released from her landlocked birthplace. Her name has already been emblazoned across her transom—MSC *Rachelle*—denoting that she will be joining the Mediterranean Shipping Company in the near future.

Standing here, surrounded by a billion dollars' worth of hardware, I can't deny the sheer magnitude of shipbuilding. Lee says that Hyundai alone has something in the region of 15 percent of the market share of worldwide shipbuilding; having launched sixty-four ships in 2004, the company hopes to produce another seventy in 2005. That may not seem like a lot, but the backlog at the yards is over two hundred vessels; that is, Hyundai has that many individual orders that customers are begging for. Between aging fleets, burgeoning economies and new guidelines for safer, more economical ships, yards like this one in Ulsan will be busy for at least another five years.

IN THE HIERARCHY of shipyards, the Koreans take the top spot, followed by the Japanese and then the Chinese. There are few commercial ships built in the West anymore, mainly owing to the costs of labour and materials. HHI produces what might be called the Mercedes or BMWs of ships, finely wrought vessels that are eagerly sought by buyers (as the backlog proves). What Asian builders have managed to do brings to mind something that Joseph Conrad wrote in 1902, in his short story entitled "Youth." While other Europeans of that era took a condescending view of the Far East, the former mariner wrote, "I have known its fascination ... I have seen the mysterious shores, the still water, the lands of brown nations, where a stealthy Nemesis lies in wait, pursues, overtakes so many of the conquering race, who are proud of their wisdom, of their knowledge, of their strength." Conrad knew that hard work would overtake vanity any day.

Once upon a time not so long ago, shipyards from Scandinavia, Germany, France, Britain, America and Canada churned out thousands of vessels in yards scattered throughout these nations. My own birthplace of Canada was once a major shipbuilding nation in its own right: Europeans began building commercial vessels there in 1606. By 1858, nine years before Canada achieved independence from Great Britain, she was sending over five hundred wooden ships down the ways to cross the Atlantic to the mother country. During the Second World War, Canada was delivering a new ship every three days, and by 1945 the nation was the fourth-largest builder of vessels in the world, with yards scattered along her coasts and throughout the Great Lakes.

A century ago, the global predecessor to Ulsan was the northeastern English city of Newcastle. Sitting astride the river Tyne, it became a place of innovation and dominance in the fields of marine engineering and construction. Vessels had been built in this area for hundreds of years, evolving from Viking-style sailers to great wooden-hulled ships and eventually steel beasts. Initially, many of these craft were built to transport Northumbrian coal south to markets in London, but Newcastle's yards also turned out everything from fishing boats to whaling ships to dreadnoughts to passenger liners. In the 1890s, those yards supplied over 40 percent of the world's vessels and were constantly at the forefront of nautical engineering. The first double-hulled cargo vessel was built there in 1844, the first purpose-built oil tanker in 1886, and the first craft powered by a steam turbine engine in 1893 (she was the *Turbinia* and could reach speeds of thirty-four knots). Some of the most beautiful passenger liners to grace the oceans were also born there, including RMS *Lusitania* and her sister,

RMS *Mauretania*. The *Mauretania* would hold the Blue Riband prize for fastest crossing of the Atlantic for twenty years and prompt American president Franklin Delano Roosevelt to say, "She always fascinated me with her graceful yacht-like lines, her four enormous black-banded red pummels and her appearance of power and good breeding. If there was ever a ship which possessed the thing called 'soul,' the *Mauretania* did. Every ship has a soul, but the *Mauretania* had one you could talk to."

In 1905, a year before *Mauretania* was launched, Newcastle's deadliest creations lay in wait just a few hundred kilometres south of Ulsan. The Imperial Japanese Navy had ordered a fleet of modern warships from the British yards, and in late May of that year they were about to test their English steel against an approaching flotilla of Russians. The two nations were bickering over control of Manchuria and Korea, and the conflict came to a head in the Battle of Tsushima, named after the straits the Russians were sailing through en route to Vladivostok. In twenty-four hours, the Japanese used their Geordie-built leviathans to decimate the enemy, sinking twelve Russian ships and forcing the Czarist commander to surrender. The consequences of this victory were far-reaching, leading to a brutal forty-year occupation of Korea by Japan, which was characterized by an almost fanatical desire to wipe out any traces of local culture while systematically stripping the country of its natural resources.

Perhaps the Koreans can take some solace in the fact that Newcastle ceased to be a shipbuilding centre of any importance decades ago. With the exception of the war years, its yards slowly closed, one by one, as demand for its creations waned. Like the workers at so many other traditional shipbuilding communities in the West, Newcastle workers were laid off, their handicrafts vanished and a piece of local culture was vanquished to the realms of county museums, replete with fading photographs and dusty models of marine history.

THE FICKLE NATURE of the shipbuilding business is something that is at the back of the mind of many Korean workers. More than a few I spoke with were aware that the current boom would not last forever. The most common response, though, was a shrug and a "What else can I do?" expression. What the future holds—as well as today's daily grind—becomes clearer to me when I spend yet another day in Ulsan's shipyards. My host this time is Jae Seong, an affable senior manager at the HMD. A nineteen-year veteran of the firm, Jae has developed a distinctiveness honed from several years spent living in New Jersey. This experience gives him the ability to bridge the East and West, so that he will be formal and reserved one moment, and then outspoken and exuberant the next.

HMD is the little brother to the HHI site, less than half the size of its elder sibling. With only four dry docks and about 6600 workers, the Mipo Dockyard concentrates on medium-sized vessels, the workhorses of the business. If HHI turns out the BMWs of shipping, HMD builds the Fords: reliable, functional and nondescript. A couple of kilometres from my hotel and HHI, the HMD yard is tucked into a narrow strip of land with green hills on one side and the busy waters of the mouth of the Taehwagang River on the other. As we drive through the main gates of the dockyard, there are two pure car carriers, or PCCs, heading to and from the nearby Hyundai Exporting Cars Shipping Docks. These odd contraptions are essentially floating boxes within which thousands of automobiles are carried, and they bear little resemblance to normal ships. Built in Ulsan, they will ferry the cars, trucks, vans and buses that we use on land, their Hyundai cargoes ending up in showrooms from Austria to Zambia.

Jae Seong is taking me down to dry dock number two to meet some of the shipwrights working on a 46,000dwt tanker being built for British Petroleum. The keel-laying ceremony for what is currently known as "Hull 0334" was held just three days earlier, but there's already an immense block in place that will house the engine compartment. This dry dock is 308 metres long and 65 metres wide, large enough that four different ships can be undergoing simultaneous construction within its concrete walls. A sign posted on the quay beside Hull 0334 highlights various important dates for the workers, such as when engines are to be installed or mechanical work completed. Hundreds of workers will be committed to completing and delivering a vessel four times the height of the Arc de Triomphe in Paris. The French took thirty years to complete that Napoleonic monument; the Koreans have just six and a half months to do the job.

Jae explains that there is hierarchy among the workers here at the yard. "When they first start, they are considered to be Level Seven. Then, after a few years, they can begin to move up the scale. Only after they have reached the age of forty, though, can they become Level One workers." A select few of these top-tier labourers may also be accorded the accolade of "Master," a purely honorific title but one that carries great prestige. "In this yard we have one Master," Jae says. "Just one. Out of six thousand employees. And I think at the other yard [HHI], they have about thirty or forty, out of about twenty thousand employees. These Masters do not get extra pay or anything, but it is considered a very important personal honour to become one."

At HMD dry dock number two, a gangway is being lowered into place to allow workers to access this first emplaced block of Hull 0334. As it is secured, a supervisor passes me and heads into what looks like a bus shelter—it is really the smoking hut—to rouse a bunch of guys relaxing there. Jae introduces me to the supervisor, a taciturn man named Kim Chung who has been working with Hyundai for twenty years. Kim began as a general labourer—a Class Seven working in the cutting shops—before rising through the ranks to his present role as a quality control supervisor. The quality of the workmanship here is one of the reasons Korea has been able to maintain its dominance in the shipbuilding industry. You can certainly find cheaper yards around the world, but for many of today's commercial ship owners, delivery cost is not as important as long-term costs, where efficiency and durability must be spread over a twenty- or thirty-year period.

"We have contracts here even for Chinese firms," Kim says through my interpreter, "though they could have gone to yards in their own country.

Our reputation is what brings them to Ulsan. We have high standards and work hard to maintain them. It is why we are so busy, right? As well as because of the demand for new vessel construction. I know that this yard will be busy for at least another five years." And after that? "Well, that is hard to say," he answers directly. "You see, this yard began as a ship repair and conversion facility back in 1975. We only began to concentrate on new building ten years ago. So, maybe we will return to more repair work in the future. With the growth of world fleets, there will be many ships in need of maintenance in the future. I think we will remain busy for a long time."

Kim goes on to assure me that the maintenance he speaks of is a normal part of a ship's life, not a reflection of the way they are built in the first place. He is eager to emphasize the level of technical expertise and workmanship that goes into each individual ship. "This is something we are proud of, that everyone here has a part in the building of these vessels. Sometimes it can seem endless, one hull after another. But at the completion there is something you can see, something you have achieved." Kim glances first at the unfinished form of Hull 0334 and then at a nearly completed bulk carrier in the adjacent dry dock. "These are great things, created by men from all over Korea. They are symbols of what we can do."

The symbols that Kim Chung and other Korean shipwrights have crafted rarely return to the place of their birth, so their final departure can be tinged with melancholy. As Kim explains, he still feels something with every vessel that leaves the yard. "You know, sometimes I see a ship that we have built on the television and I remember her. We think of the ship as a 'she'; it is like a woman. And in Korea, when a woman gets married, we use the word 'sending'; you send your daughter away." He struggles to find the words to convey his feelings to this foreigner standing before him. "You see, it is like ... the bride's family loses a member, not that the groom's family gains someone. So, for me, whenever I see the vessel delivered to the ship owner, it is like sending my daughter off to be married."

His moment of candour over, and perhaps a little embarrassed by these private thoughts, Kim hurriedly bows to my guide and me before scurrying aboard Hull 0334 to check on work and earn his keep. On the subject of pay, the shipyard workers in Ulsan are the envy of Koreans. The average worker here makes about U.S.$26,000 a year, more than double the national average. It's the main reason people come from all over the country to get a job with Hyundai, though there are few vacancies. The tradition of spending one's life working for the same firm is still a part of the culture of Koreans, something that has become an anomaly for their Western counterparts. And while Ulsan may be the most prosperous city in the nation, it is also one of the most expensive. A big problem is housing all the workers, their families and everyone else who has flocked to the city in search of a better life.

Ringing the hills that back onto the Mipo Dockyards are domino-like rows of apartment blocks, many put up by Hyundai itself (as shown by the company logo painted on the concrete walls). They are stark utilitarian towers clustered close to each other, crude edifices that remind me of workers' housing I've seen elsewhere. "Those apartment buildings," I say gingerly to my guide, "they seem sort of ... ugly. Like something from—"

"The Soviet Union?" Jae cuts in, with a smile. "Yes, they are not very pretty, are they? But demand for a place is so high here that what other choice is there? Like these ships, they are not built for beauty." One has to wonder what the neighbourhoods around these banal towers will be like in twenty years if the shipbuilding industry doesn't continue.

The many garden plots that one finds scattered throughout Ulsan are an incessant reminder that many of the apartment dwellers come from rural areas. In small pockets of the surrounding hillsides or anywhere else that's not being used for urban development are bits of green space with neatly tended vegetable patches. Thickets of bamboo stand at the edge of many plots in the hills, and after the workday is done it's not uncommon to find shipwrights hoeing and weeding and watering these tokens of a simpler life.

With noon approaching, Jae Seong has a mischievous grin on his face as he asks if I'd like to try some Korean food for lunch. I follow him to a five-storey building resembling a Holiday Inn motel, which stands adjacent to the painting shop. A string of workers make their way up the stairs to the third floor and we join them in a quiet lineup that forms outside two white doors. My guide has taken me to eat with workers at one of the yard's five cafeterias, a place he says that few foreigners bother to visit. While he's telling me this, guys begin jostling in the line, trying to get at the stainless steel sinks to wash the grime off their hands.

At some unseen signal, the doors swing open and I'm caught up in a quickly moving mass of blue denim–clad labourers streaming into the vast lunchroom. Everyone grabs a stainless steel platter, some metal chopsticks and a spoon, and proceeds to the nearest food counter. Hands scramble for some salad, plus a few dollops of meaty stew, and then a woman cafeteria worker drops a piece of smoked fish on each tray. I'm pushed along to heaping bowls of rice and fumble as I try to fill my tray; the guy behind me hesitates only a moment before reaching over me to grab his own spoonful of rice. There's no time to dally when you only get an hour off from building a ship.

A hot bowl of bean curd soup and a fresh orange for dessert round out the menu, after which I search for Jae Seong among the crowd. He's about halfway down a series of long tables that can seat a thousand, waving me to a spot he's found. Fresh bowls of *kimchi*—pickled vegetables that are a national staple in Korea—are laid out at regular intervals on the tables, so I add some to my tray and begin to eat. Around me, workers methodically devour their lunches with little or no conversation. Their faces are grimy, dirty and tired, and most men seem under the age of forty. A television is mounted high on the wall and it suddenly sparks to life with Korean-language programming. Well, it's really Hyundai Shipyard programming, beginning with a little rah-rah-rah motivational stuff: ships cruising the seas, happy workers, Korea's place in the global market. This is followed by a perky female anchor who gives us the day's news. I have no idea what she's saying, though at one point it appears we're being provided with movie reviews of new Hollywood releases. Regardless, few of the workers pay any attention to the broadcast as they chow down.

Within fifteen minutes, another wave of motion begins as workers finish their meals, gather up their trays and head for the other end of the hall. Following their example, I dump fish bones and garbage into buckets and place the dishes on a conveyor belt to be sluiced down before disappearing behind a wall. Continuing to follow the lead of the other workers, I grab a metal glass from an open cupboard and fill it with water from a faucet. It turns out the water's quite warm—I make the mistake of swallowing a gulp—and it's for rinsing your mouth out. Stumbling outside, I follow the stream of now-sated labourers as they make the most of the remaining lunch hour. Clusters of guys sit on benches and chat as they share cigarettes; here and there others recline on patches of grass and grab a quick nap. For once, the daytime din of the shipyard is muted and it's just another lunch break.

ONE PLACE THAT the activity doesn't cease is in the site office of International Andromeda Shipping, a Monaco-based firm that is about to take ownership of a new tanker. The offices occupy two spartan rooms in a low-rise building filled with other foreign shipping firms, and a buzz emanates from the half-dozen men struggling to finish all the paperwork required to get the vessel to sea. She's the MT *Emerald Star,* a 37,000dwt product/chemical tanker (meaning she can carry cargoes such as vegetable oils as well as petroleum) who is just about ready to leave Ulsan and begin her life at sea. I'm supposed to be meeting with Girish Lele, the firm's quality assurance manager, but am told he's aboard the ship, which is docked down at Quay 4. This news comes from a short, stocky man who presides over the offices in an imperious manner.

Silvano Raimond is the site manager for Andromeda here, an older Italian who used to work for the Genoa-based ship classification society Registro Italiano Navale, or RINA. Raimond has darkly dyed hair, which contrasts starkly with the white overalls he wears, and he speaks in a loud, heavily accented voice. At the moment I arrive in the Andromeda offices he is berating a Korean worker, seemingly angry about a screw-up with some engineering documents. As soon as the poor underling leaves, the Italian turns to me and says, "It's always one problem or another, no? These ships, they do not sail themselves."

Raimond does not dislike Koreans—far from it. He's been living here for a year, enjoys exploring the mountains around the city and has only the highest regard for the shipyard and its workers. But make no mistake: He's a hard taskmaster. The day I meet him is exactly two years since Andromeda signed the shipbuilding contract with HMD and only eight months since the first steel was cut for the *Emerald Star*. In that time, he has had to mediate between the owners in Monaco and the shipyard here in Ulsan, as well as deal with the local representatives of Lloyd's Register, who ensure that the vessel conforms to their standards. His cell phone is constantly ringing and I never see him sitting still for more than a moment.

"Tomorrow is the end of it all," Raimond says as he makes some espresso. "*Emerald Star* will undergo last sea trial and then, if is no problems, the final certification and ownership documents will be processed and she can leave immediately for Singapore." He takes a sip of the strong coffee and then grins slyly. "There will be *no* problems."

The spare Andromeda offices resemble those at any construction site, with hand-me-down furniture and, taped to the walls, architectural drawings alongside calendars from equipment suppliers. A fellow Italian, an equally energetic technical superintendent named Nicola Magnasco, joins Raimond. At least twenty years younger than Raimond, Magnasco is currently scowling about some engine repairs being done aboard the *Emerald Star*. A comic opera ensues as the two Italians bellow into cell phones, give lengthy orders to underlings, gesticulate in exasperation, complain loudly to themselves and stomp around the room. It's all a bit melodramatic, more bombastic than mean-spirited. From the looks on the Korean workers' faces, I can tell this is normal behaviour to be endured stoically.

The men a ship owner sends to supervise construction at a yard are all former mariners. They are well-paid troubleshooters, expected to draw upon their professional experiences and smooth out any problems a new vessel may have. The weeks leading up to final delivery of a vessel are perhaps the most intense period in her creation. Her equipment needs to be fine-tuned, a plethora of last-minute installations have to be completed, inspectors must check and re-check everything, and a new crew must become acquainted with the ship. The yard is eager to get her finished and move on to the next project (and receive final payment for the order). The owners are eager to get her to sea and begin making money. Delays of any sort can cost everyone hundreds of thousands of dollars.

At 10:07 the next morning—seven minutes late—the *Emerald Star*'s mooring lines are cast off and she is nudged away from Quay 4 into the brackish waters of Ulsan Harbour. Though she may be a bit tardy in commencing these final sea trials, the entire project is actually about three weeks ahead of schedule. A few days earlier, the official naming ceremony was held for what had previously been known as Hull 0328. A bottle of champagne was broken on her hull after the pronouncement of an age-old encomium: "I name this vessel MT *Emerald Star*. May God bless her and all who sail on her."

The *Emerald Star* is a blunt-nosed, black-hulled ship of 37,000dwt, 182 metres long and 27 metres wide. Her main deck is covered in a latticework of green pipes and tubing needed to load and discharge her fluid cargoes. The rounded prow of the vessel marks her as having icebreaking capabilities. She has no submerged bulbous protrusion extending from the bottom of the hull; instead, her smoothly curved bow can ride up on ice and bring the weight of the vessel down like a hammer. Like all vessels of her class currently being built around the world, the *Emerald Star* also has a double hull that is supposed to decrease the chance of a spill should she flounder.

Sea trials give the shipyard (and the new owners) the opportunity to put a vessel through her paces and confirm that everything operates as it should. Over the course of several days, a vessel will head to open water and undergo a lengthy series of exhaustive tests. She'll be run for hours at top speed to see how the vessel and her engines are performing. Her engines will be shut off once she reaches full speed and stopwatches will record exactly how long it takes for the vessel to come to a complete stop (in the *Emerald Star*'s case, that's about half an hour). She'll have her rudder thrown full over and be put into tight turns to see how fast she can alter course. There will be thousands of assessments done throughout the vessel, with any deficiencies to be repaired at the shipyard's cost.

Technically, the *Emerald Star* completed her sea trials a week ago, but engineers noted a few niggling problems with the main engine, so today is expected to be a somewhat routine event. Things are fairly crowded aboard the tanker, though, as she's carrying two full crews—one from the shipyard and one from the ship owner—as well another dozen inspectors, sub-contractors and engineering specialists. Until the final paperwork goes through, *Emerald Star* is still the responsibility of the Korean crew and their captain. However, since everyone expects no problems with the trials, the Andromeda crew are preparing to take over and getting acquainted with the ship. Some of the Indian crew have only been aboard for a few days; others, like captain-designate Vinay Abrol, have been here for a month.

Captain Abrol is in his early thirties but looks even younger, which may explain why he is wearing his white dress uniform as he stands on the bridge. This is an odd moment for him, as he cannot issue orders or exercise any of the authority that is within the domain of a master mariner. He can't even use his day room yet, as it's still being unpacked. For the time being, Abrol has to content himself with watching as the Hyundai captain takes the *Emerald Star* out into the swells of the East Sea.

Captain Abrol is soon joined by Girish Lele, himself a former captain who now works as a superintendent with Andromeda. A quiet man with a trim moustache and warm smile, he was also born in India but has lived in Monaco for years since coming ashore. Lele is wearing orange work overalls and still bears the hallmarks of the master mariner he once was. His hands are clasped behind his ramrod-straight back while his eyes dart around the bridge and over the control panels. From time to time he will don a pair of glasses slung around his neck and take a closer look at the charts spread out on the navigation table. He carries himself with a quiet dignity that his younger protegé is quickly acquiring. Outside the bridge windows a gentle rain is falling, masking the passing headlands in a misty haze and creating a serene tone to our departure.

The wheelhouse begins to get more crowded now, with crewmen beginning to unpack more equipment and install the stuff. A cordless power drill whines by the starboard wing as a deckhand mounts a computer printer securely to the bulkhead. The second and third officers are organizing the immense library of manuals, regulations and other shipping literature that will fill a bookcase on the port side. A booming voice from the stairwell announces the imminent arrival of Silvano Raimond, whose overall-clad form pops into the bridge with a veritable bounce in his step. He shakes hands with Captain Abrol, says hello to Girish Lele and then spies the Korean captain. "Ah, good morning, Captain, good morning. Nice to meet again," he bellows while striding over to shake his hand. "And how are you today?" Raimond barely lets the man reply before he sees me and orders me over. "Mr. Daniel, buon giorno. Come sta? Please to let me introduce you to Mr. Yu. This is the captain, commander of the ship, Mr. Yu, one of the best captains of the shipyard. Okay, so we are going to have just a little cruise today, yes Captain? Very good. Now I go to find my other colleague, okay? Ciao, ciao …"

The Italian bustles off, leaving Captain Yu and me standing alone. The Korean waits until Raimond has left the bridge before turning to me, cocking an eyebrow and shaking his head as he grins at what just transpired.

By the time we reach our trial area in waters about six nautical miles offshore, the rain has dissipated and the sun is trying to break through the cloud cover. Captain Yu, with Captain Abrol shadowing him, orders the helmsman to come around to course 030 (about northeast). Yu picks up the engine room telephone and after a short conversation he turns to Girish Lele and says, "We are ready." Lele nods and Captain Yu walks to the engine throttles, which he pushes to Full Ahead. On a 37,000dwt tanker, going from Half Ahead to Full Ahead is not that dramatic. The only real change is the motion of waves hitting us broadside as the *Emerald Star* executes the slight turn to port and we're rocked ever so slightly. For the next five hours, the vessel will trace and re-trace a circuit up and down the coast while the engineers monitor the machinery.

On the port side of the wheelhouse, Lele shows me one of *Emerald Star*'s unique pieces of equipment: an onboard system to monitor stress and fatigue in the vessel's hull. "This is something extra that we added at the shipyard," he says. "It is neither standard equipment nor anything currently mandated by IMO [International Maritime Organization] or others. But we think that it will prove very advantageous to us." Lele is referring to a piece of equipment that its English designers call SmartStress. The vessel has been built with a series of sensors running throughout it to check for longitudinal stresses, the type of dynamic strains that occur when the hull bends from the weight of its cargo or the impact of the sea. These sensors relay information to the wheelhouse computer via four white plastic boxes spaced on the main deck forward.

Fine-tuning the software is a company rep named Jim Ellis, who happens to be from Newcastle. He explains that by monitoring the hull twenty-four hours a day and recording the data on the hard drive, it should be possible to see if any structural problems are developing before they turn into something much more serious than a hairline fracture. "With this type of system, the captain can get a real-time look at just what is happening to his vessel's hull. And, of course, many of the sensors are located in places that he couldn't physically visit while at sea, so it's an important tool for him."

This ability of a master to see inside his own vessel comes with a surprisingly low price tag of about U.S.$50,000, which makes me wonder how widespread its use is. "Well, it's actually not that common," says Ellis. "I mean, you'd think it would be when you're spending $20 million or $30 million on a vessel. But I guess some ship owners just don't feel like spending that money up front; they'd rather hope nothing goes wrong for a while." Girish Lele picks up on this. "But no vessel is perfect. No matter how well built and maintained, no matter how much money you spend on its construction, a ship is exposed to tremendous forces and sea conditions. On a tanker like this, the hull stresses are not as significant as on, say, a bulk carrier. Bulk carriers face very dangerous situations and I believe that these sort of monitoring systems should be on all of them. But I am not the IMO."

Eight storeys below the bridge deck, the engineers are well into a series of tests to check the repairs done to the propulsion plant. Nicola Magnasco is presiding over a dozen guys crammed into the tiny control room— Koreans, Indians and a couple of curt Germans. Everyone wants to make sure the trials go smoothly; not only has the *Emerald Star* been equipped with a state-of-the-art stress monitoring system, but she has also been fitted with a new type of engine. Chief engineer Rahul Soman goes to great and patient lengths to detail the workings of this engine and tell me how it does not have a camshaft like traditional power plants. I struggle to keep up with the affable Indian's explanation about "hydraulic booster pumps," "high pressure manifolds" and "fuel pump solenoids," though it's difficult with all the noise being generated by the engine.

What is clear above the din of the 10,000-horsepower engine is the extreme fatigue on the faces of the Korean guys. To make the final tweaks to the *Emerald Star,* they must have been working hard. One guy is bent over the main control panel with his head in his hands, his eyes bleary and tired; another is slumped on the floor in the corner, catching a quick nap.

When Magnasco takes exception to something on one of the monitors, his Korean counterpart actually begins to argue with him, an almost unheard-of thing that even takes the Italian aback. Chief Soman winks at me and makes the OK gesture with his fingers. Tempers are frayed, nerves are on edge, but everything will be fine.

Heading back up to the bridge, I stop on Deck C and realize that this ship seems different. I've never seen a vessel so new—she still has "new ship" smell to her—but there's something else about the *Emerald Star* that's distinctive. There's a busyness aboard her, to be sure, but without the energy I would expect on a working voyage. It's more like moving day in an apartment building; people are still unpacking stuff, getting acquainted with things and preparing to start the serious business tomorrow, while others are moving out and saying goodbye. There's a sense of anticipation lingering about her.

Rounding a fisherman's homemade buoy, Captain Yu orders the helmsman to make for port: The sea trials are over and everyone seems pleased with things. The Korean master and Captain Abrol are deep in conversation and it's obvious that a subtle change is occurring; one man is relinquishing command and another is taking over. Even the Indian's body language is different and he no longer looks quite so young and ineffectual. Outside on the port wing, Silvano Raimond stands alone and—for once—quiet, staring at the *Emerald Star*'s main deck with a muted smile on his face. Girish Lele has doffed his overalls and stands by the chart table, beaming to himself as we re-enter Ulsan Harbour.

Emerald Star will not be returning to her former dockside home, not this time, not for a long time. Instead, she anchors in the outer harbour so that a launch can take her visitors ashore. Briefcases, laptops, backpacks and paperwork are gathered up and everyone heads to the Jacob's ladder on the starboard side, amidships. Named after the ladder Jacob dreamed would stretch from Heaven to Earth, it's a precarious device we're to descend to reach the tiny boat that bobs in the water beneath us. As the line of visitors leaves his ship, Captain Vinay Abrol wishes each a pleasant goodbye. Shaking hands with the man, I congratulate him on his new command and hope he and his crew enjoy a fair wind at all times.

Dropping onto the shipyard launch, I am overpowered by the wall of steel that is *Emerald Star*. With no cargo in her holds, she is riding high in the water, an imposing visage that will likely never again seem quite so immaculate. As the final passenger boards, the launch quickly veers away from the tanker and back toward the Hyundai Dockyard. Silvano Raimond, the idiosyncratic and seemingly crusty Italian, stares at the *Emerald Star* for a long time as she recedes from our view. His gaze is resolute and a smile curls at the edges of his lips. After several minutes, he turns to me.

"You know, this is a hard moment. You seek the truth about the ship, yes? Well, I will tell you right now that all new ships they have a soul and it is transmitted by people like me. I have surveyed at construction sixty-three new ships, *Emerald Star* included, and every time I feel that a part of my life is going with the ship to explore seas and countries. For me, the ship she is like a daughter and when she depart from shipyard always I have a big pain in the heart and always tears drop. The ship goes with a part of my soul. This is my feeling."

Without realizing that he'd mirrored the words of a Korean shipwright, Raimond takes a long last look at the tanker and then turns his face away from her, and from me.

3

OWNERS

Few rich men own their property.
The property owns them.

—ROBERT INGERSOLL, "GOLD SPEECH"

To most people, Monaco is synonymous with fabulous wealth, a jet-setting royal family, movie stars and elegant casinos, all encased within a magnificent setting on the Côte d'Azur. However there is a serious side to this tiny enclave perched precariously on the Mediterranean Sea. In spite of its harbours being crowded, not with cargo vessels, but rather, with expensive yachts and high-end sailboats, Monaco is an important centre in the shipping industry. This is because of the large number of firms based here—firms that operate thousands of vessels worldwide. One of these, International Andromeda Shipping, is the new owner of the tanker *Emerald Star* that I sailed upon in Korea as she finished her sea trials. Through Andromeda's quality assurance manager, Girish Lele, I have been invited to enter the rarefied world of ship owners, a somewhat secretive and elusive domain.

And so on a warm morning, by cautiously winding my way from France to Monaco, I take my first steps into the realm of those who own and operate sea-going vessels. For the uninitiated, this involves nothing more than crossing the street: With no border guards or customs check-points here, one quickly realizes that Monaco is a unique entity. Having successfully made it from one side of the Avenue des Guelfes to the other, I find that it's quiet here at this time of the year; the tourists have gone home, and without a Grand Prix or award show in sight, the locals have the place pretty much to themselves again.

The Principality, as it is properly known, occupies less than a square mile of rocky shore, surrounded by France on one side and the Mediterranean on the other. Unlike in Beverly Hills, the wealth displayed here is far more refined and restrained, perhaps the result of seven hundred years of practice. There are only about thirty-three thousand people living in Monaco proper, and of these a scant five thousand can call themselves true Monégasques. (Unless you marry a Monégasque, your family must have lived here for at least three generations before you can even consider applying for citizenship.) The rest are mostly Italian and French businesspeople, along with the ubiquitous supermodels, aging actors and other celebrities. All are attracted by Monaco's elegance, fine weather and tax-free status. It is also the safest city in the world, owing to inconspicuously placed video cameras positioned everywhere and a high number of very visible police officers.

To most people Monaco is Monte Carlo, though this is just one part of the city. I'm currently wandering the streets of Fontvieille, the west end of the Principality, in search of the headquarters of International Andromeda Shipping and one of its owners, Giangiacomo Serena. Although I'd been told that it's virtually impossible to get lost in Monaco—it's just too small—it still takes me a while to find the Gildo Pastor Center, where the firm is based. That's because everything is so discreet here; when I finally ask someone for directions, he points at the plain-looking office block behind me, the one I've passed at least three times.

International Andromeda is engaged in what most people think defines modern shipping: the operation of tankers for the international markets. Though other types of vessels are more plentiful on the seas—such as passenger vessels and bulk carriers—tankers are fixed within the public consciousness, often because of the headlines created when oil spills from a sinking vessel. Yet these leviathans quietly go about their thankless task of supplying us with the energy to propel everything from our cars to our factories. Our appetites for their cargoes are insatiable and, somewhat surprisingly, there aren't as many oil tankers plying the oceans to fulfill this demand as we might think. They number 5500 in all, but only about 3700 of the large ones would we associate with the term "oil tanker."

I know little about the way international commerce operates beyond what I can glean from periodically scanning a newspaper's business section. I've tried to educate myself as to how one puts together millions upon millions of dollars in financing to build and operate an ocean-going vessel, but it still seems like voodoo economics to me. Not the "why" of ship owning—*that* I can understand (there's potentially a lot of money to be made here, though the risks are high). What has perplexed me is whether it's possible to have anything more than a cold fiduciary relationship with the industry's assets—the ships that ply the seas.

Inside the Gildo Pastor Center a lone security guard sits idly behind his desk; off to the side is a room with a bank of video monitors providing even more security for the denizens of the building. There's a plaque on one wall pronouncing that His Serene Highness Prince Rainier III (the one who was married to Grace Kelly) had officiated at the building's opening, but the rest of the foyer is neutral in tone. Exiting the elevator several floors up, I search for the reception area of International Andromeda, which a very small sign denotes; there's nothing brash and flashy going on here. The door is locked and it takes me a moment to realize I have to be buzzed in past yet another barrier, but once I'm inside, a smiling receptionist leads me to the boardroom, asks if I'd like a coffee and then leaves me to await my meeting with Giangiacomo Serena.

A large glass table surrounded by eight comfortable chairs dominates the boardroom, with a framed map of Africa the only decoration on the walls. I sense that idle conversation is not something that goes on here; this is a place of business and decision-making. I know that International Andromeda has been in the tanker business for a decade now (a relative newcomer by shipping standards), having started as a brokerage buying and selling oil on the world market. The tanker business is a dangerous endeavour—not just because of the cargoes carried but also because of the cutthroat nature of big business—and I'm not quite sure what Serena will be like. To be honest, I've never really sat down with a titan of industry to chat about his world, least of all one who is continuing a tradition that goes back millennia.

THROUGHOUT HISTORY, ship owners have taken on many guises. There have been those who operated enterprises with hundreds of vessels, men like Samuel Cunard, the Canadian-born shipping magnate whose name still lives on today, with passenger liners such as the *Queen Mary 2* and *Queen Elizabeth 2*. There have been individuals who were both owners and captains, such as Joshua Slocum, maintaining a single vessel that had to find cargoes and customers to keep afloat. There have been the outlaws, such as pirates, who could have one, two or even a fleet of vessels under their control. And there have even been entire civilizations whose very existence depended on owning and operating ships at sea.

One very good example of the latter was the Vikings. Vessels were paramount to their culture, both symbolically and practically. While the

Vikings did use horses to move around, it was long boats that truly defined these various Northern peoples, the ancestors of the present-day Scandinavians. According to the thirteenth-century "Edda," written by the Icelander Snorri Sturluson, six wonderful objects were made for the gods, one of the most important being *Skídbladnir,* a magical ship crafted for the god Frey, a ship that was a symbol of wealth. "Frey is the most noble of the *æsir* (gods)," Sturluson wrote. "He rules over the rain and sunshine and with that the growth of the earth, and it is good to call on him for prosperity and peace. He also rules over the wealth of men." Frey's father was Njörd, who ruled the wind and the water; so, taken together, you have the god of the sea and the god of commerce in one family, an apt combination for a seafaring people.

But the Vikings seem to have been singled out somewhat unnecessarily as mere brutes and marauders when they actually brought culture and prosperity to a chaotic landscape, creating a trading region that surpassed Rome's and would not be equalled until the advent of the European Union in the late twentieth century. For three centuries, from about AD 790 to 1066, these Norse people ranged across three continents, bringing silver from Baghdad to Sweden, settlers from Iceland to Canada, slaves from Russia to Norway and the rule of law from Denmark to England. And they did it using their ships.

The Vikings learned to craft superb sea-going vessels, some over a hundred feet long, which had the ability to absorb wave energy as they sailed owing to their unique design and clinker-built construction (with the wooden planks overlapping each other). A single square-sail and rows of oars on each side allowed the long boats to be propelled in virtually any weather. Viking shipwrights carved ornate designs on the hardy vessels and fashioned a single steering oar on the sternmost right, or steerboard, side (from which the term "starboard" derives).

A hundred individuals could be carried in the largest long ships, recruited by chieftains, or *jarls,* to journey in search of riches. Their *drakkars,* or dragon boats, and cargo-carrying *knorrs* and *karvs* ventured down the Volga and Dnieper Rivers to the Black Sea, up the Norwegian coast to the White Sea, through the Straits of Gibraltar and across the Mediterranean to the Levant, and over the Atlantic to Greenland and Newfoundland.

The Viking chieftains who sent these ships forth were certainly powerful. They made their own rules, managed a trading empire with ruthless efficiency against both enemies and other Norse competitors, and seized upon the vacuum created by the decline of the Roman Empire to establish ports, shipbuilding centres, supply outposts and new markets for goods. What is rarely remembered is that the Vikings possessed a ship-owning class that was unparalleled in Europe at the time. The most successful chieftains were often ship owners, and on their deaths they would sometimes be cremated with their vessels, the souls of the *jarls* flying with the flames to Valhalla.

From one perspective, the marriage of the Vikings' skills as master mariners and their cunning business acumen would make any modern ship owner envious. Using standardized vessel designs, regular shipping routes, experienced captains, and cheap and eager crews, the Vikings created the most far-ranging mercantile economy based on the oceans yet seen anywhere. Though other seafaring communities did trade among the Pacific Islands, their impact was not as dramatic as the Vikings' in Europe; and in other cultures—such as China—it was land-borne trade routes that had a bigger economic influence. With the demise of the Norse (some say owing to their conversion to Christianity), it would be another five hundred years before international shipping regained its aura and almost a millennium before its global importance would be unsurpassed, if somewhat overlooked.

Today, shipping has reclaimed that aura and become even more important for us than it was for the Vikings. Along the way, it has also become one of the most secretive businesses around. International ship owners inhabit a rarefied world of high-stakes business with hundreds of billions of dollars in assets, employing millions of people and effectively binding the global economy together. To say they are cautious of outsiders is an understatement. Shipping has been called the most opaque industry on the planet.

There are a number of obvious reasons for this secrecy. To begin with, commercial shipping is a highly competitive business with relatively small fleets in comparison to, say, the trucking or rail industries; there are about 5500 tankers, 5800 bulk carriers and 3300 container ships all competing for customers on a daily basis. Secondly, the majority of shipping firms are privately held companies, obviating the need for public scrutiny of their dealings or accountability to shareholders. Then there is the existing level of interest shipping firms face from various international, national and regional bodies; ships, owners and crews already have to deal with customs agents, immigration officials, regulatory agencies, coast guards, navies, safety inspectors and a slew of others on an ongoing basis.

Finally, and perhaps most importantly, shipping is such a risky and dangerous endeavour to begin with that many owners are more than happy to avoid the limelight. Given the mariners lost at sea, the ships that sink each year and the environmental damage that can occur, it's only natural to maintain a low profile and go about one's business quietly.

GIANGIACOMO SERENA, co-owner of International Andromeda Shipping, slips into the boardroom while I'm gazing out the windows; I don't even notice his arrival until he calls out my name and shakes my hand. He is dressed in an immaculate navy blue suit and pin-striped shirt without a tie, sporting an expensive watch on his left wrist. Serena is tanned and fit with pale blond hair combed back and very perceptive eyes that dart about the room as he chats. But when his gaze settles on me, I find it thoughtful and honest. Though he's a newcomer to shipping, he still maintains the mariner's tradition of being reserved when first meeting someone new, checking me out much as I am doing with him. Additionally, he embodies the traits every good business executive should have; he ponders my questions and chooses his words carefully before answering in his soft Italian accent.

Serena got into the shipping business rather by accident. "Our firm began in the oil trading business in the late 1980s, chartering vessels for contracts to ship crude from the Black Sea to the Middle East," he says. When I raise my eyebrows at this—shipping oil to the Middle East—he explains that countries like Israel cannot buy crude from the major producers in the region (such as Saudi Arabia and Iran) because of the religious politics involved. Instead, they have to find more amenable sellers, and "countries like Russia and others in the Black Sea and Caspian areas were willing to do so, but did not have the tanker capacity to deliver. So we saw a market potential and soon began to charter vessels, sometimes up to twenty-five at times."

By 1992 the firm decided to purchase three older vessels, as the price was right, and by 1995 the Italians decided to set up their own shipping company here in Monaco. When I ask why they chose Monaco, Serena leans back and smiles. "Well, Monaco was an obvious choice, not only because it is a, let's say, tax-free haven, but because there is a culture of shipping with many, many ship owners and we could find all the people needed to run things. You see, we didn't have a family culture of shipping here in the firm. No one was in this business before us. Shipping is an asset business as opposed to trading, which is a service business. So it was new and we needed to be surrounded by the best. And this fit with our business plan, which is to be known as a small, first-class firm."

As well, from a purely economic perspective it made a lot of sense for Andromeda to quit the chartering business in the early 1990s. "Costs to purchase were good back then," the ship owner tells me, "so instead of paying a freight charge, we paid a bank loan. We thought it would take five years to pay back the loan on our first purchase, but the market was so good it was paid back in three. So it was a simple decision because, as a business, income and profit are what is most important."

Of course what Serena doesn't say is that there was also a bit of luck working for them back then. If all it takes to become wealthy is to buy a vessel, then there would be many more ship owners around than there are.

When Andromeda entered the tanker market, they found themselves in the right place at the right time. The global economy was booming, and the demand for oil and gas was increasing at a record pace. But there were only so many ships on hand for purchase or lease. Those who had already entered into deals, like Andromeda, quickly found the demand for vessels increasing beyond the supply available; Serena's firm began to charter its tankers to other companies, switching from being energy brokers to ship owners. Simply put, they could charge more for their ships; ten years ago one could buy a tanker for about U.S.$15 million and charge $10,000 a day to charter it out. Today, that same vessel should be making well over $50,000 a day. If one deducts the downtime a ship needs for repairs and maintenance, that's still some $15 million in annual income from one vessel.

"Ah, but it is not as easy as it sounds," my host continues. "Although many people do not think so, this is one of the most highly regulated businesses. Oil is something delicate. Not dangerous, but delicate. We're not transporting grain—if that spills, you only make the fish happy. To be a ship owner involves great responsibility. And for me, that means I wanted to know about these vessels because I started to really be attracted by this new business. Attracted because I liked the concept of transporting, from A to Z, from technical to crewing. So I really started to go on board these old vessels."

Serena goes on to tell me that just a week earlier he was in Singapore inspecting a vessel undergoing refit and spent hours crawling around the tanker's darkest recesses to get a first-hand perspective on things. I find this intriguing, that the head of a shipping firm would take such a hands-on approach, and I ask about the appeal of getting grimy and dirty within an oil tanker's innards.

Giangiacomo Serena thinks about this for a moment, sitting in front of me in his bespoke suit while staring at the map of Africa on the wall beside him. Then he turns and fixes that gaze of his on me. "Magic. It's magic, that's why I like ships. It's a drama, too. But I tell you more: I have been sailing, racing—I've done transatlantic races before I started the trading—and the sea is something that belongs to my heart. Yes, it is a business and we must, of course, make a profit. But it is also a passion. If you decide to be a ship owner, you must *be* a ship owner. You cannot stay on land, at your office. To me, to be a ship owner is not about the power of the money. It's about the knowledge of the ship."

His statement is a bit of a surprise to me, the first hint at anything vaguely romantic about ships that he's said. If there's anyone I would expect to shrug off notions of romance in the sea, it is a ship owner with his huge financial investments. But this is another example of the differences between those who make their livelihoods from the sea and those who depend on dry land for their fortunes. Looking at the captains of industry, one often sees cabals and cartels seeking to maximize their sources of income with a zealousness that can turn dark. The robber barons made their names by controlling timber, rubber, bananas, diamonds, oil, steel and even railroads. Yes, I'm sure many of them sat around in their boardrooms talking excitedly about the prospects of exploiting Indonesia, Rhodesia or the Congo, but "passion"? Of that I'm skeptical.

To be certain, the shipping industry is not made up of emotional characters clutching dreamy notions of the sea close to their hearts. It is, as has been made amply clear, a hard, cold business on one level. And there are groups of shipping companies that function as de facto cartels, trying to regulate their markets as best they can. But even at the top there is something different about the way the industry operates, a sense of independence and individuality spawned by the uncontrollable nature of the sea. No one can stop a ship from sailing from point A to point B, though many have tried. In two world wars, the German navy encircled tiny Britain, attempting to starve the island nation into defeat. A decade ago, during the embargo against Saddam Hussein's Iraq and when the might of the American navy was arrayed throughout the Persian Gulf, ships were still able to smuggle goods in and out of the Khawr 'Abd Allah near the port of Umm Qasr. Each time the attempts failed, for the oceans are just too big, something that many of us still cannot fathom.

The quality of independence imbues ship owners. Though countless regulations and laws oversee their business, as Giangiacomo Serena told me, there have always been individual owners not content to let someone else rule over them. Why should they? The oceans appear to be among the few, if not the only, venues in which commerce can reign unfettered by legal restrictions. In the middle of the Pacific Ocean there is little chance of encountering some bureaucratic functionary intent on enforcing a committee's dictates.

"But this is not quite correct," Serena tells me. "You need to respect the sea and to understand the limits that you have, because something will always go wrong out there and someone is always watching us. And we are watching ourselves, too. It is true that we [ship owners] have our clubs, but we are not all in the same club. Most of us—I think—are responsible and correct in our business dealings, because it serves our bottom line. I will agree that there are those who are … less … proper in their work." He stares out the window and his mood darkens. While rapping his fingers on the glass table he continues, "And … from one side, yes, it angers me. Because I don't see the professionality needed, but I see only to try and grab the last penny. Secondly, they ruin the reputation of the ship owners, especially with the older vessels. It was and it *is* upsetting to me. We are in the newspaper only when there is pollution. So we are always looked at as someone—an industry—that is doing bad things. Nobody realizes what we are really doing. I would never do something that put at risk what we are doing or who we employ."

WHAT SERENA IS REFERRING TO is the headline-grabbing events of sinkings, injuries, deaths, spillages and shoddy management. As with any endeavour, it's the actions of a few bad apples that have sullied the reputation of an entire group. It is something that causes many in the industry a great deal of grief—and adds to the sense of protection they feel when outsiders like me come around. It is the dark side of merchant shipping, where the malevolent power of certain owners rears its ugly head and controls the lives of mariners.

Sending an individual to sea is to ask that person to risk his life for a paycheque. With the knowledge that the sea is unmerciful, a sailor has every right to expect the best possible training and equipment with which to carry out his duties. And for the majority of seafarers—and ship owners—this is the way things are done. But the desire to cut corners and squeeze a little more profit from the coffers is an indelible part of us, with commercial shipping being no different. For the last fifty years, the biggest issue this has created is shifting the registry of ships from traditional First World maritime nations to places with less stringent regulations, usually in the Third World. The concern about flags of convenience, or FOCs, as they're commonly referred to, cuts to the core of two of the things that define the business: independence and profitability. The situation has created antagonism among owners, operators, unions, non-governmental organizations and international regulatory bodies. It is not something new, but it has become something that could change the way merchant shipping operates in this century.

To understand this issue you need to know that every commercial vessel that sets out upon the waves of the globe must have a land-bound home, a mailing address, if you will. This is one of the unique things about shipping, going back hundreds of years: Somewhere in our collective consciousness, we just *knew* that a ship had to have a home, that she could not be an orphan upon the seas. So it is that every vessel has a national ensign on its flagpole, and a home port emblazoned on its stern and duly registered in its paperwork, there for all to see. Traditionally this was the port and nation from which the ship operated on a regular basis, though there have been instances throughout maritime history of vessels being "re-flagged." Prior to the United States entering the Second World War in late 1941, a number of its merchant ships were re-flagged to other nations in order to circumvent American neutrality laws and assist Great Britain.

The predicament today is how much it costs for the honour of painting a port's name on a ship. Some nations charge higher rates for ships to fly their flag than others do, so it is only natural that some owners will switch their vessels' registry to other, more inexpensive locales. As well, different nations have different standards of safety, maintenance, crewing and operating, all of which can affect the financial bottom line. A hundred years ago, the top maritime nations—by flag registry—were Great Britain, Germany, the United States and France, with the British accounting for over half the world's tonnage. By the 1950s, Germany and France were no longer at the top of the list, and Britain and America were faced with a most unlikely competitor: the Republic of Panama.

Tiny Panama retains, to this day, the distinction of being the most widely used registry on the planet, followed by wartorn Liberia in West Africa. By offering more favourable (read "lower") taxation rates and standards of operation, these flags-of-convenience nations (also called "open registers") have attracted the bulk of the world's shipping fleets. Some other notable maritime flags seen flying from merchant vessels today include those of Tonga, Malta, Cambodia, the Isle of Man and the French Antarctic Territory (which is "populated" by about 145 researchers). A vessel need not even visit the nation where it is registered; Liberia's registration office operates from rural Virginia, and more than once I've spied a ship with "La Paz" emblazoned on its stern and wondered at the irony of landlocked Bolivia being a maritime nation.

Amusement aside, though, the issue of FOCs is dead serious. According to Lloyd's Register's World Casualty Statistics sheet for 2001, the worst three nations for ships lost at sea were Panama, Cyprus and St. Vincent & the Grenadines (all considered FOC nations), with thirty-two vessels weighing a combined 317,063 gross tonnes sunk to the bottom of the ocean. But in the strictest sense, those lost ships were not really Panamanian, Cypriot or Caribbean, for these are not places with large economies. Instead, the vessels were really operating on behalf of powerful nations, often hidden by a maze of paperwork and numbered companies. And what are the true nationalities of the ships that today fly FOCs? Well, that top-ten list includes the United States, Great Britain, Hong Kong, Japan, Germany and Saudi Arabia.

The International Transport Workers' Federation, or ITF, has been battling this issue since 1948, trying to peel back the veils of secrecy with varying degrees of success. Their concern is for the safety and well-being of mariners employed on vessels using FOCs, tens of thousands of whom endure substandard working conditions and poor pay. The ITF has created a network of inspectors based in over forty countries around the world to help seafarers in need of assistance, and in 2002 alone the federation helped win back U.S.$31 million in pay and benefits owed to mariners by unscrupulous owners, many of whom used the open registries of flags-of-convenience countries.

It must be said that not all registries are bad; they merely provide a basic level of regulation that any owner is free to improve upon. A ship owner can decide to maintain only the basic level of safety and mainte-nance as decreed by the flag registries, or go beyond the official rules and put more money into his vessels.

One of the more notorious locations for FOC registries is the Bahamas, which operates the third-largest fleet by tonnage in the world. Many of the owners of these vessels are numbered companies maintaining nothing more than a mailing address, or post box, while the real owners reside elsewhere. While visiting with designer Antony Prince in Nassau, I took time to visit with representatives of a "real" Bahamian shipping firm to gauge how they felt about some of their compatriots. Kamanna Valluri, the managing director of Dockendale Shipping, invited me into his spacious corner office on the third floor of a modern low-rise south of downtown Nassau to explain that his firm operates thirty-eight ships worldwide under the strictest protocols. When I brought up the issue of FOCs, Valluri became animated.

"In our case, it is not a flag of convenience because we are not a PO box number company. We are based here, the company is based here, we are operating the ships from here and we are maintaining in the best possible way the ships. Other companies are post box numbers, you can call them flag-of-convenience companies. They are only working substandard ships in the Bahamas and they bother us because our name gets associated with them. We try to maintain our ships in the best possible way—all our ships are ITF certified, paying ITF wages, according to ITF rules."

Like Giangiacomo Serena in Monaco, Kamanna Valluri is obviously stung by the negative publicity generated by other ship owners taking advantage of FOC rules. For instance, a few years ago there was a minor fuss in Canada when journalists discovered the shipping firm CSL International operated its vessels under foreign flags, including that of the Bahamas. What attracted so much attention is that CSL International is a unit of the CSL Group (which also includes domestic carrier Canada Steamship Lines) and the head of the firm from 1981 to 2003 was Paul Martin, the country's federal finance minister for much of the 1990s and, later, the prime minister. It was even reported that the bulk carrier *Sheila Ann,* named for the prime minister's wife, was registered in the Bahamas, not in Canada. But like Andromeda Shipping, CSL International was merely trying to remain "competitive" in an aggressive marketplace. Eventually the brouhaha faded; CSL International's fleet was—and remains—fairly well maintained and adequately crewed, albeit with foreign mariners making less than their Canadian counterparts. And given the high-profile status of Mr. Martin, it might be said the company understood the need for a degree of good governance in its daily operations.

However, FOCs are not the only thing ship owners must deal with when operating vessels. There are also the insurance companies and ship classification societies that underwrite these giants. To make an analogy, anyone can walk into a used car dealership and purchase a vehicle. But then you have to get the licence plates and insurance before wheeling down the street. Which insurance company you go with, how carefully you service the car and how safely you drive it on the road—these are all your decisions. The same applies to modern-day shipping. After purchasing a ship—whether it be new or used—a ship owner must first have it surveyed by one of a number of classification societies, the most famous of which are the Lloyd's Register (LR Group), Det Norske Veritas (DNV) and the American Bureau of Shipping (ABS). Finally, you need maritime insurance before the behemoth can cast off her lines. And just as standards of quality vary among FOC nations, so too do classifiers and insurers differ in the service they provide.

Taken together, registrars, classifiers, insurers, regulatory agencies and trade unions ought to be able to provide sufficient pressure on ship owners to maintain high standards. But with over 142,000,000 square miles of ocean surface covering the planet, a dozen, a hundred or even a thousand substandard vessels can easily hide from the authorities. This has led to several dramatic cases in which less-than-scrupulous owners have crossed the line from legal enterprises into criminal activities. One of the most notorious events in recent times was the bizarre final voyage of a Panamanian-flagged general cargo vessel called the *Kobe Queen I.*

The *Kobe Queen I* was a rust bucket of a ship built in 1976 and displacing 18,500dwt, less than half the size of the *Emerald Star.* In the summer of 1999 she was being operated by a shadowy shipping firm based in Odessa, with a crew of twenty-five Ukrainian sailors under the command of Captain Yuri Levkovsky. That July, the *Kobe Queen* loaded a cargo of 15,000 tonnes of steel in Istanbul (worth over U.S.$5 million), and was bound for the Caribbean with a stop in Senegal along the way. But sometime after leaving Turkish waters, the crew received new orders from Odessa, and the vessel began an erratic and elusive journey through the Mediterranean and around West Africa. A few weeks later, she made port in Dakar, Senegal, and 2000 tonnes of the steel were quickly sold before the ship headed out to sea once more. By now, several interested parties—

such as the owners of the cargo—were getting concerned about the where-abouts of the ship and attempted to contact Levkovsky and the owners, none of whom bothered to respond. Apparently the *Kobe Queen* had disappeared off the map, hijacked by her own crew.

The maritime equivalent of a fugitive manhunt soon began, with word sent out worldwide to port authorities, shipping agents, law enforcement agencies and others to find the *Kobe Queen*. Among those notified was Lloyd's Register (not to be confused with Lloyd's of London, which is an insurance company). Lloyd's has a network of agents in ports around the world and told these "ship spotters" that the *Kobe Queen* was now a wanted vessel with a $100,000 reward posted for information leading to her arrest and the recovery of the cargo. Throughout September and October, these spotters caught glimpses of the phantom ship, first in Cape Verde, then off Nigeria. They noticed that she had a new name painted on her transom—the *Gloria Kopp*—and was making for the Cape of Good Hope.

For two months, the *Kobe Queen*/*Gloria Kopp* wandered the South Atlantic and Indian Oceans while her mysterious owners tried to figure out what to do with the remaining cargo. Rumours of Russian Mafia or drug smugglers being involved in the case began to swirl in some quarters, but all anyone knew was that the ship owners themselves had also disappeared, leaving only an empty office in Odessa. Finally, on Christmas Eve of 1999, a Lloyd's agent in the southeastern Indian city of Chennai reported that the ship was anchored six miles offshore, and the Indian Coast Guard dispatched the patrol boat *Vikram* to intercept her. As the *Vikram* came into sight, Captain Levkovsky ordered his crew to weigh anchor and get underway as quickly as possible, intending to make for the safety of international waters in the Bay of Bengal.

While a storm erupted overhead, the coast guard boat battled through heavy winds and high seas to get within hailing range of the *Kobe Queen* and order her to stop engines. When her captain refused, the *Vikram* brought her 30mm cannon to bear and fired rounds across the bow of the cargo ship while preparing an armed boarding party to deploy. The *Kobe Queen* continued steaming at full speed until more cannon fire finally convinced Levkovsky to heave to and the coast guardsmen clambered aboard his ship, whereupon the Ukrainian crew put up a short fight before surrendering. As the prisoners were lined up on the rain-swept deck, noticeably missing was Captain Levkovsky, who had retreated to his cabin. When the Indian sailors finally broke down his door, they found the master dead: He had hanged himself with a nylon rope. The *Kobe Queen's* owners were never heard from again.

This was, of course, an isolated incident, and lest one think it means to paint all ship owners in a dark light, consider another recent event in which a ship owner—and one of his crews—defied another nation's armed warships. In late August of 2001, the Norwegian container vessel *Tampa* was bound from Fremantle, Australia, to Singapore and was cruising off the west coast of Indonesia when her master, Captain Arne Rinnan, received a call from Australian Search and Rescue about a vessel in distress. The *Tampa* made its way to the reported location and found a twenty-metre-long wooden boat named the *Palapa* crammed with over 400 Afghan refugees. The *Palapa* was wallowing in heavy swells and Captain Rinnan believed it would sink at any moment. After notifying the container ship's owners in Lysaker, Norway, he ordered his crew to help the boat people aboard the *Tampa* and give them blankets and food. With 438 passengers on his ship, including pregnant women and young children, Rinnan headed for nearby Christmas Island, an Australian territory where he figured the passengers could be put ashore and cared for. Little did he know what awaited him there.

When the *Tampa* arrived off Christmas Island, Captain Rinnan was told not to enter Australian waters but to remain offshore. Mystified, he did so for two days while radioing repeated requests for medical and food supplies, all of which were ignored. When several boats eventually made their way from the island to the ship, the Norwegians found armed members of the Australian Army's elite SAS commando unit boarding their vessel. As if that weren't enough, a couple of naval vessels took up position near the *Tampa* with their guns at the ready to prevent anyone from going ashore.

It quickly became clear that Australia had no interest in accepting the refugees and hoped that the *Tampa* would sail off to some other country, possibly Indonesia—anywhere but Christmas Island. As the Afghans began to suffer from dehydration, fatigue and exhaustion, they became more agitated at their plight. So, too, were the *Tampa's* owners in suburban Oslo; Wilh. Wilhelmsen ASA knew the container ship was unequipped to care properly for the Afghans and asked the Norwegian government to pressure the Australians to resolve the standoff. The owners' concerns were for the safety and well-being of the refugees, and reflected the company's commit-ment to humanitarian concerns. (Since 1977, the company's ships have helped more than 1300 people in need of assistance.)

Eventually, as international pressure mounted, the Australian govern-ment relieved Captain Rinnan and his crew of the Afghans. The refugees were promptly sent to the remote South Pacific nation of Nauru while the *Tampa* was allowed to continue on its way. For their heroic efforts in saving the Afghans and standing up to the Australians, Captain Arne Rinnan, his crew and the ship owners were later presented with the Nansen Refugee Award by the head of the United Nations' High Commission for Refugees. (Some of the refugees eventually settled in New Zealand and a select few were allowed into Australia. The plight of the rest seems lost and forgotten.)

With enough ship owners willing to risk the lives of their mariners, their vessels and their cargoes, the issue has been the impetus for count-less high-level meetings between leaders of industry and those who keep an eye on them. It's one of the reasons that all single-hulled oil tankers are currently being phased out of operation, replaced by a new generation of double-hulled vessels built to much higher standards. And in the aftermath of the terrorist attacks of September 11, 2001, a variety of governments are taking a much closer look at just who are the real owners of the leviathans bringing such strategic supplies as crude oil to the heartlands of the West.

It's a little ironic that it took a terrorist attack by passenger jets on office towers to finally focus government attention on the shipping industry. But the libertarian freedom of the seas may finally be coming to a close, or at least coming under a higher degree of global control. There have been far too many incidents involving sea-going vessels for the public to ignore, especially given the prevalence of televised images when something bad happens. From the sinking of the tanker *Torrey Canyon* off southwestern England in 1967 to the *Exxon Valdez* disaster off Alaska in 1989 to the loss of the M/V *Prestige* off Spain in 2002, awareness of the environmental impact of shipping has increased. The plight of seafarers working on substandard FOC vessels remains less well known. David Cockroft, the ITF general secretary, wrote about this in an issue of the organization's *Seafarers' Bulletin:* "When we have a culture that values seafarers' lives as highly as the more telegenic suffering of seabirds, then perhaps the ongoing harvest of environmental damage and preventable deaths will end."

Given all the various bodies that purport to regulate shipping, why are some facets of the industry so poorly run? Good question. On the other hand, shipping industry insiders were quick to remind me of Enron, WorldCom, Tyco, Global Crossing and other firms willing to "push the envelope" in their business dealings. In the end, I suppose any business can succumb to the lure of the almighty dollar if left unfettered. "Corporate social responsibility" is a relatively new term in the lexicon of international commerce.

Commercial shipping is on the cusp of changing the way it's been doing business for the last half-century. The last boom period in shipping, in the 1970s, coincided with the early years of the environmental and international labour movements, but little real pressure was placed on owners at that time. As the industry went into a slump following that period, economic pressures squeezed many ship owners and some allowed their standards to fall. Today, though, business is once more booming and an entire generation of newer, safer vessels is being launched each week. The technology exists today to safely and efficiently operate sea-going vessels, as well as to track their movements throughout the globe. And there is a demand for highly trained mariners to operate these ships and protect the owners' financial investments.

One could argue that shipping is being given a second chance, a clean slate to start anew and improve the industry as a whole. It's a unique opportunity, and if merchant shipping doesn't take advantage of it, the industry may not get another chance for at least twenty or thirty years. As well, if the industry doesn't do something to fix things on its own, it may finally find itself facing very real and very serious attention from the various, disparate regulatory bodies. One way or another, the laissez-faire years may be coming to an end.

So whose responsibility is it to improve the situation in commercial shipping? International Andromeda's Giangiacomo Serena is blunt in answering this question: "It is our [the ship owners'] responsibility. I cannot, in my heart, send a poorly trained crew out on a badly maintained vessel. And I tell you this: We believe that the human factor in this business is the most important. If you look at all the big oil pollution cases, most of them come from human error. Low maintenance of vessels is second. Weather is last. And this is something we have learned through our experiences. We had this experience in the beginning, where one of our first vessels was Malta-flagged, Filipino and Croatian crew. OK? Now, Malta flag—flag of convenience?—disaster. Because most of the majors [customers] were reluctant to use that. The register was a disaster. Cheap, but … And the Filipino crew? They would disappear when the ship went into port."

In order to attract the types of customers Andromeda wanted—larger firms—the company switched from using a Maltese flag to what is called a Norwegian second flag (the same as that used by the container ship

Tampa). Andromeda didn't want to hide behind a flag of convenience. The company also began using Lloyd's Register in London, because its higher standards would be attractive to clients. Finally, Serena tells me that the firm decided to use officers and crew from India. "Why Indian [crews]? They were more expensive than, say, Filipino. But what I liked was the British maritime culture they had. They don't drink alcohol, which can be a problem on other ships. And they have loyalty. Filipinos, for $20 more—they jump ship. So put it all together and what does a customer choose? They choose the best. But not just the vessel. The ships may be all the same, so the customer looks also at the flag, the officers, the crew, the registry and the organization."

A skeptic might wonder whether Serena is merely spinning some good public relations here, and it certainly wouldn't be the first time someone in the shipping industry did this. But I know that International Andromeda has a pretty good record in terms of vessel operation. They have retired all their older vessels and are currently taking delivery of a new generation of tankers from Asian shipyards, built to the highest international standards. While awaiting these new additions to their fleet, they have continued to pay the salaries of some of their Indian mariners as the sailors sit at home. With a worldwide shortage of experienced crews, the last thing the firm needs is to have poorly trained seafarers handling these multimillion-dollar investments. As well, Serena has chosen to situate himself in the open, here in Monaco, not hidden behind a numbered company in Liberia. It's easy to think that if the firm were running a shoddy operation, their compatriots in this exclusive Principality would not look kindly upon them and, in Monaco, appearance is everything.

Finally, I also know that Giangiacomo Serena sits on the board of the London Steam-Ship Club, a P&I (protection and indemnity) group that meets regularly to look into shipping disasters and the risks that mariners and owners face. He has chosen to involve himself actively in the world of commercial shipping instead of sitting back and taking a passive role.

As our interview winds down, Serena sits back in his chair and stares out the window again. "You know, I am proud to be a ship owner. Very much. I am proud to be even more than a ship owner, I am proud to do what I am doing. It's not about going around and saying 'I have ten, twenty vessels, I am the king.' I don't care about that. And our ships? To me they are beautiful. Absolutely. Absolutely." I must look skeptical, because he continues, "Yes, beautiful. It's something you have created, from scratch, and that you have been trying to make work. You have five hundred people, speaking of crew, working on your vessels. That means, for us, you are sustaining also five hundred families. It is very special."

When Serena walks me to the lobby, I ask if he feels there is something soul-like about his vessels, prompting him to give me an odd look. He fingers his jacket for a moment while thinking of a response. "I don't understand exactly the term 'soul.' But I would say that if we enlarge the concept to the vessel with the crew—definitely, yes. Because you cannot think of the vessel without the crew, this is my way of looking at it. A vessel is a piece of steel. It's a big box with a few pumps, and heater and whatever. It's a very easy vessel compared to passenger vessels. I do not consider passenger vessels to be anything to do with shipping. They are hotels. I cannot think of the vessel without the crew on board. And our crews, they think of the vessel as having a soul. It's like a soccer match: You cannot think of a soccer match without the players."

In the warm Mediterranean sun outside Andromeda's headquarters, I ponder Serena's thoughts about the inhabitants of his vessels, and what they bring to each ship they sail in. And I think about something written in the mid-1930s by the Australian mariner, photographer and author Alan Villiers. Years ago I stumbled upon a book of his in the back of a small shop in lower Manhattan. His exact words elude me here in Monaco, but I remember him saying that anyone can read books about ships and the sea, and cut and paste what is written; but to really experience the sea and understand why individuals set out upon its turbulent waters, you have to begin by getting into a ship. A day-long trip on a brand-new ship isn't enough. The time has come to find a ship and meet her crew.

4

MASTERS

Knowledge can be communicated, but not wisdom.

—HERMANN HESSE, *SIDDHARTHA*

I n today's world, the number of individuals with the legal power to make life-and-death decisions over others has—mercifully—diminished from times past. Heads of state, military personnel and police are the most common arbiters of this authority, but to this list I must add ship captains. A ship captain retains absolute control over a vessel and its inhabitants: He can arrest people and discipline them; he can order his crew to do things that could imperil their lives; and, yes, he can still perform marriages at sea.

Within the hierarchy of seafaring, no other individual carries as much responsibility, power and respect as the captain or has as complicated a relationship with his charge. He may love that ship, he may hate her, he may even be indifferent to her, but no matter what his personal feelings, the captain must care for the vessel, his crew and the cargo with all the zealousness he can bring to bear. As long as he is contracted to be captain, the master will relinquish control of his ship to only one other person, and then for the shortest time possible.

That one other person is a pilot, another mariner with special expertise in navigating harbours, rivers and canals, and on a sultry Friday afternoon, I'm getting a first-hand look at the interplay between him and a merchant captain. The MV *Antwerpen,* a cargo vessel laden with tonnes of coal in her holds, is currently outbound from Providence, Rhode Island, to the main shipping lanes of the Atlantic and then on to Portland, Maine. Before we reach the open sea, though, the vessel must transit Narragansett Bay, and things are getting tense.

The captain of the *Antwerpen* is staring intently through the forward-facing bridge windows, his pale blue eyes taking in a massive fog bank that has suddenly loomed up ahead. The wheelhouse is silent except for the sporadic chatter of other vessels on the radio and a periodic command from the harbour pilot, who is assisting the captain to leave port.

"Dead slow, Captain, dead slow," the pilot says with a note of concern in his voice.

"Dead slow," the master relays to the chief officer who throttles the engine telegraph back with his bear-like hands.

"Foghorn, please," the captain adds as an afterthought, and a deep drone begins to reverberate through the bridge every minute and a half.

As the commands are relayed, the chief officer, who is also known as the first mate, makes detailed notations in the ship's log of each change in course or speed.

According to the wheelhouse indicator, we're now making barely five knots. The second mate has been dispatched to the forecastle (the forwardmost part of the ship) to keep a lookout for any small boats, but he is barely visible from the bridge, so heavy is the fog. A tugboat farther down the channel radios in that "it's thick out there."

The captain wanders over to one of the two radars on the bridge, checking to see what the electronic eyes are picking up. There's minimal commercial traffic in the bay today beyond one other freighter inbound, several nautical miles away. He's more concerned about the sailboats and Jet Skis, and the approaching Newport Bridge with its immense steel tower piers. If the *Antwerpen* were to have an accident there, it would be the captain who would shoulder the blame.

Suddenly the Newport Bridge begins to materialize before us, rising from the fog like a ghost. Cars carrying vacationers en route to their weekend homes whiz a hundred feet overhead.

"Make course 177," the pilot tells the helmsman, followed quickly by, "Midship … port ten … port twenty."

The helmsman responds, "Midship, aye … port ten … port twenty."

And then we're through the narrow shipping gap and can make out Newport itself off to our port side. As the tension in the bridge abates and the fog lifts slightly, the pilot radios to a boat waiting to take him off and then instructs the captain to set a course for a series of rocky shoals called the Dumplings. As the ship approaches the rendezvous area, its engines are throttled back, the pilot packs up his gear and shakes the captain's hand goodbye. From the starboard bridge wing, the *Antwerpen*'s captain watches the pilot gingerly descend a rope ladder and jump the last few feet to the deck of the pilot boat. Then, after a quick wave at us, he speeds off in the launch toward Providence and another vessel in need of pilotage. With a clear sky now ahead of us, the captain turns to me, grinning, and says, "Good. I have my ship back."

To GET TO THE POINT of being able to watch this little interaction on the bridge of a working commercial ship had not been easy. I'd already witnessed day-long sea trials in Korea, but now I wanted to get aboard ship somewhere closer to my home in Canada, to see what life was like on the Atlantic. I undertook months of negotiations with a variety of shipping firms in the hope of finding a ship whose schedule and company policies would allow me to get to sea. It seemed a pretty straightforward request: Could I sail in a ship to learn more about the lives of mariners?

There was a time, not that long ago, when cargo ships often carried passengers as they plied their varying routes. In the post-9/11 world, however, passengers on commercial vessels are becoming decidedly less welcome. Worries that terrorists could use a ship to attack a port or other centres has made shipping companies nervous about strangers calling them up and asking to ride along on their vessels, however well intentioned those strangers may be. And various governments, that of the United States in particular, have come to regard merchant vessels and those who sail on them with the same degree of paranoia applied to aircraft.

Eventually, an expatriate Canadian living in New England smoothed the way for me to spend a few weeks with the *Antwerpen*. Robert Abraham works for SMT Shipmanagement and Transportation, a European-owned firm with head offices in Cyprus that operates twenty-three vessels worldwide, mostly off the eastern seaboards of North and South America. Coming from a family with a long history in shipping and having started out as a deckhand on freighters in the Great Lakes, Abraham knows how the world of the modern mariner has slipped from our collective consciousness.

Driving me down from Boston to join the *Antwerpen* in Providence, he fills me in on the ship and its crew. "She's what we call a 'self-unloading dry bulk carrier,' meaning she has her own cranes and conveyor system that can discharge cargoes like ore, gypsum or limestone, though she's now laden with high-grade coal from Venezuela. After offloading part of that cargo in Providence, she's to make for Portland and then Halifax. There she picks up some gypsum to take to Florida, then heads back to South America for more coal and will do the whole thing all over again."

Antwerpen, he tells me, is a tramp, a term that describes not her appearance, but her itinerary. Because they tramp from port to port in search of various cargoes, the captains of these vessels may, at times, not know what their next destination will be until they are at sea. (The other main type of commercial operation are liners, which operate on fixed schedules from fixed ports; think of a line drawn between two points on a map.)

"This is an older ship," Abraham continues. "She was built in 1979, in Belgium, as her name suggests; about 40,000 deadweight tonnes, so one of the more common-sized vessels in her category, and she flies a Cypriot flag since that's where she's registered. But *Antwerpen* is very well maintained. She has to be, because American and Canadian officials have really tightened the screws lately when it comes to issues of safety."

The officers and crew are all Polish, thirty-two in all, and they work contracts ranging between four and nine months at sea. The company uses Polish mariners because of their professionalism and work ethic. "These guys work hard," Abraham says. "It's a dirty job on a bulk carrier and the turnaround time in port is usually quite short. Sure, we could use cheaper labour from Third World countries, but we really feel the Polish guys are more productive."

He goes on to explain that SMT maintains an office in Gdansk, Poland, the historic port that was once part of the Hanseatic League, a group of trading centres on the Baltic Sea whose power was based on economic strength, not military capabilities. The firm chooses the best seamen available, with the junior officers often coming straight out of the Polish Merchant Academy. SMT even takes cadets still completing their studies on their vessels, an investment in future employees.

After clearing security at the Port of Providence's main gate, we pull up in front of the bulker where I get my first look at what will be my home for the next little while. The MV *Antwerpen* is, well, unassuming. I mean that not as a slight against the *Antwerpen,* but because she appears to me as typical a merchant ship as you can imagine.

Her hull is painted an ochre red below the waterline and black above it, with her name, *Antwerpen,* visible near the bow and "SMT—MARIAC" inscribed on her side (these are acronyms for the corporate entities that own and operate the ship). Her white superstructure sits aft of the main hatches, rising six storeys high, topped by a rectangular black funnel. *Antwerpen's* two giant gantry cranes are unloading coal from the holds onto a conveyor belt system that ferries the cargo to shore where it is dumped onto the piles. She has a lifeboat on each side of the superstructure and, beyond that, nothing that would cause you to glance twice at her.

Hefting my sea bag over my shoulder, I follow Robert Abraham up the gangway and into the house, where the living quarters, offices and bridge are located. Up three flights of stairs and just below the wheelhouse, we come to the officers' deck, where the captain's day room is situated. Abraham knocks on the open door and Captain Jacek Wisniewski beckons us to enter.

The master of an ocean-going vessel is universally known as "The Old Man" in honour of the maturity needed to command men on the seas and the loneliness that goes along with that position. The stereotype of a wise older man with a trimmed, salt-and-pepper beard and a crisp white shirt embellished with the four gold stripes of a captain on the epaulettes has been embedded in the public mind through countless movies, books and paintings. But when I first meet *Antwerpen's* captain, it's clear I'll have to revise some of those stereotypes.

Captain Jacek Wisniewski is sitting behind his desk dressed in a blue polo shirt and blue jeans as we enter his office. His desk is strewn with paperwork, and a spreadsheet is open on his computer monitor. Captain Wisniewski stands as introductions are made, and when we shake hands, I note his pale eyes beneath a receding hairline. He's about my age, early forties, and speaks excellent English in a quiet voice (though he will apologize frequently for perceived inadequacies in what is his second language). Wisniewski exudes calm and relaxation, two of the many traits that a master mariner must have to be successful. He seems somewhat indifferent to the fact that a writer is tagging along, as though he is holding something back and waiting to assess my character.

After ordering a steward to bring us some coffee, the captain and Robert Abraham discuss business matters. Wisniewski's office is not dissimilar to that of a plant manager at a mid-sized factory: dark brown, fake wood panelling, an L-shaped desk and three IKEA-style sectional sofas. When the office was furnished back in 1979, it must have seemed quite modern. Now it has a certain retro look to it.

Behind the captain's desk are shelves lined with file folders, three-ring binders and technical manuals. There's a photo tacked to a corkboard—presumably his wife and daughter. We are sitting on one of the sofas arranged around a coffee table that is strewn with shipping magazines. In one corner are a small television and a stereo system; a large, framed art print occupies one wall, while portholes on the other two open to the starboard and forward directions, pale golden curtains diffusing the morning sunlight. A number of plaques hang on one wall, commendations for work accomplished and such, and a few geranium plants are placed about the captain's day room, human touches in an otherwise workmanlike environment. His sleeping quarters are adjacent to this office area.

Abraham lets me introduce myself and I launch into an explanation of why I'm writing a book about mariners and commercial shipping. When I finish my little speech, Captain Wisniewski raises an eyebrow and quietly says, "That sounds very interesting. People do not usually take notice of us. Welcome aboard." After further small talk, it is clear that the captain needs to get back to his paperwork. Robert Abraham prepares to say his goodbyes when Wisniewski asks for something from me: my passport. It's normal practice on ships for the captain to retain the passports of all who are aboard his vessel, as he is our guardian. Still, it's a little disconcerting to hand over my documents to him. But it's also the first part of trusting this man.

EIGHT HOURS AFTER I've boarded *Antwerpen,* she leaves Narragansett Bay and the heavy fog behind her, and enters the open waters of the Atlantic Ocean. With the captain now firmly back in charge, a quiet routine seems to take over the vessel. From the bridge I see deckhands securing things on the main deck hatches, the mates checking our course on the plot table and a crewman washing down the windows. There's no sense of excitement among these guys about going to sea; they do it almost every day.

At 1800 hours—the ship operates on the twenty-four hour clock—Captain Wisniewski stops by the wheelhouse to check on things and, seeing I'm still here, invites me to join him for dinner. Wordlessly we make our way to the officers' mess located on D Deck, one down from the main deck (there's another mess for the crew on the other side of the deck, with the galley in between). I'm introduced to the steward, Rafal Winczo; with his short, skinhead-like haircut and lumbering gait he could be intimidating were it not for his voice, a falsetto that makes me do a double take when I first hear it.

Captain Wisniewski seats himself at the first of two long tables firmly anchored to the floor and gestures for me to sit beside him. Another officer is at the other end of the table, heartily wolfing down his dinner. There are a couple of others sitting at the second table, silently eating their own dinners. The mess is spartan and workmanlike, with a painting of the *Antwerpen* on her maiden voyage and a photo of her at sea the only adornments. The steward brings us soup and I wait for the captain to begin before picking up my spoon.

Almost immediately, a man enters the mess and sits down opposite Captain Wisniewski. He's older than the master and bears a striking resemblance to the American actor-dancer Fred Astaire. Wisniewski pauses from his soup.

"Uh … Daniel, this is Chief Engineer Janusz Ostrowski," he says, while explaining what I'm doing aboard *Antwerpen.* "The chief, he is in charge of engines. And this is Chief Officer Slawomir Bordon," he adds, gesturing down the table. "He is first mate of bridge."

Ostrowski smiles at me and shakes my hand, while Bordon merely nods in my direction. It would appear that suppertime conversation is not something that regularly occurs on the ship. The captain and chief engineer finish their appetizers in, what seems to me, record time, and then silently wait for the main course. Since it's Friday and the officers are from a Catholic country, the main course is fish. The meal continues in complete silence; when the younger officers leave, no one says goodbye or good night. When Ostrowski is finished, he wipes his hands, nods at me and heads off, along with Chief Officer Bordon.

Captain Wisniewski lingers as I continue to eat, grabbing a carafe to pour himself a cup of tea. "Is good?" he asks, and I nod in reply. He quietly sips his tea and I begin to feel more uncomfortable. After a few minutes, he sets the cup down, glances at his wristwatch and tells me he has work to do.

Left alone in the mess hall, I pick at my meal and wonder if I haven't gotten myself into something difficult. These sailors, these professional mariners, are aloof, distant and cautious. Unlike the others I've so far met on my travels, they seem closed to me and I have no idea how to pierce their armour. So, after thanking the steward, I retreat to my cabin to wait and see what tomorrow brings.

To SLEEP ABOARD a ship, a working commercial ship, is quite unlike anything I've ever experienced. It's not an uncomfortable thing and my mattress is certainly pleasant enough. But it takes some time to get used to the constant throb of the *Antwerpen*'s engines, which makes the bulkhead walls and dresser drawers rattle throughout the night. My bunk resonates to the cycle of the power plant's pistons driving up and down endlessly as they propel the ship forward.

The Atlantic swells brush against our hull, creating a slight roll from time to time that I soon find to be reassuring. The cadence and rhythm of *Antwerpen* at sea are workmanlike, not gentle and inconsequential. They signify a purpose, a destination to be sought out, as opposed to some less practical recreational foray onto the water. I awaken periodically throughout the night just to listen to the ship, lying there in the dark to enjoy the muted industrial cacophony that lulls me back to sleep.

By dawn I am stirred by daylight streaming through the curtains of my starboard-side portholes. Based on the course I'd seen plotted yesterday, the *Antwerpen* should be somewhere off the eastern shore of Cape Cod, steaming north toward Portland, Maine. Outside my portholes, I glimpse low-lying fog hovering over the calm seas, waiting to be burned off by the morning sun.

At just past 0730, I return to the officers' mess for breakfast, which is served until 0830. I find the mess busy with a dozen guys quietly chowing down at the two dining tables. Rafal Winczo, the young steward, greets me in his falsetto voice and gestures to my assigned place at the head of the table. Rafal asks what I'd like for breakfast: Coffee? Tea? Eggs? Toast? Cereal? I opt for some scrambled eggs and coffee, the latter of which turns out to be the instant kind. For some reason, *Antwerpen* seems to lack the ability to make a good pot of coffee.

Captain Wisniewski enters the mess, along with Chief Engineer Janusz Ostrowski, and they sit beside me, facing each other. In his deep baritone voice, the captain asks how I slept my first night at sea and seems pleased at my response. The steward quickly reappears and hovers over the captain to take his breakfast order. As Rafal brings our food, everyone begins eating breakfast, again in silence.

Finishing my eggs, I break the silence by asking the captain if it's all right to wander around the deck and up to the bow.

"Yes, sure, is no problem. We have excellent seas, good weather. Watch out for some of the crew, they are doing some work on the forward hatches, but is OK. We should be in Portland by evening. I think we take pilot aboard around 1600. If you want, you can come on the bridge again. You can go up any time you want." Then he looks at his watch—he's been here barely ten minutes—and says he has to check emails from head office in Cyprus.

After the captain and the chief leave, the steward comes over to take my plate away. "You like it, yes?" he asks, and I nod energetically.

Rafal continues, "Um … Daniel, do you like *flaki wolowe*?" I stare at him dumbly: I have no idea what *flaki wolowe* is. I mumble something about my father being Croatian and the lad grins at me broadly. "Ah good. Then you will like *flaki*. We are serving it for lunch today." Closing the door to the mess behind me, I can only wonder what lies in store for me.

I stop off on the bridge to check on our position, still trying to put thoughts about what *flaki* might be out of my mind. It's almost eight o'clock and Chief Officer Slawomir Bordon is just finishing his morning watch—he came on duty four hours earlier—and is chatting by the chart table with the third mate, who's relieving him. Their main concern is that we're transiting through an area where northern right whales migrate and we must report any sightings to the American government's National Oceanic and Atmospheric Administration (NOAA). A U.S. Coast Guard circular has been taped to the wall behind the chart table to remind the crew what to look for with the endangered mammals. Otherwise, Bordon tells me that it's quiet right now, meaning there's little other vessel traffic to worry about.

Wandering out to the starboard bridge wing, I see that the morning fog has disappeared and the Atlantic is calm and peaceful under a cloudless, blue sky. From this height—seven storeys above the waterline—the horizon line is the only break in the vista, and if I look at it carefully, I can just discern the slight curvature of the Earth, proof that our planet is indeed round. I ask Bordon just how far away the horizon is from our ship and he furrows his brow while trying to gauge the distance.

"Is maybe eighteen mile. Ya, I think eighteen nautical mile. Can be less when visibility is reduced, but today we have clear weather."

The mate then gives me a brief explanation of just what a nautical mile is. A nautical mile, he begins, does not equal a terrestrial mile. Rather, it is a measure of the average distance on the Earth's surface represented by one minute of latitude, latitude being the east–west lines used by navigators (the equator is zero degrees latitude), and longitude being the north–south lines (zero degrees longitude is the prime meridian that cuts through Greenwich, England). Through international agreement, a nautical mile is defined as being 1,852 meters, or about 243 meters longer than its terrestrial kin.

Like so much of seafaring, these terms are yet another thing that separates the lives of mariners from us landlubbers. Mariners speak a completely different language, though they use the same words. A nautical mile is not a statute mile. A ship's speed in nautical miles per hour is not the same as a truck's speed in miles per hour.

Leaving Bordon to finish his watch, I wind my way down to the main deck and forward to the front of the superstructure. Facing me are the seven large holds containing our precious cargo of coal. There's a front-end loader strapped to the deck here that the crew can lower into the holds to help in the offloading process. A couple of guys are working on its engine and one gives me a shy smile as I pass by.

After the confined spaces inside, the open expanse of the deck hatches is refreshing, much larger than a football or soccer field. In these calm waters, with no pitch or roll and only the slightest of breeze, it almost feels like we're still in port, except for the sparkling blue seas that surround me. In contrast, the steel hatch covers, crane supports—well, pretty much everything up here—are all painted drab ochre. There are frequent signs of touch-ups on the metal, and a couple of deckhands are washing down the forward hatch covers with a hose, both signs of the unceasing battle to fend off the corrosive attacks of rust.

Scattered here and there throughout the monotonous ochre blandness are painted-yellow markings that denote where walkways, ladders and low overhangs protrude. Following these yellow highway markers, I'm amidships when I spy a couple of gulls perched on a hatch cover, though there's no land in sight. The birds barely notice me as I continue forward and climb off the last hatch cover onto a short ladder that leads to the forecastle deck itself.

I've always liked the archaic term "forecastle" and especially its English mariner's diminutive: fo'c'sle (pronounced "fawk-sill"). This is the working area at the front of a ship, usually raised a bit to fend off waves and protect the anchor equipment. The origins of the word "forecastle" go back to ancient times when fighting vessels had wooden structures built on the forward and after parts of the deck, which were painted to look like stone castles. "Aftcastles" got lost somewhere along the way.

The forecastle deck narrows to the very prow of the *Antwerpen*, which draws me like a moth to a flame. I stop to look down the hawse pipe, the opening through which chains descend to the heavy steel anchor that lies dormant and menacing, its flukes silhouetted by the bow waves. For the first time I notice that the sounds of the ship have vanished, replaced by the sound of the sea, which I think is being funnelled up the hawse pipe. But as I walk to the stem of *Antwerpen* I realize that the ocean envelops me. The wind carries the scent, the sound and the feel of the salt water; it surrounds me with a freedom that comes from being in this place at this time.

At the stem of the ship is an empty jackstaff, which I grasp with one hand while hauling myself up better to see the waves below me. The bulbous bow of the ship, an unnatural, submerged chin-like protrusion, lies just beneath the surface of the water. As it cuts through the sea, it rises with the timbre of *Antwerpen*, cresting the surface of the Atlantic for a moment before diving beneath the waves once more.

Mesmerized, I trace the steel mass of the bulbous bow battering its way through the indigo seas. In scientific terms, the blue of the ocean comes from the reflection of the sun's rays on the surface waters; the red wavelengths of light are most quickly absorbed, while the blue end of the spectrum travels deeper. But science cannot do justice to the palette of hues that make up even the smallest portion of the sea. On my right it's grey-blue and cold; the shallow swells ahead are highlighted with brilliant azure, warm and inviting; to my left the seas are a cobalt blue that resonates with the strength of the ocean.

Looking that way, toward the unseen shore of Massachusetts, I spot two darting shapes that streak toward the *Antwerpen* like torpedoes fired from a submarine. As they get closer, I realize they are dolphins swimming with a grace and speed that is amazing. The two mammals circle the prow of the ship and then begin to escort us, one dolphin to port, the other to starboard. Gripping the railing, I peer over the edge as far as I can, barely five metres above the duo as they frolic and play beside the bulbous bow of the cargo ship.

The smile the dolphins bring to my face is universal, for they have energy and—dare I say—speed that resonates within all of us. As they swim in front of the ship and leap with careless abandon in front of me, I have to remind myself that these marine creatures are travelling faster than *Antwerpen* is, easily matching the output of our powerful engines. Their blowholes open and close in the second or so they are aloft, their mottled brown backs and rainbow-coloured bottoms identifying them as Atlantic spotted dolphins. After a minute or so the two partners suddenly take off to port again, as though frightened away. And, at that very moment, I hear a voice behind me say, "So, you have found my private place."

Turning, I find Captain Wisniewski standing there, grinning with his hands on his hips. He joins me by the prow and continues, "I like to come here at least once a day, if possible, and be alone. Just me and the sea." He smiles at this and gazes at the ocean around us, his blue eyes mirroring the colour of the water. I tell him about the dolphins. "Yes, they come to visit many times, many times. They are good ... how do you say?" He pauses for a moment to think in Polish. "Yes, omen. Omen? Is that correct?" I nod and we both silently take in this special place of his.

"Ah, you see? They come back." Sure enough, the pair of dolphins has returned, bringing the rest of the pod with them, seven in all. Of the seven, two are younger mammals, one barely two feet long and sticking close to its mother. This one easily matches the speed of its parent, leaping when she leaps, turning when she turns. The zigzag of the animals around the bow of the *Antwerpen* is wonderful to behold, like a dog-fight in the air. As our bow crashes through the gentle swells, the dolphins leap from the foaming waters—one, two, four of them at a time—gasping for air and then slicing back into the sea. This goes on for about five minutes and then the pod grows bored with us and the dolphins swim off to starboard, heading out to sea.

"There, you see," the captain says in his quiet voice. "There is romance in the sea. Standing here, watching the waves and the dolphins. It is special, yes?"

It is indeed. In the aftermath of this display, I take the chance to ask how he became a mariner, and he pauses to think for a moment before turning to me. Jacek Wisniewski has a stern look on his face and I fear I've offended him somehow until I realize he's trying to organize his thoughts into English.

"You know, I always had interest in the sea when I was even a child; I would make the model ships and talk with my father who was captain of a fishing vessel. But I thought I would like to become a doctor because I like to help people. And I talked with my father about this and he told me that whatever I decided to do with my life was my decision. But he also suggested I consider becoming a sailor. Because, you know, at that time in Poland things were very strict. You had the socialistic system and travel was difficult. My father told me that if I became a sailor, I would see the world beyond my borders, see the capitalistic system, and the chance to make more money would be available to me as a Polish seaman. So I thought about it and then changed my mind from becoming a medical doctor. And I do not regret it. Not at all."

Wisniewski explains to me that he entered the Polish Merchant Academy in the early 1980s, when the Communists still ruled his country. While a cadet, he sailed on the tall ship *Dar Pomorza* (meaning "Pomerania," a region of northwestern Poland), a three-masted, steel-hulled, sail training frigate built in Hamburg in 1909. This experience of training on a sail vessel is a rarity today for merchant mariners, many of whom receive nothing more than a few weeks', or months', classroom preparation for the profession they are about to begin. To crew aboard a sail ship creates a different type of sailor, one with a greater appreciation for the vicissitudes of the sea. I ask the captain what it was like.

"I think is very important experience to do that. Because you learn to work as a crew, like a team, with all the lines and ropes and the sails. It is also important because you have the young men and you need to develop a certain ... bravery. I remember the first time I looked up at the masts and I thought, 'How am I going to climb up there?' But you have to do it. There is no option. So I climb the mast and, you know, work with the sails. The first time it is scary, very scary. But it gets easier and soon you do not think about it. Except maybe when the weather is bad and the ship is rolling from side to side. Then—you think about it."

The cohesive entity of a crew that is created aboard sail vessels like the now-retired *Dar Pomorza* brings to mind a quote by the writer Joseph Conrad. Though better known for his novella *Heart of Darkness,* Conrad was a merchant mariner before he ever put pen to paper; and he used that experience to describe sailors as "a small knot of men upon the great loneliness of the sea" in his book *The Mirror of the Sea.* Conrad was, like Jacek Wisniewski, a captain of men and ships at sea, albeit in the late nineteenth century. And, like my captain, he was also Polish: Conrad was born Jozef Konrad Korzeniowski before moving to Britain and anglicizing his name.

The captain and I stare at our own lonely sea, now that the dolphins have disappeared. Perhaps aided by the contemplative nature of this solitude, Wisniewski continues to recount his early years as a sailor. His time as a cadet included one of his most memorable voyages to date, a trip to Antarctica to re-supply a Polish research station on King George Island. His eyes light up as he remembers the ice, the clear blue waters, the penguins, whales and the snow. "It was like ... how do you say in English? It was like being an explorer, for the first time walking where no one had ever been. Like an astronaut on the moon, looking at my footsteps on the snow. I found some whale bones on the shore and brought one back home with me, which I still have."

After graduating from the Merchant Academy in Gdynia in 1986, Wisniewski found himself unemployed in socialist Poland. The waning years of communism in Eastern Europe saw the emergence of free-market economies and with those came layoffs and decentralization, so Wisniewski left Poland for Holland, where he tried to get permission to emigrate to Sweden or Australia while making ends meet by cleaning flower bulbs in a nursery. Returning to Gdynia empty-handed, he recounts that he was surprised to find a job waiting for him on a ship; it seems that so many Poles were jumping ship once they reached ports in the West that there was a shortage of seafarers.

After that, Captain Wisniewski's nautical career followed a fairly standard and time-worn path, one that has the ability to transform the youthful energy of individuals into mature figures empowered with the discipline to take command. Essentially it involves giving young officers more and more tasks to accomplish while the mates above them eye their progress. A third mate, usually fresh out of school and in his mid- to late twenties, is the safety officer and responsible for the deck equipment. The second mate, usually in his late twenties or early thirties, has more navigational work to do. (In today's world, commercial ships do not have a navigator per se, or a radio officer; these roles have been made obsolete by technology.) The chief officer (a.k.a. first mate to some) has the most work to do of the three, as he is the captain's right-hand man. He oversees the actual loading and discharging of the cargo when in port. Most chief officers already have their Class 1 Certificate of Competency, known to mariners as "the ticket" (Wisniewski got his in 1997, at the age of thirty-five). It's one of the most prized pieces of paper in the profession: the document required to be a shipmaster. What the chief officer doesn't yet have is a command; that doesn't normally happen until he's closing in on forty years of age.

It is said that the difference between a third and second mate is minor, as is the difference between a chief officer and captain. But the leap from second mate to chief officer is perhaps the most important event in a seafarer's life, except for taking command of his first vessel. If an individual makes it to the chief mate's position, he—or increasingly, she—will be deemed worthy of eventually becoming a captain.

And what does it take to be a captain? I ask Wisniewski about this and he again puts on his thinking face for a few moments. "From the very beginning, you cannot show the crew that you're a friend to everybody. The company gives you the vessel, worth millions of dollars; the company gives you the lives of the crew. So you must be strict, but not too strict. You have to be uncle or father to the men. It comes down to your character and I think I have the character that can communicate with the people and to listen to them. I never think that my word is always the best. I listen to the chief officer, I listen to the chief engineer—but my word is always the last, because somebody must make the decision, take the responsibility. So, I think the captain must have a strength—yes?—to know that this decision is the correct one. It is very hard. The captain is always alone."

The pressure of being a captain and the loneliness that goes with that command can age a man quickly if he is not prepared for it. Luckily, most shipping firms have a process for weeding out those who cannot handle the weight that is placed on the shoulders of senior officers, so individuals like Wisniewski have been observed and tested for years before ever being made captain. My captain, as I now think of him, was watched throughout his career and had his ticket in hand for several years before being given his first command two years ago: the *Antwerpen*.

To be correct, his true title is "master mariner," an honorific steeped in tradition and respect. Individuals like Captain Jacek Wisniewski are members of an exclusive fraternity of about fifty thousand shipmasters spread throughout the world's oceans, seas, lakes and rivers. He has far-ranging powers, the most obvious of which is the control over the human lives he is entrusted with.

A walkie-talkie crackles to life and Captain Wisniewski pulls the device from his pocket. Speaking quickly in Polish, he responds to some query from the bridge and tells me that duty calls. "It is something about the pilot we will take aboard in a few hours' time. More paperwork, probably.

There was less paperwork when we did not have computers. Now—bah! So, I must go."

A FEW HOURS LATER, I enter the officers' mess to find the omnipresent steward, Rafal Winczo, waiting for me with a broad grin on his face. "Daniel, we have *flaki*." I'd forgotten that I was to be served something different. "You know, it is a specialty in Poland and my favourite. You will like." Well, I certainly hope so, since there are a half-dozen others already seated here and I have no doubt they are watching with eagle eyes to see my reaction.

Rafal returns with a tureen and ladles a watery soup into my bowl before taking a step back to watch me enjoy this hometown favourite of his. A few vegetables float in the liquid, along with some long strips of white, meat-like stuff. I begin with the veggies and find them spicy, or at least the broth is. Finally, after finishing them off, I delve into the meat. I gnaw on the rubbery tissue and note a strong taste, which I've never encountered before. A glance over my shoulder reveals the steward keeping his watch on me, so I go back to the meaty things. I get them down as fast as I can, hoping they will pass over my tongue's taste buds with minimal effect. Soon I have finished the bowl of mystery and push it ever so slightly away from me.

"You like?" Rafal asks before I've even taken a breath. I tell him it was great, but when he offers seconds I decline, saying I'm not too hungry today (even though I'm famished). He looks mildly disappointed but the entrance of Captain Wisniewski distracts him. As the captain sits beside me, the steward speaks to him in Polish and I can deduce that he's mentioning today's special is *flaki*. Wisniewski waves his hand dismissively and Rafal fetches him a plate of potatoes, cabbage and sausage—the main course. I look on in envy as the captain digs in before asking him what *flaki* is.

"Ah, *flaki*. Is the stomach of animal. You call it tripe, I believe. I do not like it very much. When I joined my first vessel as apprentice, the *flaki* was one of my favourite meals. Cook prepared it each Sunday so I always ate it double until one day I said 'Never more.' After so many years I still feel its taste. But never more." I let the captain finish his feast in privacy and pop my head into the galley where the cook and Rafal are chatting. After introducing myself to the master of the *flaki*, I thank him for the meal and he laughs. "No problem, no problem. But you should eat more. You are too skinny man. We can add twenty kilos to you!" I ask about dinner and am told that salmon is on the menu, causing me to heave a silent sigh of relief.

By 1500 hours, preparations are underway to begin our return to land. I pop my head into the captain's day room and he tells me we'll take pilots aboard in about an hour to guide us into Portland Harbour. *Antwerpen* is to offload the remaining 18,000 tonnes of coal there, something that will take a couple of days to complete. As he finishes some paperwork for American officials, he suggests I head up to the bridge and go chat with the chief officer.

In the wheelhouse, Chief Officer Slawomir Bordon is talking to the second mate, who's introduced as Jakub Rosicki. Fresh charts are on the navigation table showing the approaches to Cape Elizabeth, Casco Bay and Portland Harbour. The seas are still fairly calm, though the wind has picked up a bit. We're holding steady on a course of 327 and outside the windows there are dozens of seagulls flying around the ship.

Slawomir Bordon is about ten years younger than the captain and a large man with a barrel chest, powerful hands and a short, scruffy beard, one of the few Polish mariners with facial hair aboard *Antwerpen*. He's not really fat; he just has what some would politely call an ample girth and a healthy appetite. But the chief officer also has a shyness about him that is noticeable when I ask how he ended up here on a cargo ship off the coast of the United States.

His pale blue eyes stare out the forward windows and then a reflective smile crosses his face. "I always wanted to be sailor. Even when I was a kid. Always. I remember my father took me out on a small boat, a sailboat, when I was about eight or nine. That was my first experience with a boat and water and I loved it. I still remember it."

His dad, however, a lieutenant colonel in the Polish Air Force, was hoping that the young boy would follow in his footsteps and become a flyer. When Bordon was about twelve, his father took him for a ride in a small plane, seeking to spark an interest in flying, but the child remained unconvinced by the experience. "When we landed I turned to him and I said, 'Nope, I do not want to be a pilot, not even a fighter pilot like you. You are crazy to fly this metal thing, it doesn't seem right.' And I told him that I would rather be a sailor. Later, after I began working at sea, my father told me that he thought *I* was crazy, to take a ship out into the ocean, far from home. So, maybe my father and me, you know, maybe we're both a little crazy."

I've heard that a surprising number of officers in the merchant marine have pilots as fathers. Maybe this instills a sense of freedom and a yearning to escape terra firma, which, when coupled with teenaged rebellion, manifest themselves in a desire to go to sea. I'm not sure. Most of Bordon's childhood was spent moving from place to place as his family followed their jet-fighter father to various military bases around the country. This experience, the Polish equivalent of being an "air force brat," was good preparation for his present career, since it was not unlike travelling from port to port.

He hoped to join the Polish navy and become an officer—"Maybe to please my father a little bit"—but that nation's naval forces were too small, so Bordon opted for the merchant academy, joining at nineteen and spending five years studying on land and at sea. He joined the *Antwerpen* in 2000, initially as second mate before being promoted to chief officer. With no wife or children back home in Poland, he says he finds the four months of sea time easier to cope with than some of the others.

"I get to see many places I never thought I would see. New York, South America, Florida, even Canada. And I think sometimes that my father, you know he flew advanced fighter aircraft, like the MiG planes, and he would fly even faster than the speed of sound. Yes? But he never really saw much of the world. Not like me. So I think this is better life."

THE *ANTWERPEN* has almost reached her rendezvous point with the pilot boat, so Bordon joins Captain Wisniewski and the helmsman near the ship's wheel. We're now within sight of land—Cape Elizabeth is off our port beam—and the captain instructs the second mate to go below and prepare the Jacob's ladder. This is a wood-and-rope ladder that will be draped over the starboard side near a midships opening, and the pilots will use it to climb aboard the ship from their smaller boat. I join Wisniewski on the starboard bridge wing to watch the operation. Our vessel will slow to six knots but not stop, and the pilot boat will come alongside and match our speed.

I can see the pilot boat swinging in an arc off our starboard quarter and quickly closing in on our larger shape. There is always a bit of tension with this operation, as our hull creates a region of suction on either side that can smash the smaller craft and even overturn it. Luckily the seas are easy right now; I've heard so many stories of pilots struggling to get on or off commercial ships in rough weather that you have to wonder why anyone would bother with the job. This time the small boat eases ever closer and I can see two men making their way on its foredeck to the Jacob's ladder. There's a bit of chop being created by the *Antwerpen,* and the pilot boat bounces up and down in the wash.

The pilot boat helmsman skilfully manoeuvres his small craft alongside the *Antwerpen*'s hull, fighting the suction of the larger vessel and the chop of the seas. His first attempt brings him side to side with us, but the wash created showers the pilot boat's deck, making it impossible for anyone to jump aboard. The helmsman pulls away from us and tries a second time.

He now brings his bow toward the bulker, coming from an angle such that his stern is separated from us by several metres of water while his nose is nudged tight against our hull. Like a remora and a shark, the pilot boat is joined to the *Antwerpen,* if only momentarily, matching our speed with a precision born of years of experience. For a few minutes the smaller boat is held in our embrace and a couple of hands reach from *Antwerpen* to help the men aboard. Then the pilot boat quickly motors off.

Antwerpen will be entering Portland with two pilots. One is the ship's pilot, who will guide us in through the outer waters of Casco Bay. The other is a docking pilot, who will manoeuvre us through the harbour to our berth. Captain Wisniewski has never been to Portland before, so he will have to entrust his ship to these two men he has never met.

The two pilots enter the wheelhouse following the second mate, and Captain Dave Germond introduces himself and his partner, Docking Master William Gribbin, to Wisniewski. Germond is a blond-haired man in his forties wearing a polo shirt and khaki pants who, like most pilots, doesn't speak much while working. Pilots board so many vessels in a day and bear almost as much responsibility as the ships' masters that small talk isn't really part of their nature. Their job is to get a ship in and out of port as quickly and safely as possible, then move on to the next one.

The bridge is somewhat crowded now; besides the two pilots, the captain, chief officer, second mate and a helmsman are present, as well as the itinerant writer trying to stay out of the way. Wisniewski stands off to one side of the bridge and lets the chief officer deal with Pilot Dave Germond's orders. I can tell that my captain is somewhat uneasy at letting someone else dance with his girl, and he paces about in a small circle, glancing at the pilot from behind sunglasses.

After checking the *Antwerpen*'s present course and speed, Captain Germond quickly assesses the ship's navigational gear. Based on his own experience in this harbour, he notes a slight error in *Antwerpen*'s equipment, about a degree and a half. It's nothing serious—all ships have slight errors in navigational calibration—but he'll have to factor this in as he gives orders to the wheelhouse crew.

"Starboard easy to 322," orders Germond, and the helmsman repeats the new course heading back. The pilot picks up the ship's radio and calls the local shipping traffic office. "Security call, security call, channel 13. This is bulker *Antwerpen* just passing West Cod Ledge, we're inbound for the rolling mills dock in Portland Harbour by way of Willard Rock, officer traffic. *Antwerpen*." He then repeats our intentions on another channel and turns his attention to a fishing boat that's heading our way.

On this glorious late afternoon, numerous sailboats, powerboats and fishing vessels are beginning to crowd the harbour approaches. Entering the confines of Casco Bay, we pass remnants of the Civil War, Fort Williams and the old Portland Head lighthouse on our port side and Fort Scammel on an island dead ahead. Two tugboats are making for us, ready to assist *Antwerpen* in docking. Germond and Captain Wisniewski are still keeping an eye on the outbound fishing vessel. A 40,000-tonne vessel like *Antwerpen* has little room to manoeuvre in the narrow shipping channel here, so the pilot radios the smaller boat.

"Call to fishing vessel just coming up on Catfish Buoy ... what's the name of your fishing vessel?"

"Anna Maria."

"OK, *Anna Maria,* we'll see you starboard to starboard if that's OK with you?"

"Roger, roger."

Captain Wisniewski picks up a pair of binoculars and watches the approach of the *Anna Maria* while we continue the slow journey into harbour. It'll take us another hour to swing left into the Fore River and past downtown Portland to the discharging docks. I see the other pilot standing on the port bridge wing and join him outside in the late-day sunshine. Captain Bill Gribbin is older than his colleague, sporting a broad-brimmed hat and windbreaker and talking with the relaxed accent of this part of New England. He initially takes me for another Polish crew member and is surprised to find I'm a Canadian travelling aboard a bulker. Gribbin has nothing much to do until we get into the harbour, when he'll take over from Captain Germond and ease us into our berth.

"There are different kinds of pilots everywhere—river pilots, ship pilots like Dave, harbour masters like me," Captain Gribbin says. "But we all bring a local knowledge that ship captains often don't have. There are also all kinds of regulations that say that, for instance, foreign vessels must have a pilot when entering certain waters. Even if this ship had an American master and American crew, she'd still be required to have us aboard because she's flagged." He turns to the stern to check *Antwerpen*'s ensign. "OK, she's Cypriot."

Each port or waterway, he explains, has different criteria for deciding who becomes a pilot. In places like the Mississippi River, for instance, the pilots don't have to be licensed as sea-going master mariners; they just have to know the way of the river. Here in Portland, though, the pilotage authority requires that its guys have some sea time, as well as experience as tugboat captains. Captain Gribbin has both.

"I did my time at sea, I got my second mate's licence, but wanted to come home. Because it gets harder as you get older, being away all the time. So I actually left a good job, returned to Portland and started again as a deckhand on a tug, worked for nine years at that. Then I was a mate for a year and a tug captain for another five years. So it's been a long process."

We're now getting close to Portland itself. The downtown core is off our starboard beam and Gribbin gets ready to take over from Captain Germond. The docking master mentions that I'm Canadian to his compatriot and Germond gives me an odd look, a sort of "What the hell are you doing here?" thing. When I explain I'm writing a book on commercial shipping, he seems nonplussed, but I ask him how he became a pilot anyway.

"I was a tanker captain out west for ARCO Marine before returning home," he tells me while staring straight ahead with arms crossed over his chest. That's interesting, I say, since I was on an old ARCO Marine tanker being broken up in India recently, a ship that used to do the Valdez run.

"Yeah, I used to do that route." He still seems uninterested in conversation but asks after a few moments which vessel I was on. When I mention her name—the SS *Sag River*—he turns and stares at me, his brow furrowed.

"I was captain of her for a few runs."

I'm flabbergasted. We both are. I can't even fathom the odds of being on a dying ship in northwestern India, wondering about her life, and then encountering one of her masters in the wheelhouse of another ship half a world away.

"She was a good ship," he continues. "Well run, no problems. I, uh, I don't really know how I feel about her being scrapped. I mean, that was a while ago I was with her and all ships have to go sometime. I suppose a lot of ships I sailed with have gone somewhere like that. You don't really think about it. This job is always about moving on."

I guess I thought he might have more of a connection to the tanker, something personal that her memory would elicit. But as Germond said, he only sailed with the *Sag River* a few times; she was but one of many ships that make up his seafaring career, and the crew that took her to India would have been from another shipping firm. It's rare—very rare—for a mariner to spend more than a few years with any one vessel nowadays. Owners, schedules, promotions, layoffs, family commitments, other job offers—all conspire to keep sailors constantly rotating among different vessels.

Merchant mariners are less concerned with nostalgia about former vessels than they are with the present state of their floating home. This is amply evident as I watch Captain Wisniewski pace the *Antwerpen*'s bridge. We're approaching the Portland Bridge, a drawbridge that spans the Fore River, connecting the north and south sides of the harbour. The two tugboats are trailing in our wake, eager young puppies following their lumbering master. They hang back a bit as we get closer to the bridge.

Captain Wisniewski's unease arises from the fact that we're about to thread a needle by taking his thirty-metre-wide ship through an opening with about ten metres of room to spare on either side. An ocean-going vessel is at its weakest in situations like this, hemmed in by a narrow channel, facing an immense concrete barrier that looms in front of it, and getting only one chance to do the transit properly. I can hear the warning alarm scream out from the bridge as the central sections begin to rise for us. Wisniewski stands on the starboard wing and stares at the obstruction that, to him, is as dangerous as any hurricane. The wheelhouse gets very quiet the closer we come to the narrow opening.

"Starboard ten," Docking Master Gribbin asks.

"Starboard to ten," answers the helmsman, and once the rudder reaches that position, he confirms this to the pilot. "Starboard ten." The orders ring out in repetition as pilot and helmsman run the ship.

"Easy to five."

"Easy to five."

"Midship."

"Midship."

"Starboard five."

"Starboard five."

"Starboard ten."

"Starboard ten."

"Slow Ahead." This last command comes from Captain Wisniewski himself, as instructed by the American who now stands beside him.

"Slow Ahead," Wisniewski repeats, louder; the chief officer wasn't fast enough in responding and my captain is glaring at him.

"Slow Ahead," Bordon responds.

"OK, Captain, steady as she goes," says Gribbin as we inch closer to the edifice, its two steel spans in a near-vertical position, open like the palms of a giant's hands. Passing through the gateway, we hear the noise of *Antwerpen*'s engines funnelled around us, echoing off the concrete battlements. The bridge-keeper waves at Gribbin and then we're through. Captain Wisniewski turns to me and raises his eyebrows above a sheepish grin. "Don't tell the crew I was nervous. I am supposed to be like a rock."

Once past the bridge, *Antwerpen* comes under the care of the two tugs, one fore, the other aft, and we prepare for the docking dance. I'm told that the one off our stern, the *Vicki M. McAllister,* is a new-generation boat, driven not by traditional propellers and rudders but by azipod drives. Known as Z-Drive tugs, such vessels use two self-contained pods that hang beneath the hull and can turn in any direction, like a rotating fan. This may be the future of nautical propulsion, and similar mechanisms have been installed on such large ships as the passenger liner *Queen Mary 2.*

What hasn't changed, though, is the use of a tug's whistles to communicate. As *Antwerpen* is pulled into position at the rolling mills docks, Captain Gribbin radios his instructions to the tug captains. They, in turn, respond by tooting their horns; this is simply easier than picking up their radios and affirming the instructions. As I stand on the open bridge wing, the pips of first one, then the other—one high in tone, the other lower—welcome us in. There's a reassuring fondness to the tugs' whistles, though I can't say I've ever actually noticed the sounds before in other ports I've visited.

After tying up, the pilots depart and the crew immediately set to work preparing to discharge our cargo here in Portland. It'll take a day and a half to offload 18,000 tonnes of coal, with the crew working around the clock to finish the job. The crew can't simply dump the coal into piles on the wharf as they can at other ports; instead, the gantry cranes will scoop the coal out of the holds and onto *Antwerpen's* conveyor belt system, which feeds a hopper on the shore. There, dump trucks will be loaded with the fuel and take it away to a nearby power plant, a slow and boring process. I can see the American drivers smoking and chatting beside the line of trucks waiting for the first coal to arrive, while the chief officer and second mate are already walking on deck to begin supervising the work. The *Antwerpen* is beginning its transformation from sea-going vessel to shore-bound factory.

THE AMERICAN DEMAND for coal surprises me, perhaps because so much attention is focused on ensuring secure supplies of oil and gas for the West. Having essentially fought two wars in little more than a decade to safeguard Middle Eastern oil reserves (regardless of proclamations about democracy or terrorism or weapons of mass destruction), Americans have actually most increased their coal consumption in the last few decades: Since 1970 American coal consumption has almost doubled. And it's ships like the *Antwerpen* that quietly circulate along the coast and even inland to the Great Lakes, keeping America warm in the winter months while soldiers tough it out in the deserts and cities of Iraq.

Captain Wisniewski mentions he was also surprised to be carrying so much coal to the United States from South America. "You know, before I came to *Antwerpen,* I had no idea that the United States used so much of it. I thought they only used oil and nuclear power. But it's good for us. It keeps us busy. And I like the coal cargoes. They are better than the gypsum we will pick up in Halifax."

I don't see much of the captain while we're in Portland, as he's busy solving a variety of problems that must be dealt with while we're here. There's a mechanical repair that needs to be done to one of the conveyor belts, documents to be prepared and sent to Canadian port authorities and, of course, the endless paperwork. I do stop by his day room to ask permission to leave the ship and wander around Portland for a bit, and he grants it. Noticing the photo by his desk again, I ask if that's his family.

"Yes, that is my wife and my daughter, Martina. It is at a weekend house we have, by a lake. I have a son, too, but no photo here. He is a teenager." I tell Wisniewski that his daughter looks just like him and he chuckles. "That is very important for the seaman. Thank you, thank you. It is better if your children are similar to you. Because if his children do not look like him, a man begins to wonder ..."

Grinning, I leave the captain and walk into town for a few hours, find a coffee house and end up at a shop selling nautical antiques and knick-knacks. The place is crowded with tourists browsing among the ships' nameplates, naval uniforms, old navigation equipment and other souvenirs from the sea. A teenager idly flips through some postcards of passenger liners while an older couple is looking at used books. The man pulls out a history of the merchant navy at war and shows it to his wife, who gives him a bored look and walks away. I wonder if any of these mingling tourists with their passing interest in nautical lore would think to leave the sanitized confines of the shop and walk down the street to where *Antwerpen* lies berthed—to see a working ship instead of memories of long-gone forebears. Not likely. And I'm positive no one will stay up to watch us leave later this evening.

As midnight approaches, the crew has almost completed discharging the coal. The last thing is for teams of men to descend into each hold and, using brooms and shovels, sweep out every final bit of anthracite. They become temporary coal miners, scouring all the darkened nooks and crannies for lumps of rock, until they emerge with blackened faces and can secure the hatch covers, cranes and other equipment in preparation for departure. They pay particular attention to Number Four Hold, the middle one, which will be filled with seawater after we clear the harbour's headland. This will act as ballast to give the empty ship better handling in the ocean. Before we enter Halifax, the ballast water will then be pumped out. (It was ballast water from European ships that accidentally introduced zebra mussels into North America's Great Lakes in the 1980s, causing great environmental damage. Regulations concerning what types of water may be used for ballast have since been tightened.)

The skies are clear and filled with stars as Docking Master Bill Gribbin and Ship Pilot Dave Germond return to *Antwerpen*'s wheelhouse. Chief Officer Bordon has calculated the amount of water to be pumped into the Number Four Hold, allowing *Antwerpen* to ride lower in the water and reduce the drag created by our profile.

At 0230, the order is given to throw off our lines, and the bulker is eased away from the dock by the two tugs. Captain Gribbin must coordinate a ninety-degree turn to bring *Antwerpen* into the middle of the Fore

River and line her up with the drawbridge. Any impression that clearing the bridge will be easier a second time around is missing. Instead, Captain Wisniewski and the rest of the wheelhouse crew are even tenser, as we're making the transit in the middle of the night.

The Z-Drive tug, the *Vicki M. McAllister,* scoots past us and takes up position off our starboard beam, using one of her powerful searchlights to illuminate the channel buoys leading to the bridge. Once more the sirens wail from the bridge and the steel spans open toward the heavens. Making dead slow ahead, we pass through the gateway and glide past the sleeping city. Gribbin's work is done and he shakes hands all around before following the second mate below to disembark to the tug *Vicki M. McAllister.*

Captain Germond issues instructions to bring us into Casco Bay, passing a tanker that's unloading its crude under the arc lights of the Gulf Oil Terminal in South Portland. *Antwerpen* makes a graceful turn to starboard around Break Point and into the bay. The sweep of the lighthouse at Portland Head picks out a bunch of fishing trawlers inbound with fresh fish, which pass us silently as we slink out of town. Half an hour later, Captain Dave Germond radios for the pilot boat to come and meet *Antwerpen* so he can go home for the night. He wishes the captain luck, as there are reports of fog hovering over the Atlantic between here and Nova Scotia.

Sure enough, almost as soon as the pilot has left, I can see low-lying fog begin to surround us, initially rising only a few metres above the glassy, calm water. The outside temperature begins to drop and I can make out a massive bank of fog on the horizon. As she enters the ghostly haze, *Antwerpen* is enveloped and the captain orders the foghorn switched on. The horn resonates deeply and powerfully, broadcasting our presence to any small vessels that may lie in our path. Wisniewski checks the waypoints plotted into the autopilot, and then asks the chief officer to send the helmsman to bed. The last piercing rays of light from the house at Portland Head struggle to penetrate the fog behind us, and we are then alone in the night on the sea. I glance at my watch and see it's almost four o'clock in the morning, so I say good night to the captain and descend to my cabin, collapsing onto my bunk and quickly falling asleep.

SHORTLY BEFORE TEN O'CLOCK the next morning, I awaken to the comforting throb of *Antwerpen*'s engines. My closet doors make a rhythmic patter akin to some sort of base tribal drumming. One could create a musical score by using the fake wood enclosure as a metronome. Groggily, I peer out my portholes but barely register anything as I pull some clothes on and make my way down to the mess in search of coffee. Rafal Winczo, the steward, is there and mercifully gets me a mug of instant coffee while saying that few of the crew got much sleep. I immediately feel a tinge of guilt, since Rafal not only has to serve the meals here—meaning he has to be in the mess before seven o'clock—but is also a deckhand responsible for the aft mooring lines when we enter and leave port. So the poor kid tells me that he only got two hours' sleep.

Taking my instant coffee, I stumble up to the bridge to check on our position and am surprised to see Captain Wisniewski slumped in his chair, wearing the same clothes from last night, or early morning. He looks tired and haggard, and is staring at the radar screen with deep bags under his eyes and a vacant gaze.

"Good afternoon, Daniel," he mutters politely, though it's not even 1100. I look around the bridge and suddenly notice that the fog has not lifted; in fact it appears worse, with the bow of the *Antwerpen* invisible from here. I ask Captain Wisniewski if he's been here all night. Without taking his eyes off the radar screen he says, "Yes, the captain must remain all the time when there is fog like this. It is my responsibility." Then with a sardonic grin, he quietly adds, "Now the company gets their money's worth from me." I ask him the longest he's ever had to stay on the bridge and he sighs. "One time I think I was on the bridge for almost four days. We had fog that would not end. I hate the fog. Sorry, but you are speaking with a little bit tired captain now." Thinking I should leave him be, I prepare to go when he says, "No, stay. Is good to have some company."

The radar screen in front of him is empty of any other vessels, excepting a small fishing boat off our starboard quarter (behind us and to the right). We're still in American waters but sailing through the German Bank off Nova Scotia's southwestern coastline, quickly approaching the unmarked line that demarcates the Canadian domain. Wisniewski has already faxed off an official request to enter Canadian sovereign territory. He jokes, "I am taking you home."

The moniker "The Old Man" comes to mind as I watch my tired captain. "Yes ... the old man. The crew does call me this, I know, but not to my face. They call me *stari* in Polish. But I think I'm a very young old man." Fatigued, he opens up a bit to me as we stare at the foggy blanket embracing us.

"You know, this is a hard life sometimes. Being away from the family, being tired. But somebody has to be a sailor. And I think there are many people who work hard, on the land. But I will be happy to go home soon. I leave next week, did you know? And then I will see my wife, my daughter, my son ... it will be good."

Wisniewski tells me that spending four months at home and four months at sea creates an interesting relationship with his wife. "It is like getting divorced and remarried every four months. It's a good thing, I think. And I have a routine when at home. I live in a city that is very close to Gdynia and the first two months, I never think of the ship or the crew, just my family. But by the third month, I begin to think of *Antwerpen* from time to time. And then, by the end of the fourth month, I cannot wait to get back here. My wife is ready to see me go then; she says I am sometimes talking in my sleep, giving the orders."

Changing the topic, Wisniewski rises from the captain's chair and opens a small cupboard beside the navigation table. "Let me show you something," he says while pulling out a small wooden case not much larger than a shoebox and placing it on the chart table. "I bet you did not know we still have these things."

Unclasping the top, the captain reveals a golden sextant cradled inside, just like seafarers have used for hundreds of years. Wisniewski gingerly removes it from the box and screws a small telescope atop the brass device. "We are required, by law, to keep two of these aboard the vessel, in case all other navigation equipment were to fail. This is for the true seaman."

He holds the sextant in his hands like a prized possession and then, surprisingly, offers it to me. It is a beautiful piece of engineering, elegant and refined, the brass cold to my touch. I run my fingers across its burnished sides and see that it was crafted in what used to be known as the German Democratic Republic—East Germany. Hesitantly I place the telescope against my eye but can see nothing through it. Though it seems complicated, Captain Wisniewski explains that the sextant is actually a fairly simple device.

Invented in 1731, the sextant allows mariners to plot their latitude at sea. When the sun is at its highest position in the sky, at noon, you look through the sextant's eyepiece at that burning star of ours and move a semicircular armature beneath the telescope to reveal a degree of angle. "But, this only tells you where you are in terms of north or south of the equator. We also must maintain a ship's chronometer," Wisniewski says, pointing to a clock on the other side of the chart table, recessed beneath a glass cover. The chronometer maintains Greenwich Mean Time, also known as Zulu Time or Universal Time Coordinated (UTC), an unchanging, constant time zone unaffected by daylight saving time or other worldwide vagaries. "The chronometer shows us how far we are from London, where the prime meridian is located, and this gives us our longitude east and west. So, we do some mathematical calculations with the observations from the sextant and the chronometer and then we know exactly where we are."

Of course, what Wisniewski has just told me glosses over hundreds of years of trial and error, disasters at sea and the work of thousands of scientists and mariners to come up with a foolproof system of plotting position.

IT'S ALWAYS BEEN fairly easy to determine latitude, how far north or south you are on the planet: At noon, local time, on any given day of the year, the sun above Anchorage, Alaska, is in a different position than if viewed from Mexico City. The real problem was always figuring out where the hell you were in terms of longitude: At noon in Philadelphia, the sun is in about the same position as if viewed at noon from Denver. For mariners, this problem came to a head in 1707, when four Royal Navy ships floundered on the Gilstone Ledges off the Isles of Scilly, killing almost two thousand men. The cause was discovered to be bad navigation techniques, so a few years later a reward of £20,000 was offered to the first person to come up with a dependable means of plotting longitude (the sum was equivalent to £2 million today, or about U.S.$3.8 million). And everyone knew that the only way to ascertain longitude was by standardizing the measurement of time from a fixed point on the planet. The competition being British, the point decided upon was the Royal Observatory in Greenwich. Quite simply, someone had to come up with a dependable clock, which had not existed until that time.

The competition led to a flurry of activity as individuals came forth with various solutions to the problem, some more bizarre than others. One of my favourites is a macabre operation utilizing a mystical element called the "powder of sympathy." The theory goes something like this: You first convince someone to let himself be stabbed with a knife. Once you've removed the blade from the wounded victim, you then sprinkle it with the powder of sympathy, magically empowering the knife. This will cause the unfortunate subject to feel pain again, in a voodoo-like manner, even though the knife is no longer embedded in his flesh. The proponent of this theory also suggested gathering a bunch of dogs, stabbing them with the same knife and placing the animals on British ships. At noon each day in Greenwich, the knife would be plunged into a bowl filled with the powder and the dogs would all yelp in pain, no matter where in the world they were. Thankfully, the Board of Longitude rejected this idea.

As the top minds in Great Britain and Europe struggled to come up with a solution to finding longitude at sea, a lowly carpenter from Yorkshire was preparing to best them all. John Harrison began to tinker with clocks in his spare time and then became obsessed with developing the perfect timepiece for mariners. His eventual result was the "H4," a silver timepiece the size of a pocket watch that, in 1761, became the first dependable chronometer and solved the longitude problem once and for all. To this day it still keeps time in a display case at the Royal Observatory. And, at 1300 hours (1:00 P.M.) in Greenwich, an aluminum time ball still drops from the tower above Harrison's clock, so that any ships moored on the nearby Thames River can set their chronometers.

Until just a few decades ago, the sextant was still a regular part of the process of navigating at sea. But the advent of the global positioning system, or GPS, has made this handsome device all but redundant. GPS uses a system of satellites that feed data to small receivers, such as the one mounted above the chart table, and every seafarer alive today is grateful for the technology. Still, as I take a last look at the German sextant before returning it to Captain Wisniewski, I feel a little sad that this wonderful device should have become an afterthought in today's world.

As he carefully returns the tool to its sea box, my captain has little time for nostalgia. "Yes, it is an interesting piece of equipment. But I will gladly take satellites and computers over it any time."

A LITTLE LATER, the chief officer enters the wheelhouse and I note that he's also looking exhausted. Bordon has been able to catch some catnaps on the sofa in his office, but he's also been on duty most of the time since we left Maine, giving Wisniewski small breaks to sleep, though the captain doesn't leave the bridge. It's obvious that Bordon is checking on the captain, making sure he's not too exhausted. The two men chat in Polish to each other and then Bordon checks the most recent weather update, a fax that sits on the navigation table.

The chief officer tells me that both men will not get any rest for a while, as the weather report says the fog won't clear until we reach Halifax Harbour itself, which will probably be around 0500 hours tomorrow morning. As well, once we do tie up in Halifax they'll be busy supervising the loading of 39,000 tonnes of gypsum rock bound for Florida. Bordon will have to resume his duties supervising the deck crew, while the captain will be called upon to move the *Antwerpen* a few times, as the loading cranes at the port can't reach all the cargo holds.

After Bordon leaves, Wisniewski jokes that a few more days like this and his chief officer will start losing weight because of not getting a chance to eat. When I say something about it being a good thing that Bordon didn't become a pilot, the captain looks at me quizzically. So I explain that the chief officer's father is a retired air force fighter pilot who wanted his son to follow in his footsteps. "I did not know that," Wisniewski says. "It is the unfortunate part of my job. I cannot be friends with everybody. I must remain separate. To tell you the truth, I do not know much about the private lives of my crew. But," he checks the radar screen again, "I tell you that it is interesting that his father wanted him to be pilot. Because I think that in my next life I would like to be an airline pilot." Why? "I do not know. Why not? I have already been the seaman. I think it must be easier to be the pilot."

We both stare glumly at the fog outside. I can see deckhands walking to the forecastle, disappearing into the haze as they pass Number Two Hatch. "Captain," I ask, "do you think a ship has a soul?" Wisniewski rests his chin on his hands and thinks long and hard.

Finally, after several minutes, he answers. "You know, I have some answers to your question here in my head. But I do not want to say them yet. Because what you are asking is, I think, an important question. And I am tired, as you can see. Let me think about this for a few days, if that is OK with you?" I can't tell if he's dodging my question or genuinely concerned about it; it just slipped out of my mouth. Regardless, I'll give him as much time as he wants to collect his thoughts.

In the meantime, Captain Wisniewski suggests I go seek out the chief engineer, Janusz Ostrowski. "You should spend some time with him, go below to the engine room, if you want to know more about the spirit of this ship. Besides," he glares at the fog, "there will not be much to see up here." Another pause to privately curse this weather condition that has him bound to his chair on the bridge and he turns to me. "Did I mention that I hate fog?"

5

ENGINEERS

A man must keep a little back shop where he can be
himself without reserve.
In solitude alone can he know true freedom.
—MICHEL DE MONTAIGNE, *ESSAIS 1588*

F ollowing the advice of Captain Wisniewski, I go in search of Chief
Engineer Janusz Ostrowski, the keeper of the nether regions. He is
responsible for the engines as well as the maintenance of all the deck
equipment, such as the gantry cranes. Known universally as "The Chief,"
Ostrowski is technically the equal of the captain in the hierarchy of the

vessel, but in practical terms Wisniewski is the boss. There is a benign rivalry between The Old Man and The Chief as to who is really more important for the operation of a ship at sea. A hundred years ago, the role of the engineer was just emerging as mechanical power came to supplant wind power. Lost in the dark bowels of a ship, the engineer lived a world apart from the traditions of the sea, more concerned with fuel intake and engine output than the ability to use a sextant. The captain was the eyes and ears and the brains, the engineer the brawn. This has changed as automation has increased aboard vessels, and the day when the two roles are combined into one may not be far off.

Below the bridge, on the officers' deck, The Chief occupies an identical set of quarters to the captain's, but on the port side of the vessel. Unlike Wisniewski, though, The Chief is rarely to be seen in his quarters; most of the time he seems to be either in the engine room or checking the deck equipment, and today is no exception. Heading back to my cabin, I run into the steward, Rafal Winczo, and ask if he's seen The Chief around. "Yes, I think he is checking equipment on the forward deck," he replies, fatigue still etched in his eyes from a night of little sleep. He's heading to his little cabin to grab some much-needed rest.

Donning foul-weather gear in my own cabin, I head on deck and into the fog that still surrounds us. (OK, an admission: My "foul-weather gear" is actually a set of Canadian miner's gear, a rubberized bib and jacket, but it does work just fine, so long as things are warm and not too foul. The rest of *Antwerpen*'s crew is outfitted with professional Helly Henson–style clothing.) It's early afternoon, but you wouldn't know it because my entire world is grey. A couple of deckhands are cleaning up a storage locker by the fantail of *Antwerpen,* but there's no sign of The Chief there. I head forward, to the bow, walking across the damp hatch covers and feeling the cool air. In the haze ahead of me I can see some figures huddled around the conveyor belt that's on the port side, the one that is hoisted over the side to offload cargo but is secured into a cradle when we're at sea. At closer range, the figures materialize into The Chief, the third engineer and a couple of motormen. They're examining a part of the cargo conveyor system, a drive belt or something. I stand off to one side as the four guys do what so many workers do when they have a problem of some sort: They stare at the machinery with arms crossed over their chests. Eventually The Chief says something in Polish to the guys and he leaves them to start the repairs.

I catch his attention and Ostrowski beams and comes my way, hand extended. The Chief always seems to want to shake my hand for some reason, a gesture I make certain to return. In heavily accented English he tells me, "We have problem with equipment. Is … roller. Ya, ya, roller. Under belt. Not function good."

Walking back toward the superstructure with The Chief, I ask him if it might be possible to visit the engine room. Unfortunately, his grasp of my mother tongue is not as adept as I think, and he merely stares at me blankly. I repeat my query more slowly, and he raises his eyebrows and smiles. "Ah … visit engine? Yes, is OK." I ask when that might be arranged and he pauses for a moment before answering, "Um … would you like to go to Halifax with me?" Now it's my turn to stare dumbfounded. But of course he means, "Would I like to be in the engine control room when we enter Halifax Harbour tonight?" At least, I'm pretty sure that's what he means, so I tell The Chief that would be great, and he says to meet him on the bridge at 0100 hours. Since we're due to arrive in Halifax around 0400, it looks like another late night is in the offing.

THE ONE THING that is always apparent when you're at sea on a merchant vessel is the throb of the ship's engines. No matter where you are, there is a cadence to the *Antwerpen;* nothing stands still. As I walk through the corridors, the hand railings vibrate ever so slightly as I grasp them. A door left ajar will swing as though a breeze were catching it. Every enclosed space resounds with an ambient soundscape twenty-four hours a day. Even outside, on the decks, the steel plating shivers beneath your feet, a motion additional to the roll and pitch of the ship.

All of this emanates from the power plant hidden below, which is the most sheltered and protected space on *Antwerpen*. The body of this ship has three distinct elements. Her seven holds are her great lungs, breathing in the cargoes that are her reason for being. The wheelhouse is the de facto head of the ship, from which her sense of direction comes. And the heart of *Antwerpen* is her engines. Without their great pistons pumping up and down, she is merely tonnes of useless steel, lifeless on the water.

Without a doubt, the development of mechanical propulsion has been the single most dramatic innovation to seafaring in the last two hundred years. The advent of the steam engine altered thousands of years of sail-powered dominance of the seas, though it didn't happen overnight. We may think of the nineteenth century as the era of sailing ships—which is essentially true—but it was also the century in which engines appeared. And the shipping industry was at the forefront of their use during the Industrial Revolution.

Most historians consider the first reliable steamboat to be the *Charlotte Dundas,* designed by the Scottish engineer William Symington. She first sailed over two hundred years ago, on January 4, 1803, towing barges on the Forth & Clyde Canal. In 1812 another steam-powered vessel, the *Comet,* was making regular passenger runs from Glasgow to Greenock. By comparison, the first practical steam locomotives were not in use on Britain's railways until the 1820s. Within a few decades of that, the brilliant English-born son of a French engineer, Isambard Kingdom Brunel, began unleashing his maritime creations: the steamers *Great Western, Great Britain* and, finally, in 1859, a true behemoth of the seas, the *Great Eastern,* a ship that was four times larger than anything else afloat and in theory capable of carrying four thousand passengers. None was particularly profitable, and all had numerous mishaps and tragic accidents, but the groundwork had been laid.

The advantage of mechanical power was obvious to any nineteenth-century mariner: It was another means of dealing with the untameable ocean. The image of a clipper ship underway with all her sails set, running before the wind, belies the great difficulty in controlling these majestic vessels. To leave a port and reach the open seas, one didn't merely hoist sails and throw off the lines. It could take days for a British merchant sailer to slowly make it through the sheltered waters of the Irish Sea after leaving Liverpool, working herself this way and that until through the St. George's Channel separating Ireland and Wales. Later, in the doldrums of the mid-Atlantic, a vessel could find herself becalmed, the crew forced to tow her by rowing in the lifeboats. And it was not unheard of for ships to require weeks or even months to make it around Cape Horn off South America. In every case, those sailing ships lived and died at the mercy of the winds.

Ironically, as steam-powered vessels replaced sailing merchantmen throughout the nineteenth century, one of the last uses of the merchant-men was to supply the precious coal required for their new masters' engines. Many of the vessels that had once carried wool from Australia, tea from China or wood from Canada found themselves ferrying loads of coal to remote parts of the world, ready to be stockpiled in anticipation of the arrival of steamers hungry for the fuel. In a way, it was not unlike *Antwerpen* and her journeys between Venezuela and New England.

By MIDNIGHT I'm staring out the portholes of my cabin; there's not much to see, as it's pitch-black and I can't tell if the fog's lifted or not. On the bridge, the sea chart seems to indicate we're passing St. Margaret's Bay on the south shore of Nova Scotia, not far from the approaches to Halifax. There's a curtain that surrounds the chart table to keep light from spilling into the main part of the bridge. This is necessary because the only way to see if there's another ship out there—besides the radar—is to keep watch for another vessel's running lights. And light travels surprisingly far in the darkness of the sea.

Pulling the curtain back, I plunge into the blackness of the wheelhouse. After a few moments, my eyes adjust and I make out the captain and chief officer standing near the wheel. Wisniewski turns my way and greets me, still sounding tired. The fog has lifted a bit and there are faint glimmers of light off our port bow. They could be fishing boats, buoys or even homes on the shoreline.

"So you are going down below with The Chief tonight?" Wisniewski asks. "You will find it different from up here. Much different."

"Do not ask them about automobiles," Chief Officer Bordon quizzically adds, chuckling.

Chief Engineer Janusz Ostrowski enters and confers with the other two officers in Polish for a bit. Unlike the captain and chief officer, Ostrowski is wearing white overalls, albeit slightly dirty ones. They are the mark of his office, the closest he ever comes to wearing a real uniform.

"So ... you are ready?" he asks with a smile, after shaking my hand. And then off we go, descending from the wheelhouse into his mechanical lair.

To get there, The Chief leads me through a maze inside *Antwerpen*'s inner spaces. First we wind our way down the staircases toward the mess halls on D Deck. Around a corner I've not yet explored is a passageway that ends at a yellow steel door with a large "No Admittance" sign posted on it. Through this we enter a warm, narrow space that surrounds the engine room itself. The walls are lined with orange work overalls hanging on hooks to dry after being laundered. Just past the line of cleansed work clothes we come to another heavy door, this one painted white and marked "E/R," which Ostrowski opens before beckoning me to follow.

Stepping into the heart of *Antwerpen*, I am surrounded by an engine room that occupies a space six storeys high. We're about halfway up the enclosed cavern on a landing that is level with the top of the main engine. I can feel the heat given off by it and hear a deafening roar from the engines, a sort of chugga-chugga like the sound of old steam locomotives. From my pockets I pull two foam earplugs and work one into one side, then one into the other. They dampen things only a little.

The Chief has already descended a ladder to E Deck and is waiting for me to follow, but I continue just to stand there, transfixed by the sense of power that emanates from every corner of the room, this space from which our floating village maintains its independence.

I make it down the ladder without stumbling—barely—while The Chief stands there grinning proudly. Though the engine room is noisy and hot, it is also one of the cleanest and brightest parts of the *Antwerpen*. The bulkheads and ceilings are painted white, the floor plates and engine parts a dark shade of green; and a latticework of pipes, conduits and wiring hovers above me. Looking around, I see no oil stains or piles of rags or general signs of disorder such as you might find in an auto mechanic's garage. If given the choice between the sun-bleached main deck and the engine room floor, I'd eat a meal off the steel grating beneath me here. The Chief runs a tight ship down here.

The main engine is behind him, a green monster that has been trapped and confined in this industrial bestiary, along with a trio of smaller generators and various other equipment required to maintain a ship on the high seas and in port. I ask Ostrowski about the particulars of his baby and he shouts answers at me.

"Is Sulzer engine. You know Sulzer? With six cylinders." He holds up six fingers to emphasize this. "It can generate ... um ... 14,400 horses of power. Over there is three Daihatsu generators, diesel, for auxiliary power."

He walks around the Sulzer engine and bellows statistics over the din of the machinery. The main power plant is fuelled by a thick type of marine diesel that has to be heated up before being injected into the firing chambers. The days of coal-fired steam engines with their immense water boilers are long gone. Instead, what you have essentially are really, really big truck engines like this one, a "straight six," with the cylinders in a line. Each piston is five metres high, as shown by a spare one that stands off to one side. The three smaller generators are aft and I can see someone fumbling around beneath the middle one. I follow Ostrowski as he climbs down to a narrow catwalk where a crewman is labouring to put an access panel back in place. The Chief shouts some instructions to the guy, a motorman about my age whose hands are coated in thick grease and oil. He is contorted into an uncomfortable position, with one arm in the open portal and the other grasping a portable light better to see what lies inside the engine. Still, he manages to give me a weak smile before The Chief leads me off to explore more of his world.

Farther aft and down another level, I see the propeller shaft itself. Almost a metre in diameter and open to view, it doesn't spin as quickly as I had imagined it would. The shaft runs from the main engine through the back of the hull to the blade, a 14,800-kilogram piece of bronze with six blades on it. Chief Ostrowski explains that the shaft turns in a clockwise manner, and to keep seawater from flooding in, a casing of heavy oil and a series of O-rings form a barrier.

But all that information is inconsequential; for I am the closest I can get to seeing the reason for this vessel's existence. The engine, of course, is vital to propelling us through the seas; the bridge and its equipment provide our sense of direction; and the crew, of course, keeps everything working. But without the spinning propeller blade, *Antwerpen* would be adrift on the seas; this cylindrical armature gives us vitality, essence and freedom. It sits here, day and night, toiling away unseen, each turn taking the bulker somewhere new.

Tearing myself away from the shaft, I'm led to the starboard side, where a machinists' shop for doing repair work is located, fitted out with a lathe, drill press and other gear. Forward of the shop is the desalination plant. I've always been fascinated by how a ship at sea can sustain its freshwater requirements, and Ostrowski gives me the layman's explanation. Seawater is actually 96.5 percent pure, the remaining 3.5 percent being dissolved salts (so a litre of ocean water has about thirty-five grams of salt in it). The *Antwerpen* takes in salt water, through outlets in the hull, which is then boiled inside the desalination plant, creating freshwater steam that is then siphoned off and allowed to cool before being pumped to the water bunkers for use in the showers, toilets and even as potable drinking water.

We've completed an entire circuit of the engine room and The Chief now leads me into the portside control room. Once inside, we remove our ear protectors and I say hello to the second and third assistant engineers who are manning the controls as The Chief talks with them. The room has a large window along the inside wall, facing into the main engine compartment, and a four-metre-wide panel festooned with gauges and dials takes up most of the space. There are sixteen pressure gauges on one half of the panel, along with the tachometer, rudder indicator, temperature readers and the main engine control itself. The other half of the panel has three banks of switches and looks like an audio mixing board in a recording studio.

The most noticeable feature of the control room, indeed of the entire engine compartment, is that no windows or compass or anything else provides a glimpse out into the real world or any sense of direction, except for an indicator on the panel that shows whether the propeller shaft is turning in a forward or reverse manner. This is also the one place in the ship where there is neither day nor night, only an artificial fluorescent-lit timelessness. The only thing that matters here is to keep the *Antwerpen* functioning by caring for the main engine and its smaller siblings.

A red light on the bulkhead near the windows flashes and The Chief picks up the telephone to talk with the bridge. It's just past 0130 and he tells me that the pilot is coming aboard shortly. We've been steaming full ahead at a little more than fourteen knots but will reduce speed for the pilot boat to come alongside. Ostrowski takes up position in front of the control panel, with his back to the engines, while the second engineer stands by on the other side.

The *Antwerpen*'s engine controls are somewhat antiquated in terms of technology; most newer vessels have fully automated systems linked to onboard computers that allow the wheelhouse to directly control any changes in speed. Not here. Instead, the orders from the bridge are transmitted via a ringing bell that warns the engineers of a command, and a telegraph on the panel that shows exactly what is required. Then, an engineer has to manually effect whatever the captain has asked for, such as a change in speed from Full Ahead to Half Ahead.

Like the recess bell in school, the first warning comes from above. The telegraph asks for Slow Ahead and the second engineer adjusts the control accordingly. Besides having no window to the outside world, the engine room has another anomaly—no indicator registers speed in knots. The engineers are more concerned with the propeller's rpm, or revolutions per minute: Full Ahead is 90 rpm, Half is 55, Slow is 45 and Dead Slow is 35. The duty engineer tweaks the load—the amount of fuel fed to the main engine cylinders—by turning a small dial, and there is an audible change in the tone emanating from beyond the windows as we slow down.

It will take several minutes for *Antwerpen* to slow and the pilot to transfer aboard her, so everyone relaxes a bit. The Chief tells me it takes *Antwerpen* 3840 metres to come to a dead stop from Full Speed Ahead, or about twenty-nine minutes. While we await the pilot, the third engineer wanders over to an ad hoc lounge in the corner, nothing more than a couple of chairs and an electric kettle beside a battered-looking desk. He flops down into one of the chairs and, to kill time, he pulls out a Polish automobile magazine from the desk and begins flipping the pages. Within seconds, Chief Ostrowski joins him and grabs his own magazine, and they start talking about cars. Even though I don't speak Polish, I know the international language of boys and their toys.

"What car do you have?" The Chief asks me. When I tell him I don't currently own a vehicle (besides my bike), he seems disappointed, so I quickly add that I used to own a Toyota. That cheers him up and he peppers me with questions about the make and model while searching for the section of the magazine on Japanese cars. He then proceeds to show the type of Opel he owns and tries to translate the engine capacity and fuel consumption into English for me. When he makes some sort of mistake, the third engineer joins the fray to correct him, and soon the two men are in a heated discussion about the differences between litres per kilometre and gallons per mile. I try to change the subject by asking The Chief how much fuel *Antwerpen* burns.

"The vessel uses 30 tonnes of fuel each day. It is a type of diesel fuel, heavy bunker." Though this may seem like a lot, he gestures with his arms to indicate what that would look like; he is very precise. According to Ostrowski, 30 tonnes works out to an amount equivalent to a space two metres high by three metres wide by five metres long, or about the size of a compact car. "Um, in practical terms, a cubic metre of fuel weighs about .98 tonne. A cubic metre of ocean, the salt water, weighs 1.18 tonnes. And a cubic metre of fresh water weighs 1 tonne."

He then goes on to give me a convoluted explanation of why a steel-hulled ship doesn't sink. Although the explanation's a bit hard to grasp due to his poor English, Ostrowski manages to use a calculator and a pencil and paper to educate me about how the water displaced by our hull weighs more than the weight of the hull, allowing the ship to float. When a vessel like *Antwerpen* enters fresh water, she actually sinks a bit because salt water is denser. And, hypothetically, were the ship to be placed in a liquid lake of gasoline—which weighs less than any type of water—she'd sink like a rock. Preferring not to think about this last point, I query him on how he ended up being an engineer.

He shrugs and then says, "We must all have a job. I do not know, it was not … anything particular. Maybe I could have been a captain instead. But I always liked motors, especially as teenager. I went to school first to become mechanic and did repairs on automobiles. But then I decided to become a mariner—the pay was better—and so it was natural that I would be with the engines."

The Chief has an innate sense of his engines. He's barely finished telling me about his background when he notices something and wanders over to where the second assistant is standing. Without a word, the second engineer and The Chief cock their ears and listen to the engine for a moment. Then the junior officer tweaks the rpm ever so slightly.

But this connection with the engines' performance extends beyond the control room. Both The Chief and the captain have told me about instances when they have been awakened from a sound sleep in their bunks by some change in the tenor or timbre of the ship. Maybe it's a burp in the engine output or a change in the vessel's momentum caused by wave actions. Regardless, they will be up in a flash to check on what's happened and, hopefully, to reassure themselves that it's nothing serious.

As the *Antwerpen* slows from 90 rpm, the ship begins to shake much more dramatically for a few minutes. I must look perturbed, because Ostrowski comes over to stand beside me and explain what's going on.

"When engines reach this point, at this rpm, there is created a sort of … resonating. Yes? Do you understand? And then is the vibration you feel." There is a sign posted on the control panel I have just noticed, stating, "Critical speed—engine not to be used continuously between 73 and 81 rpm." After a few minutes, the vibrating ceases and the duty engineer once more fine-tunes the engine output.

As he does this, I notice that he—like all the engineers—has dirty fingernails. This, of course, is to be expected from people who work with motors and oil and whatnot. But it is also something of a marker, a point of individuality among mariners. The deckhands working with the equipment up top often wear gloves, so they may have dirty hands but not like this. And the wheelhouse officers certainly don't have to worry about grease on their navigation charts. No, you can always identify engineers by their hands.

Chief Ostrowski puts on his ear protectors again and slips outside the control room to check something or other. When he returns, he scans the gauges and dials as we slow to take the pilot aboard. With the plastic ear protectors pushed up on top of his head, The Chief looks like some bizarre insect with two bulging yellow eyes.

The bridge telephone rings and we're told that the pilot is now aboard and we'll be making for the approaches to Halifax Harbour. The rpm of the engine is increasing as we rev up to full speed again. As this happens,

The Chief makes an entry in the engine room logbook. Like the one kept on the bridge, this logbook officially records all engine orders and the time they were executed.

For another hour little happens as we motor our way past the unseen communities of Portuguese Cove and Herring Cove, somewhere off to port side. The guys read their magazines or stare blankly at the engine controls. I ask The Chief if he ever gets bored with his job.

"Mmm ... yes. Of course. You see, like at the present there is not much work to do. But I must still be here when we are coming to the port. It would be easier to be doing this work if it was in the day, in the daytime hours. But the sailor has no choice. It is the schedule of company which we must follow."

Does he feel like *Antwerpen* is *his* ship? I wonder.

"Ah, this is interesting question, ya. Is she my ship? Well, I like to think this is so. But I know the captain," he gestures toward the upper decks, "he thinks she is *his* ship. It is of us both, you know. We must protect her. And the crew, too." The Chief pauses for a moment and furrows his brow. "But there is something else, I think. I have been with many ships as sailor and each vessel is different to me. I think, for me, there is not so much of this ... mmm ... romance thoughts about the ship. Is maybe a more practical thoughts. You know? We have no windows here with which to watch the sea passing us by. So I don't know if I am answering your question, but this is my impression. I am practical man."

And it's true that all the romantic impressions of the sea are written from the decks of ships, not the belly. Perhaps this is what makes engineers so much more practical, as The Chief seems to be saying. They are the unseen caretakers of ships at sea, working in the purgatory below.

When one thinks of the sinking of the RMS *Titanic* in 1912, the tales of Captain Edward Smith stoically going down with his ship come to mind. Or the heroism of the wireless operators, the junior deck officers and even the ship's band playing their instruments as the liner slipped beneath the North Atlantic's waters. But what of the men in the engine rooms? Rarely is any thought given to their actions, which helped keep the lights on and the power going for the pumps seeking to slow the crippled vessel's demise.

For the record, the chief engineer of *Titanic* was named Joseph Bell, who, along with thirty-five other men below decks, had no say in the course charted or the speed selected but nevertheless fought valiantly to keep the ship from dying. All sacrificed their lives that April morning, leaving eighteen widows and twenty-six fatherless children back home.

Maybe I'm thinking about *Titanic* because the largest number of victims of that disaster are buried in Halifax, 150 out of over 1500 who died. Also, it's almost two-thirty in the morning here in *Antwerpen's* engine room, about the exact time the great ship ended her brief life. Yawning, I fix myself a cup of coffee in the "lounge" and look at a notice conspicuously posted on the bulkhead. It's a fleet notice from SMT's head office, warning of the dangers of illegally discharging oil from the ship into surrounding waters. American authorities have, in the past, sentenced engineers to prison terms and fined companies millions of dollars for dumping oil in U.S. waters. SMT's policy is pretty strict, warning in no uncertain terms that any employee caught doing this will be fired immediately.

I hadn't even noticed our progress into Halifax Harbour—how could I from down here?—but I do see that The Chief is pacing back and forth now, though he doesn't seem nervous at all. We must be passing the downtown of Halifax on our port side and her sister city, Dartmouth, on starboard. I can imagine the Angus Macdonald suspension bridge that connects the two looming in front of *Antwerpen,* but I know that there's plenty of room beneath it for ships to manoeuvre. After passing under the bridge, we enter The Narrows, barely five hundred metres wide, and our speed is yet again reduced as we approach the second suspension bridge over these sheltered waters, the Murray MacKay.

The Chief tells me we're heading for the National Gypsum terminal in the Bedford Basin, a large bay at the north end of the harbour that makes

Halifax such a natural port. We must be getting close to it, since the bridge commands are coming much more frequently now. *Antwerpen's* making 45 rpm, Slow Ahead, and executing a gentle turn to starboard as we swing into the basin. The bridge telegraphs Dead Slow Ahead and the rudder indicator shows Starboard 10, then it swings to midships as our engines rev down some more.

The Chief comes around and stands behind his two junior officers, scanning the control panel. No one speaks. Then the bridge telegraphs a command to Stop Engines and the rpm indicator spools down to zero. Ostrowski looks at the duty engineer for a moment and then fixes his gaze on a gauge that monitors compressed air.

Antwerpen is capable of five "stop–starts," as pilots call them. To restart the main engine, compressed air is released into the six cylinders, forcing the giant pistons to begin moving. The concern here is that there is only enough air in the compressor tank for five stop–starts in a short time; it takes several minutes for the machinery to recharge itself. Though it's highly unlikely the tank would ever completely run out of compressed air, The Chief still monitors the amount in reserve and makes a note in the logbook.

The bell rings again and the wheelhouse orders Dead Slow Ahead. The duty engineer then depresses the black Start button and the pistons begin to move again. As we nudge ever closer to our berth, another Stop Engines command is telegraphed and we again idle in the water. I assume there must be a tug, or two, outside pushing on our hull, but can feel nothing from down here.

The Chief turns to me and says, "Daniel, would you like to start the engine?" Well, sure. So I move beside the duty engineer and place my hand where The Chief tells me, near the Start button. "Ummm … when I give command, you push the button, ya?" The two other engineers are eyeing me cautiously, as though I'm about to launch a ballistic missile. The bell rings, Dead Slow Ahead is ordered, and I release the compressed air into the cylinders. It's fairly anti-climactic; there's no sense that anything has occurred. But Ostrowski still beams at me like a proud parent.

For the next twenty minutes the ship moves gently along and twice we reverse engines to slow our progress. Finally, at 0345 by the clock on the wall, a final command to Stop Engines is issued and everyone relaxes. Another note is made in the engine log and then a light flashes, signalling the Bridge is on the phone. Chief Ostrowski speaks to the chief officer briefly before hanging up. "They are finished with the engines. We are done."

There's not much more to see now. There are notes to be made in the logbook, and some of the equipment needs to be checked, but otherwise the engine staff is done for the night. I thank them all and The Chief escorts me out of the engine room to the narrow companionway where the crew dry their laundry. He is, I note for the first time, tired. It occurs to me that The Chief is one of those people who never seem fatigued, who know how to pace themselves. But at this early hour—passing four in the morning—Chief Engineer Janusz Ostrowski is letting his exhaustion show as he shakes my hand, less vigorously than usual. He will return to the control room, make a final check on things and then head for his bunk to grab a few hours' sleep before awakening to watch the cargo-loading operation.

AFTER THE CLAUSTROPHOBIC ATMOSPHERE in the engine room, I head for the main deck to get some fresh air. It's well after four in the morning, closer to five even, and the air is warm and inviting after the atmosphere below. Our starboard side is moored to a long concrete jetty and flood-lights are washing over *Antwerpen* from the shore. A few crewmen are already preparing to begin the loading process—I can hear the crackle of walkie-talkies and deck gear being unlashed. I wander toward *Antwerpen*'s stern and sit myself on one of the steel posts known as "bitts," which are used for securing the hawsers, or mooring cables.

Our stern is pointing southwest into the middle of Bedford Basin, and Halifax is quiet at this hour. Though I've been to Halifax many times in my life, I've never actually arrived via the sea and on a ship. I realize, for perhaps the first time, that this community would not exist were it not for its natural harbour. Oh, I might have been taught that in school, but it was always an intangible sort of statistic: "Halifax founded as a key British port in the New World." As early as 1715 the site had been identified as a good harbour "most convenient for trade," though when Edward Cornwallis first arrived here back in 1749, in a sloop of war called the *Sphinx*, he was unable to sail into the bay. Instead, the *Sphinx* tacked back and forth aimlessly until a commercial vessel happened by, outbound from Boston, with a sailor who knew the local waters aboard. So it was that a merchant mariner piloted the British navy into these waters.

Viewed from the *Antwerpen*'s fantail, the commercial importance of Halifax is still evident. I can see headlights of transport trucks moving along the highway that skirts the basin, hear the whistle of a freight train somewhere behind me and notice a container ship unloading her cargo at the terminal across the way. I watch the eastern skies, looking for the first signs of daylight, urging the sun to move faster and enlighten my vista.

I've always found the last hour of nighttime, those sixty minutes before dawn, to be somewhat magical. To watch a city awake always holds the promise of something new and the memory of something passed. It is a time of reflection, and I spend it this morning on the fantail of a bulker. To some this may be an inglorious locale, but to me it is as near to peace as I can imagine.

Walking to the stern railing, I stretch tired arms and legs while peering over the edge of the hull. *Antwerpen*'s propeller lies motionless somewhere down there in the black waters, at rest after incessantly performing its heroic task of urging us on through the seas. The rudder, too, is asleep; a silent sentinel standing a watch from its sternpost that no one sees. Just above my head, the ensign of Cyprus hangs limply from the flagpole. It only appears when we are entering or leaving a port; the rest of the time it is neatly tucked into a small box on the bridge, along with all the other signal flags and national ensigns that ceremony and regulations require.

The mooring lines to my left are taut, snaking from the capstans through the chocks to the bollards on the wharf. The land does not clutch us so much as we grasp at it, these tentacles reaching out to restrain *Antwerpen* from fleeing back to her normal home. Mooring lines are neatly coiled on the deck plating and, indeed, the entire fantail is ship-shape and tidy. I like this display of organization and always have. My hometown of Sault Ste. Marie—or, at least, the first of many places I would call home—sits upon the St. Mary's River, through which Lake Superior drains and upon whose waters lake freighters and ocean vessels transited the locks on their journeys. For a youngster struggling to comprehend the big picture of life, these ships were an early lesson in what constitutes a "society." They were easy to understand: They had a beginning, a middle and an end; there was a crew led by a leader; they had set paths to follow, predetermined destinations to reach; there was nothing uncertain about them, no shades of grey. It all seemed so simple. They seemed organized.

Yawning, I'm about to head to my bunk when the first rays of daylight appear from the east as 0600 nears. With a speed that always surprises me, the sun makes her reappearance known to all and etches the skies over Dartmouth with subtle shards of orange light.

I remember a childhood weather rhyme: "Red sky at night, sailors' delight. Red sky in morning, sailors take warning." The prognostication is based on the usual weather patterns in this part of the world, in which systems generally travel from west to east. Seeing clear skies on the western horizon as the sun sets is supposed to bode well for the next day: There are no storm clouds swirling your way. Whether or not that will hold true for us remains to be seen. Regardless, we'll be here for a few days loading crushed rocks into *Antwerpen*'s holds.

As the sun rises higher, it illuminates the waters of the Bedford Basin, which are glassy and calm. Off to the northwest I can see some submarines tied up. They are old Oberon-class boats recently decommissioned by the Canadian Navy after over thirty years of service. Farther along past the subs is the navy's munitions wharf, with reinforced concrete bunkers lining the hill above it. There's a Canadian warship tied up at the wharf, which turns out to be HMCS *Toronto,* a newer frigate. She's just returned from a six-month deployment overseas in the Arabian Gulf as part of the war on terror and the actions against Iraq, and I have no doubt that her homecoming included brass bands, flag-waving crowds and the smiles and tears of loved ones reunited.

How different from the experiences of merchant mariners. The solitude of their time at sea extends to their personal lives, in which homecomings and departures are distinctly more private events, bereft of fanfare. Some of the crew of *Antwerpen* haven't seen their homes or families or friends in seven months, and won't return to Poland for two more. Naval or military personnel can spend six months or a year, or more, overseas, and we appreciate their commitment and sacrifices. They will be away from their homes for lengthy periods, forced to rely on their own skills and those of their comrades, facing boredom and solitude, to say nothing of life-threatening dangers. Pretty much the daily life of a merchant mariner.

During this warm late-summer dawn in Nova Scotia, I realize that mariners and military personnel share many bonds. Both foster a closed society, off limits to outsiders; both operate on codified rules of daily existence, with a clear delineation of leaders and followers. It can be no other way when one's life is in the hands of one's comrades. This is not melodrama but reality.

The life experiences of each community have forged a sense of identity that we civilians find hard to comprehend. And centuries of trying to explain this to us has left both groups exasperated, such that they rarely bother opening up to us anymore. Why should they? We often don't seem to care, as the experiences of Vietnam War veterans have so vividly shown (a three-decade-long conflict that involved not just the Vietnamese and the Americans, but tens of thousands of French, Laotian, Cambodian, Korean, Japanese, Canadian, Australian and New Zealand soldiers and civilians). But at least those who don the uniforms of our various nations' armed forces seem to be getting a little more respect of late. The profession of arms is one in which individuals can expect to be injured or killed, and for that, we honour them. If only the same were true for merchant seamen.

During two world wars, the very waters of the Bedford Basin here behind *Antwerpen* teemed with cargo ships lying at anchor, ready to move into convoy formations and cross the perilous North Atlantic bound for Britain. That ocean was perilous not just because of the threats posed by Mother Nature, but because of the malevolent threats posed by humankind, in which U-boats, armed cruisers and attack planes lay in wait to kill and maim. In fact, sometimes the price of duty occurred right within this very port. The route that *Antwerpen* just took into the anchorage followed the course taken by another merchant vessel almost nine decades ago, a journey that was to be short and exceedingly deadly.

Just past 0830 in the morning on December 6, 1917, the French munitions vessel *Mont Blanc* was making for the Bedford Basin to join up with a convoy bound for Europe. *Mont Blanc* was laden with four hundred thousand pounds of TNT in her holds, as well as various other explosives and ammunition packed on her deck. At about the same time, the SS *Imo* was leaving the basin, bound for New York to be loaded with relief supplies for Belgium. *Imo* was about two-thirds the size of *Antwerpen* and had been a cattle carrier before the war, part of the White Star Lines' fleet, which also included the *Titanic*. At the time the two ships were approaching each other, Halifax was a main transshipment point for men and supplies being sent to wartorn Europe, with dozens of vessels coming and going through the harbour each day.

This was an era before radio communications and traffic control were as regulated as they are today. The *Imo* and the *Mont Blanc* approached each other in the Narrows, head-on. The ships were supposed to pass port-to-port—that is, left side to left side, as on most automobile highways—but the Belgian relief ship was moving too fast and veering close to the French munitions vessel. Like two cars on a narrow country road, the *Imo* and the *Mont Blanc* were stuck in a deadly game of chicken: Who would make the right move? In the end, neither did. At about 0845, the outbound *Imo* rammed her bow into the *Mont Blanc*. Sparks flew as metal careered off metal, igniting the explosives on the deck of the French vessel.

For the next fifteen minutes or so, confusion reigned. The *Imo* drifted toward the northern shore of the Narrows, near Dartmouth, while the crew of the *Mont Blanc* fled their burning vessel for the lifeboats. Aflame in the waters of Halifax Harbour, the *Mont Blanc* began to drift toward the south shore and Pier Six as crowds gathered to watch the event. At about 0900, the munitions vessel was close alongside the pier when the TNT exploded.

Within seconds, the *Mont Blanc* erupted in an explosion that would be the largest one made by humans until the atomic bombs were dropped on Japan in 1945. A mushroom cloud like none ever seen before filled the sky above Halifax; the *Mont Blanc* disintegrated into 3000 tonnes of shrapnel worse than anything seen in the trenches of Europe; the buildings on shore were flattened, ships were thrown on their sides and most every window in the city was shattered. Over 1600 people died instantly; within days the toll would rise to 11,000 people seriously injured or killed. It was said that, for a moment, you could see the bottom of the harbour as the water exploded upward. The devastation was beyond comprehension.

To this day, the Halifax Explosion remains little known outside Canada. Part of the reason for that is the news blackout that surrounded the event when it occurred; the Allies did not want Imperial Germany to hear of the disaster and feared it would demoralize the civilians in Canada and her troops fighting abroad. I pause for a moment to think what it must have been like for the mariners on those two vessels, especially the crew of the *Mont Blanc,* who knew what lay in their ship's holds.

The price paid by the merchant mariners of all nations in the last two world wars was atrocious. There really is no other way to describe what these mostly unarmed men endured feeding the war effort. When it comes to a nation's power at sea, the image of a cruiser, destroyer, battleship, aircraft carrier or submarine springs to mind. The term "navy" refers to the ships of war of a nation, and though we might assume "navy" to mean merely fighting vessels and their uniformed support ships, this definition ignores the importance of commercial shipping in times of conflict. Indeed, when nations go to war, they can transfer their commercial ships— by law—to the "merchant navy," a fleet of vessels tasked not with supporting economic interests but, rather, the strategic interests of a country.

To be a merchant mariner in either war meant you were far more likely to die than if you were serving in uniform on a naval vessel. To give you an idea of the dangers, consider that 534 Allied merchant ships were sunk in the Second World War just from enemy mines alone. That works out to about 1 in every 10 ships lost, because over 5000 cargo vessels were sunk in that war. In the Atlantic Ocean alone, fifty thousand civilian mariners died between 1939 and 1945; they died of horrible burns caused by explosions, were gunned to death as they clung to flotsam, or drowned alone in the frigid waters of the North Atlantic.

For their heroic service in helping to defeat the enemy, many merchant mariners found that once the war had ended they were treated as second-class veterans, denied pensions and other benefits accorded to their naval brethren. In Canada, it took until 1998 before these men received official government recognition and compensation. Unfortunately, little has changed. When it comes to war, the role of mariners remains as invaluable to governments today as it has throughout history, but their contributions continue to be overshadowed by others'. Rarely has a conflict been waged without the support of sailors manning cargo vessels, be it the Trojan War, Napoleon's conquests, the Korean conflict or the struggle to remove Saddam Hussein. When Roman triremes headed across the Mediterranean toward Egypt, cargo ships filled with amphorae followed them. The Spanish conquistadors in the Americas shipped home their plunder on merchant galleons that were attacked by the English navy.

Most recently, the two wars waged against Saddam Hussein would never have been fought without civilian support vessels. However eager President George W. Bush might have been to depose Saddam Hussein in 2003, he could not begin the military campaign until his forces and those of the other members of his "Coalition of the Willing" had everything they needed to wage uncontestable war. One of the reasons the invasion took so long to begin had nothing to do with international diplomacy and everything to do with simple logistics. The United States did not have enough ships to carry the implements of destruction across the seas.

To overcome this shortfall, the Americans (and the British) hired commercial ships to transport the guns, food, medical supplies, spare parts, mobile hospitals, Coca-Cola, Apache helicopters and anything else imaginable that could not be carried on a U.S. Navy vessel. So, while United Nations investigators wandered around the deserts of Iraq and as endless speeches were made at UN headquarters in New York, hundreds of ships were being quietly loaded at ports in the United States, Great Britain and elsewhere. It wasn't until the last stevedore had finished loading some unknown ship that Saddam Hussein realized the end was truly near.

In peace and in war, ships have always left port laden with their cargoes, the sailors resigned to their fate, trying not to think about the madness of the seas and the maliciousness of the human beings that might await them. The wheelhouse officers will plot a course, the engineers will get speed up and the deckhands will cast off the lines. And if anyone is going to get swept overboard, burned or injured, it's likely to be an OS, an ordinary seaman, or an AB, an able-bodied seaman, the rank and file of the merchant-shipping world.

6

DECKHANDS

The fair breeze blew, the white foam flew,
The furrow followed free;
We were the first that ever burst
Into that silent sea.

—SAMUEL TAYLOR COLERIDGE,
"THE RIME OF THE ANCIENT MARINER"

S everal days after arriving in Halifax, the bulk carrier *Antwerpen* is
returning to her natural habitat, steaming south through the Atlantic
Ocean toward Jacksonville. While in Nova Scotia, the crew worked

around the clock to fill her seven holds with 38,000 tonnes of gypsum rock bound for some factory in Florida. This entailed dumping clumps of dirty white rock into each individual hold, a process that soon caked the ship in a film of dust. It was on the decks, in the corridors; you could even feel it smearing your clothing. Along with the ever-present sound of the gypsum crashing down, the dust made our brief communion with land a somewhat unpleasant and annoying event.

Now that we're back in Neptune's embrace, a quiet sigh of relief has occurred. The routines of shipboard life at sea have resumed, watches are kept, the decks have been hosed down, maintenance is done, clothes have been laundered and a quiet sense of order envelops the ship.

From the fantail, the seas look deceptively calm, with moderate swells that *Antwerpen* handles easily. We appear to be alone out here, with no land in sight or any other vessels on the horizon. It's midmorning of some day, either Tuesday or Wednesday, but I've lost track of which one, as days themselves are unimportant here. Ten o'clock offers a fifteen-minute "tea break" for the crew, and three deckhands clutching mugs soon join me at the stern to watch the churning wake of *Antwerpen* froth and disappear as we plod southward.

I've seen them together often—they share a cabin on my deck—so I introduce myself and ask if they speak English. Maciej Urbanski, a good-looking guy who appears to be in his late twenties, answers for all three. "Yes, we all speak. Some better than others." He smiles at his friends. The other two are Michal Fasiczka and Wojciech Jeschke. They're all about the same age; Urbanski and Jeschke tell me they're marine fitters, responsible for operating the deck machinery, while Fasiczka is a sand-blaster whose duties include maintenance of the holds and internal tanks.

Like most of the crew, the trio hails from northern Poland, near the Baltic Sea. Urbanski says they've been mariners for several years now. Thrown together as crewmates, they will spend eight or nine months aboard *Antwerpen* before returning home for leave. That's a long time to be confined in a small space and you had better be able to get along with your fellow sailors or things could get tense. Jeschke, the other fitter, picks up on this.

"We are away from home for long times, very long times. And it is not easy. We are young men, hard workers, but we get along. Yes?" He nods at his shipmates, who agree. "We have ... rules, I think you say. You know, we have to maintain our—"

"Privacy," Urbanski answers for him. "There are limits between us. This is very important. We do not steal from each other or like that. We have a code, not something that is written, but something you learn when is first a sailor. You must understand, this ship can be like a prison with no escape." His friends nod solemnly at this last comment.

To cope with this claustrophobic environment, seafarers uphold privacy and order as paramount. One generally doesn't enter another's cabin unless first invited; times for meals and work details are clearly delineated; and when someone is off-duty and his door is closed, it probably means he wants to be left alone. I have no doubt that seafaring has always been like this, ever since the first vessels appeared between five and seven thousand years ago. Removed from the strictures of land-based communities, sailors have had to create their own cultural parameters in order to maintain some sense of order. Because the sea remains an unpredictable and dangerous environment, there is little room for laziness on a ship.

Maciej Urbanski stares at the seas surrounding us before turning to me. "Why do you come here? Why do you travel with us? We hear that you are writing book on ships and sailors. Is this true?" I tell him it is. "Mmm ... another one looking for 'romance of the sea,' perhaps? It is just water, you know," he chuckles. Michal Fasiczka says something to Urbanski in Polish, and the guys finish up their tea and chuck the last drops overboard. Tea break is over and the guys have to get back to work, so off they go after saying goodbye.

Four decks up, in the wheelhouse, Captain Jacek Wisniewski and Chief Officer Slawomir Bordon are deep in conversation with the third mate, while the second mate is huddled intently over the navigation table, a set of dividers in one hand and a pencil in the other. It's odd to find all the deck officers up here at the same time, so I ask the master what's going on.

"We have some 'weather problems,'" Wisniewski tells me while looking at a weather fax. "It could be a rough ride coming up; there was a tropical storm lying off the southern American coast. It was supposed to go inland, but the weather reports say it is turning to the north and picking up strength. So maybe, Daniel, maybe you will get your first sea legs, see what the crew sees, yes?"

Wisniewski makes this last comment with a somewhat sombre smile on his face. At the chart table, Second Officer Jakub Rosicki is plotting a course update for the captain. A taciturn man with curly dark hair and a penchant for talking to himself, Rosicki yanks open a drawer by his knees and pulls out a couple more charts that he flings onto the table while continuing to mutter quietly in Polish. He keeps glancing at some faxes and then the ship's clock on the wall in front of him before grabbing a pocket calculator that he verily hammers at with his fingers. With whatever result the little computer gives him, he quickly picks up the calipers again and runs them across the chart in a series of swinging arcs until he arrives at some position that he duly marks with the pencil.

As the mate takes in the sea chart, he twiddles the pencil and keeps talking to himself. I realize that Rosicki must be doing what sailors have done for millennia: trying to figure out where a storm is, where it's supposed to be in a few days, where we will be at the same time and whether or not the approaching storm will put us in harm's way.

Though I'm a little hesitant to interrupt Rosicki's concentration, I nevertheless ask him where the tropical storm is currently situated and he looks up from his computations. "Tropical storm? It is no longer a storm; it is now called Hurricane Alex. And it is … here." He stabs a finger at a position off the coast south of us and continues, "It is supposed to go to the northeast. Now, we are here and our course was supposed to take us along this route, to the southwest." He traces a path across the chart that seems to indicate we'll be meeting Alex's edge in a day. "But, no, I think it will pass beside us and be no problem. But only the captain will decide our route."

As the second mate goes back to his navigational work, I glance at the weather report, a high seas forecast from the National Weather Service in Washington with an update of a storm that was lying off the Carolinas, and read:

PAN PAN

NORTH ATLANTIC NORTH OF 31 N TO 67 N AND WEST OF 35 W WARNINGS.

... HURRICANE WARNING ...

HURRICANE ALEX 35.8 N 74.6 W

AT 2100 UTC MOVING NE OR 40 DEGREES AT 15 KT. MAXIMUM SUSTAINED WINDS 85 KT. GUSTS TO 105 KT. TROPICAL STORM FORCE STORM WINDS WITHIN 90 NM NE ... 90 NM SE ... 75 NM SW ...

Oh, crap.

"Daniel, you look ... concerned." Captain Wisniewski is at my elbow as I look up from rereading the weather report. "So, now you know. There are some concerns about this storm, but we have decided to risk it. It was supposed to come ashore in United States but has turned northeast, for some reason. We think it will not affect our passage." Then, in an offhand manner he adds, "Do not worry about it. We do this all the time. We are mariners."

To reassure me, the captain says he receives regular weather updates from a private firm that collates information from various sources, such as the National Weather Service. While in Halifax, Wisniewski was in contact with the firm, as well as with SMT's head office, to determine if the ship should postpone its journey to Florida. In the end, it was decided to change our course slightly so we'll run closer to the American coast, keeping the hurricane (hopefully) well off our port beam. Besides, we are a relatively large, heavily laden ocean-going vessel built to take rough seas.

GOOD SAILORS NEVER underestimate Mother Nature's fickle personality; Captain Wisniewski's seeming nonchalance about Hurricane Alex is born out of professional experience that reflects thousands of years of seafaring in which men have learned how to cope with the worst that Mother Nature throws at them.

Hurricane Alex—so named because hurricanes are designated alphabetically and it's the first one of the season—has a radius of about eighty-five nautical miles, within which one could expect high winds, heaving swells, pelting rain and low visibility. Like most such storms in this part of the world, the hurricane was born somewhere off the coast of Africa before migrating slowly westward toward the Americas. Along the way such storms pick up momentum and increase in size until they descend on the Caribbean. They may blow themselves out down there or make landfall along the coastline of the southeastern United States, where they will lose momentum and slowly die. But sometimes these storms won't die out.

Though we will not encounter the worst of Hurricane Alex (I hope), we will be skirting its extremities. The storm has been classed as a Category 2 Storm on the Saffir-Simpson Scale, meaning it's considered "moderate." Hundred-mile-an-hour winds are what the experts think of as moderate. The same scale calls a Category 5 Storm "catastrophic," with winds in excess of 155 miles an hour (Hurricane Katrina, which devastated New Orleans in August 2005, was a Category 5 storm at its peak).

Along with their siblings, Pacific Ocean typhoons and Indian Ocean cyclones, Atlantic hurricanes are Earth's greatest meteorological phenomena, capable of a diameter in excess of five hundred miles. These Atlantic maelstroms get their name from the ancient Maya and Caribs; the word "hurricane" has its roots in the languages of these indigenous peoples, who variously called the storms "evil spirit," "storm god" or "devil."

They are beautiful in their own deadly manner, furious creations that are beyond human control, unstoppable forces of nature from which we can only flee. Composed of the central eye, the eye wall that surrounds the centre, and the spiral bands at the outside, these storms spin counter-clockwise during their brief lifespan—two weeks at most. Scientists still don't know for certain how the eye and the eye wall are formed, but they have calculated that the heat energy contained within a typical hurricane could provide enough electrical power to supply the United States for about three years.

Centuries ago, at a time when meteorology was more fiction than fact, mariners throughout the globe had acquired a broad knowledge of weather patterns and forecasting techniques. They knew where major systems developed and which tracks the storms would take; they were aware of the cyclical nature of various conditions and which months were worse than others; and they were aware of the relationships among wind speed, depth of water, air temperature and landmass obstructions. That is how Arab traders knew to use seasonal monsoon winds and the North Star to sail their dhows from East Africa to India, away from the sight of land. Or how the Vikings were able to cross the Atlantic in four weeks and establish colonies in the New World.

But this knowledge remained hidden from outsiders, protected like a state secret in countless different cultures and societies. There were no nautical charts available for purchase at the local ship chandler, no weather updates available via fax, no satellite imagery. The ability to read the skies, like the ability to find fish or the ability to venture where no one had gone before, was the only thing that made a captain—and only the senior officers really had this ability—into a "commodity." Captains were the guides that led men to sea, ships to ports and nations to new lands.

The knowledge that master mariners held within their fold remained a singularly secret wisdom until the mid-nineteenth century, when an American naval officer named Matthew Maury began to collate it for greater use. Just prior to the American Civil War, Lieutenant Maury began to improve upon the early work done by an Englishman, James Rennell, in standardizing wind and current charts. He did this by convincing ship captains to keep logs for him so that he could compare their data and come up with compilations, first published in 1847. Eight years later he released a compendium entitled *The Physical Geography of the Sea,* which is still considered one of the primary works of oceanography.

Lieutenant Maury's ability to induce seafarers to keep notes and reveal professional secrets was a singularly important advancement in the field of marine navigation. Many had tried this before him, but the American's timing differed fundamentally from his predecessors'. By the mid-nineteenth century, the globalization of economies was spreading as European nations consolidated their far-reaching empires. This was the first true era of multi-national trade, as opposed to the more protective period that had come before, in which the Spanish zealously guarded their trade routes to the Caribbean, the British their North American colonies, and the Portuguese their Brazilian conquests. As Asia and Africa were variously colonized, goods now flowed from all corners of the planet, usually back to Europe, and the means of maintaining this trade was commercial shipping.

So, in the end it was the demands of business—of nascent capitalism—that compelled mariners to come together and help Maury create marine roadmaps that would safeguard the valuable goods in the holds of their ships. Australian wool could now be shipped to Britain's textile mills more efficiently; Chinese porcelain could adorn the mantels of fashionable Parisian townhomes; rubber could be brutally extracted from the Congo for use in Belgium; and emigrants could leave Eastern Europe bound for the New World and new lives. The mercantile power of a nation meant as much as its military and naval might. (Though it's interesting to note that, as a Southern patriot, Matthew Maury would resign his U.S. Navy commission to serve in the Confederate navy during the War Between the States.)

Since then, the oceans have been scanned, mapped, probed and plumbed using each generation's most up-to-date inventions. But the modern tools available to mariners—even satellite imagery—remain just that: tools with which the master mariner augments his own instincts. No amount of software, hardware or textbooks can properly prepare a mariner for the challenges of foul weather. The mariners' collective wisdom might be summed up in the words of one of the captain's instructors at the Polish Merchant Academy: "When the truth ends, the meteorology begins." Even after all the facts have been checked and the weather reports analyzed, the data can be rendered worthless within minutes by the unpredictability of Mother Nature.

Within twelve hours of our hearing the news about Hurricane Alex, *Antwerpen*'s roll has increased with the approach of the storm's extremities, and portholes in the officers' mess have been closed and dogged as a precaution against heavy seas. Captain Wisniewski gives me a weather update and, for once, he seems a little concerned. The storm appears to be moving farther to the east, out of our path, but it's behaving erratically. The most recent forecast has the hurricane position shifted considerably from the last report, the captain says. "Maybe someone made a mistake and put it in the wrong place on the ocean. I don't know; these storms can be unpredictable."

In the galley, steward Rafal Winczo sits alone listening to a CD on a boom box and smoking a cigarette, oblivious to the vessel's movement. He invites me to join him for a cup of tea and asks how I'm enjoying the trip so far. He's in a relaxed and jovial mood tonight, and goes on to tell me about how he ended up here.

"I was born in Slupsk, a city about one hundred kilometres west of Gdansk and Gdynia," Winczo begins in his falsetto. "It is not far from the [Baltic] sea. But I am not a true sailor, I think. I do not come from a sailor family. But this is a good job for me, very good. For five years now I am steward. And why I am here is easy question to answer: money. Simple, yes? I can make in one month here what would take eight months for me to make back in Poland. And I can save a lot of money. I do not pay for meals. I have a bed to sleep in. Things are very cheap here. So for me it is a very good job."

I'm momentarily stunned by what Rafal has told me. Eight months' wages in one month at sea? To put this in perspective—and keeping in mind there are vast societal differences—it's like making U.S.$20,000 every month for the guy. In Poland today the average income is about U.S.$11,500 a year. So Rafal Winczo makes about $7600 a month here on *Antwerpen*. When he says it's simple why he's here, he is not understating things.

Rafal goes on to tell me that he works five months on, three months off, and will be returning to Poland in about four weeks' time, something he's looking forward to. He also reveals his dream: "I do not want to be on ship for rest of my life. No. I think I would like to do this for maybe a few more years and then open a bar or something near my home." The steward has a smile on his face and a faraway look in his eyes. With the reappearance of the cook, the steward stubs out his cigarette and gets back to work washing dishes, so I leave him, hoping that his dream never fades.

The next few days find *Antwerpen* dealing with the outer edge of the hurricane. Each night I'm awakened in my cabin by the sound of things falling, of closet doors crashing open, of my desk chair rolling back and forth. The tempered, methodical cadence of *Antwerpen* to which I've grown so accustomed has been replaced by a slightly more erratic rhythm. My sleeping quarters, which have the look of a motel room circa 1975, take on the feel of a midway ride as we pitch up, then down, rolling to the right, then back the other way. I can feel the propeller cutting into the water, throwing its six blades into combat. Deep, sonorous thuds reverberate throughout the ship as seemingly every millimetre of her steel hull is straining to keep out the sea. The chief engineer told me that *Antwerpen*'s hull is about twelve to thirteen millimetres thick; that's a sheath of metal barely the width of my little finger, a disconcertingly thin margin of safety that stirs me to ever more vivid thoughts.

A daytime view of the storm from the bridge reveals a great wall of grey lying like a curtain across the southern and eastern horizons. There are scattered clouds above the ship—the third mate says we're keeping as far from the hurricane as possible—but the barrier edge of Alex blots out everything behind it. The ship's timbre remains unsteady and she's now encountering three-metre swells and headwinds. By the chart on the navigation table, we're passing North Carolina's Cape Hatteras, in an ocean more than 1500 fathoms deeps—that's almost three kilometres of cold water beneath us.

The third mate says the captain has altered course again to accommodate Hurricane Alex; we're running a bit closer to the American coast while the storm is veering farther out into the Atlantic. We can expect some rough seas for the next twenty-four hours, but nothing that most merchant mariners would consider abnormal, so, with the mate's permission, I decide to head to the fo'c'sle.

Even with radar, weather reports and satellite updates, the speed with which the weather can change at sea is uncanny. As I leave the superstructure and begin walking across the hatch covers, the sun is shining and a warm breeze blows toward me. I can see dark rain clouds, part of the extreme edge of the hurricane, but they appear to be far off in the distance. I walk in a slightly unsteady manner, trying to match the pitching rhythm of the ship as she deals with the ocean swells. With no handholds on the hatch covers, I stagger as though slightly inebriated: a bit to the left, a bit to the right, then a two-step forward. Each hatch cover is separated from its neighbour by a metre-wide access space that runs the breadth of the ship. There are intermittent walkways over these crevices, painted bright yellow, which I head toward, preferring not to jump from hatch to hatch.

It takes me fewer than two minutes to make my way forward, but by the time I reach Number One Hatch, the wind picks up and I can see large waves breaking over the bow and spraying the exposed deck sections. Suddenly I hear thunder and turn to see that the sun has disappeared and that it's begun to rain. Within seconds I am being soaked in a heavy downpour that hides the bridge windows from view. The speed of the *Antwerpen* combined with the swiftly moving edge of Hurricane Alex has put us in the hurricane in just minutes.

I scurry toward the fo'c'sle workspace, a sheltered area that is the only refuge from the elements up here. Stepping inside, I find the three young crewmen I'd met earlier—Maciej Urbanski, Michal Fasiczka and Wojciech Jeschke—watching me with amusement. Urbanski grins as I stand there dripping on the deck. "You got a little wet, huh? It's better inside here."

The workspace is a crowded metal room lit by a few bare bulbs, containing storage lockers for tools, paints and deck equipment. From within the enclosure, the sound of rain and thunder reverberates along with the crash of the waves as the bow plows through the seas. The guys are relaxed, since the rain has given them a break from their deck work, so I ask Urbanski more about his life here on *Antwerpen*. He tells me that he has been a sailor for almost seven years now, though not out of any love for the sea. Making the universal finger-rubbing gesture for money, he simply states, "I do this because it is a good job. Good pay. I used to work in the shipyards in Gdansk, but there are very few jobs there now. So I went to sea. I fix the equipment. I save some money. But I will tell you, it is hard when you are gone five months, six months ... I wish the time was shorter here."

While the four of us watch the rain, Urbanski falls into the natural habit of sailors when asked about the weather: recounting tales of ever more dangerous conditions. As anyone who has been in the company of small-craft sailors can attest, the stories of storm-tossed journeys—some truthful, some inflated—seem to come out of the woodwork as the rum and beer are consumed dockside. But the difference between recreational boaters and professional mariners is simple: Most of the former can head for a nearby port when things get ugly; most of the latter don't have the option. And merchant mariners tend not to brag.

Except in truly bad conditions, commercial vessels must strive to maintain their schedules no matter what the weather. They will, as the *Antwerpen's* master has done, plot a course around storm fronts to avoid the worst of things, but rough seas are part and parcel of the job description for men like Maciej Urbanski.

"I remember some bad storms in the Pacific Ocean," Urbanski says as he looks out the doorway at the clouds. "You know, big waves crashing on the deck. But the worst one I saw was in the North Atlantic, in wintertime. I was on a container ship and the seas were bad, very bad. You know, waves like ten metres high, for three days. The crew, we could not work. Just lie in bed and try to sleep. This," he gestures outside, "this is nothing. *Antwerpen* is good ship. We can handle it."

In answer to my question about whether a ship has a soul, the young deckhand looks at me blankly and then translates for his friends. After a short conversation in Polish, Urbanski turns back to me. "You know ... I do not think this is a good question. The ship, this ship, it is just steel and things, you know? Remember, I worked in shipyard and even there it was just a job for me. I like *Antwerpen,* she is a good ship to work on with a good crew. But I do not love her. My next time I could be on another vessel, then another. We do not choose the ships." Maybe the ships choose you? I ask. He smiles slightly. "Maybe. But then it would have some sort of soul, yes? No, I do not think this is so. The company chooses for us."

Wojciech Jeschke, the other marine fitter, pipes up: "When ship is good, all is OK. The food, the work, the captain. Yes? These make it good. When ship is bad, then maybe is something wrong with the people. It is the people who make the ship. Without us, it is nothing."

We stand there thinking about Jeschke's comment, three Polish mariners and a Canadian writer huddled near the forepeak of a ship fending off a hurricane in the Atlantic Ocean. In many ways, the crewmen's relationship to *Antwerpen* is as fleeting as mine; it's a temporary place to work before returning home to friends and families. Jeschke, Urbanski and Fasiczka appear to have no vested interest in the ship, no connection with the seminal lore of the seafarer. Yet this entity must shelter and protect them, a fortress against the dark forces that rage just off the horizon line.

"Well, OK," Maciej Urbanski concedes, "the ship is important. It is, as you say, a fortress for us. But maybe while we are here we do not like to think about it too much. Sometime I go to the back of the ship, you know the fantail? In the night, before I go to sleep. And there I think about things. But not now. Hey, ask me when I have grandchildren." Glancing at his wristwatch, Urbanski says something in Polish to the other two deckhands and then turns to me. "Come, it is almost tea time."

Then the three men begin to head aft, with me following closely behind. We make for the conveyor belt on the starboard side after a quick look at the hatch covers reveals a wet, rolling surface buffeted by wind and rain. Using the rubber belt as rain cover, we duck beneath it and crab walk aft for about five minutes, the deck awash the entire time. Periodically the water is ankle-deep and we time our progress to the rolls of the *Antwerpen*, when the liquid sloshes toward the scuppers and into the sea. By the time we reach the house, we are all wet. A warm mug of instant coffee never sounded better.

As we continue to get past the last of the hurricane, Captain Wisniewski is spending more time on the bridge, just in case. Outside the wheelhouse, the seas are still angry. I can see waves breaking over the bow, sending up spumes of water that form into brief clouds before crashing down again. Periodically the seas crash so heavily that the masthead at the bow and then the whole forecastle disappears in a grey mist of salt water. The motion of the *Antwerpen* in these seas is amplified by the height of the bridge; as the bow pitches down and digs into the water, I can feel the plunge, the thud and the slow rise upwards in my knees. But there is a safety here in the wheelhouse, surrounded by the captain and mate, warming with a coffee, dry from the elements.

During this afternoon watch no one is at the wheel itself—the ship is still on autopilot—so I wander over and stand in front of it. The ship's wheel itself is barely larger than a supper plate, mounted at waist level on a console centred exactly amidships. Above it, hanging from the deckhead, is an illuminated circle that shows the rudder position. As we are being controlled by a computer, the rudder seemingly moves on its own— a few degrees to port, then amidships again—to compensate for the rolling of the ship.

As Captain Wisniewski comes over to join me, I ask him about worstcase scenarios: What would happen to us if things became dire out here? At first he tries to mollify me.

"To begin with, we have constant communication with the shore, even out here. If the engines should fail or something bad happen, we would be able to contact the coast guard quite quickly. Now, how long they would take to reach us? Well, that is something else, something I cannot say. But at this time of year, in this part of the world, it is very good."

Then he surprises me. "You know, I am not so much afraid of the storms. I am certainly cautious about them, but they are not the worst thing that could happen. For me, I think that fire is the worst. To have a fire at sea is very, very bad. I have never been on a ship that had a fire, and I hope to never see it."

Should a fire break out on *Antwerpen,* the first priority—after dealing with the blaze—would be to protect the engine room. Without power, Wisniewski adds, the vessel would be dead in the water. The engine room is a self-contained section of the ship, separated from the remainder of the vessel by watertight doors and special vents that can be used to protect this mechanical environment. If a fire broke out in the engine room, fire dampers—air vents that reach to the main deck—would be closed, the engineers evacuated and, on the captain's command, the chief would release CO_2 gas into the area to snuff out the fire by denying it oxygen.

I assume that if something such as a fire occurred, the captain would make for shore so that it would be easier to abandon ship or get help. But this turns out to be incorrect. "No, being close to the shoreline is very dangerous," Wisniewski tells me. "You could have shoals or reefs or rocks or shallow water. And if the engines should fail, that could be a disaster. Instead, I would take her to deeper water, where there is more room to manoeuvre. I would rather have a thousand metres of sea beneath me than be in sight of land and have only a few fathoms."

The captain is staring out the windows now, his eyes focused on something I cannot see. "I remember my father had a fire on one of his ships," he says quietly. "He was off the coast of Argentina with this trawler. It was about 100 or 120 metres long, half as long as *Antwerpen*. And it had a crew of about one hundred. These were deep sea fishing trawlers, like factories. But something went wrong in the engine room, not caused by human error, and a fire spread to the electrical wiring. Soon my father's ship was without power and drifting. A Russian trawler came near to them and he threw a line to my father and towed the ship out to sea. And after some time the engineers repaired things enough that they could get into port. But my father said it was a scary time."

In return for saving the ship, the Russian captain had only one request: Would the elder Wisniewski reveal his secret fishing locations marked on the Polish mariner's private charts? To a commercial fisherman, these were more valuable than any monetary reward. My captain's father gladly gave the Russian whatever he wanted.

I'M NOT SURE if Captain Wisniewski's thoughts about fire are related to our current position, but I do know that we're currently steaming close to the sight of a recent tragedy. On February 28, 2004, the chemical tanker *Bow Mariner,* a vessel almost the same size as *Antwerpen,* was heading from New York to Texas after having discharged a cargo of 3.2 million gallons of industrial ethanol. Yet she still had 193,000 gallons of fuel oil and 48,000 gallons of diesel oil aboard when something went terribly wrong. While the vessel was about fifty miles off the coast of Virginia, an explosion suddenly ripped through her hull, causing wing tanks on both the port and starboard sides to open to the seas. Within minutes, the tanker began to sink and the crew abandoned ship, jumping into the frigid waters. Though a nearby bulk carrier rushed to the scene and a U.S. Coast Guard helicopter was dispatched from North Carolina, only six out of a crew of twenty-seven survived.

Fires, explosions, foul weather, faulty equipment, human error— these are but a few of the dangers facing the merchant mariner today as he puts to sea. They are the dark side of maritime traditions, going back thousands of years. To cope with the dangers of seafaring, maritime nations have set up a fairly comprehensive system of rescue coordination centres around the world. They are known by the acronym JRCCs (for Joint Rescue Coordination Centres). *Antwerpen* has already transited through three of their sectors—Halifax, Boston and Norfolk—and will soon enter a fourth, Miami. Hundreds of these rescue centres are scattered about the globe, but each does essentially the same thing: It looks out for the safety of mariners and their vessels.

The JRCC in Halifax, Nova Scotia, is typical of this global emergency system. While *Antwerpen*'s crew were loading her cargo of gypsum in that port, I paid a visit to the RCC. Located in a nondescript building within the Canadian Navy's main Atlantic base, it resembles a war room, but then, that's exactly what it is: This is where men and women do battle to save lives, albeit in an area covering 4.7 million square kilometres and encompassing over 29,000 kilometres of coastline.

The middle of the room contains a large map table of the North Atlantic sector for which this centre is responsible. Surrounding it are a half-dozen computer workstations; there are also tinted windows that look out onto the harbour, and a giant projection screen above the map table. The operations room is not unlike a police or ambulance dispatch centre, with Canadian Coast Guard officers and air force personnel working side by side here. When a distress call comes in from a vessel, the JRCC staff can call upon coast guard or naval vessels, air force helicopters and fixed-wing aircraft, and even other merchant ships that may be able to render assistance. They deal with about 2500 "incidents" each year, everything affecting pleasure boats to fishing vessels to passenger liners to aircraft—anything that transits on, above or below the waters of this sector.

Paul Rudden is a coast guard officer who's been working here at JRCC Halifax for years, and I ask him how bad things really are for seafarers today.

"How dangerous is it to be a mariner today?" Rudden takes a long moment to think before answering my question. "Um … very. The average mariner out there is on a ship that may be questionable, does things that may be questionable. It's a very dangerous job. For example, last week there were two guys on a Portuguese fishing dragger and something let go on the deck and cut the legs out from under the both of them—they both had broken their ankles. We had to go out and get them. And that happens all the time. The risk of injury at sea is just so much higher.

"This job tends to be somewhat seasonal," he continues. "Like in the winter things are usually more serious—the weather's worse, the ships tend to be farther offshore. But in the summer we see more stuff, we're steady busy. A lot of small boats getting in trouble, and a lot can go bad quickly with a small boat. Just a few days ago we got a call from a fishing boat out on the Grand Banks [off Newfoundland]. A guy was experiencing chest pains. If he'd been on land, he would have just gone to the emergency room and been tested. But you can't do that when you're on a ship at sea. So something small can become a big problem."

Rudden should know. He's worked on everything from buoy tenders to icebreakers and has twenty years' experience in search and rescue. As a cadet in the Coast Guard College, he hauled bodies out of the Atlantic after the offshore drilling rig *Ocean Ranger* sank in a violent storm in 1982. But even if no one is injured or killed when a ship sinks, it's still a sad event. Paul Rudden says, "Any mariner you talk to that's watched a ship sink, everybody just goes quiet. It's like watching somebody die. Even here at RCC."

He goes on to tell me about the sinking of a bulk carrier similar to *Antwerpen*, a ship called the *Gold Bond Conveyor* with a crew of thirty-three.

In March of 1993 she was about a hundred nautical miles off Cape Sable, Nova Scotia, in the same vicinity where the American fishing boat *Andrea Gail* had sunk two years earlier (the *Gail* was made famous in Sebastian Junger's book *The Perfect Storm* and in a film of the same name).

"We have video of her, shot from an air force Aurora plane," Rudden continues. "And you could see her fighting in these seas. Whenever we watch that tape, everyone goes quiet in the RCC. One of the air force guys, the pilot, told me that he just watched her sink right in front of him. Like, they were talking to the ship and they turned their plane around to make another pass and then all he sees is the stern of the bulker up in the air, her propeller still turning, and then the ship just slid under. No survivors. Any time I've seen even video of a ship sinking, it's hard for me to watch."

As it turns out, the *Gold Bond Conveyor* set sail from the same pier *Antwerpen* had used to load her cargo of gypsum, and both vessels chose pretty much identical courses to head south.

LUCKILY—FOR ME and for the crew of the *Antwerpen*—the waters off the eastern seaboard of the United States are among the safest in the world. This is due in no small part to the extensive resources the United States makes available for merchant safety. On average, the United States Coast Guard responds to about five thousand cases in the waters we're currently traversing, and the loss of life is about fifty per year. But most of these tend to be recreational sailors getting themselves into dangerous situations.

From the bow of the bulker I can make out a sailboat tacking toward the shoreline of Georgia, which is still over the horizon somewhere. Otherwise, we remain alone on the Atlantic. Well, that's not completely true, of course. The oceans of the globe teem with more life forms than can be found on dry land, and most of those marine entities are clustered in the top layer, the two hundred metres or so that the sun's light is able to penetrate.

Take the surface of the sea, which can seem devoid of fish and other sea creatures at first glance. It is actually crowded with tiny plankton and algae that make up the very bottom of the food chain. And then there are the ocean's waves, for instance, mesmerizing to watch and undeniably beautiful. I realize that like snowflakes, no two waves are the same: Some have a fierceness about them, like shards of cut glass constantly thrusting at me, threatening me; others reach out languidly, reassuring me they mean no harm. Spindrift explodes from atop some of the waves, the fine spray reaching skyward like the plume on a lady's fancy hat. Still other waves curl their whitecaps forward as the kinetic energy pushes them ever onward on their ceaseless voyages.

The sea's fingers continue to reach out when the water beneath me suddenly erupts into small explosions. A school of flying fish shoots from the water to escape the *Antwerpen's* onslaught, their iridescent blue forms scattering like shotgun pellets, their fins now wings. I can count to six on more than one occasion as the larger fish skim across the surface of the ocean like stones skipped on a pond by a child.

These planktivores use their large eyes to hunt down surface plankton in the neuston layer of the ocean, the top metre of water. Their brief flights are a means of evading predators, and as I watch the dozens of fish return to their submarine domain, I catch sight of a large shark no more than ten metres away, its dorsal fin tracing a path away from us. A smaller shark swims off the starboard bow, quickly moving out of the way of this lumbering behemoth.

Now awakened to the life that surrounds me, I begin to notice passing orbs that had seemed invisible only moments before: Jellyfish, too numerous to count, whisk past the bow as we are propelled onward. Smaller than the size of your fist, these opaque brown creatures are everywhere around the ship, their gelatinous forms well suited to the pummelling they take as our wake thrusts them rudely aside. Above the jellyfish are streams of sargassum, the floating seaweed common to the waters here known as the Sargasso Sea. Resembling tufts of grass ripped from your front lawn, they litter the sea like so much flotsam.

Even in the darkest night, the Atlantic reveals she is far from lifeless. Standing by the stern under a starry sky, I catch with my peripheral vision patches of dim light off to the sides of the ship, in the ocean itself. They're the phosphorescent glow given off by small marine organisms, sometimes referred to as the "cold light" of the sea. Whatever you want to call it, it is an absolutely magical thing to see, mysterious and enchanting. The mere sight of it causes the hair to rise on the back on my neck. Emitting an ethereal luminosity, these masses of minute life pass astern of us effortlessly, the glowing sea clouds fading quickly, but softly, into the night.

Charles Darwin, the father of evolutionary biology, saw this same phenomenon while sailing on HMS *Beagle* off South America and wrote about it in 1839:

> While sailing a little south of the Plata on one very dark night, the sea presented a wonderful and most beautiful spectacle. There was a fresh breeze, and every part of the surface, which during the day is seen as foam, now glowed with a pale light. The vessel drove before her bows two billows of liquid phosphorus, and in her wake she was followed by a milky train. As far as the eye reached, the crest of every wave was bright, and the sky above the horizon, from the reflected glare of these vivid flames, was not so utterly obscure as over the vault of the heavens....

I wonder if there's any connection between the green of the phosphorescent glow of these organisms and the origin of the term "Fiddler's Green." Fiddler's Green is the sailor's heaven, a place of bountiful rum, beautiful women and anything else he wishes for. This is the mythical place of lore where mariners go when they die on land (those who pass away at sea are relegated to Davy Jones's Locker). Maybe I'm just being romantic about the sea, as Maciej Urbanski alleged. But, on the other hand, he did say he likes the ship's fantail at night as a place to think about things.

AFTER ANOTHER TWELVE HOURS of plodding southward, *Antwerpen* has finally been able to put the remnants of Hurricane Alex well behind her. Making anchorage off the coast of Florida, the bulker lies quiet; we're a couple of miles from the mouth of the St. Johns River, lolling in gentle swells under a warm mid-August sky. Landfall is in sight—I can see buildings on the shoreline—and three other ships sit idle in the waters around us, also awaiting permission to head upriver to Jacksonville. According to the crew, we should be heading into port in a few hours. Meanwhile, there's a little downtime on the ship.

I run into one of the young fitters—Wojciech Jeschke—who excitedly beckons me to come outside and see something. A group of deckhands are clustered around Mariusz Blok, a tall ordinary seaman in his mid-twenties who is holding a small shark in his gloved hands, a broad grin creasing his youthful face. The two-and-a-half-foot-long animal flops from side to side as the crowd peers cautiously at its mouth. The shark is dull brown on top and white below with few teeth to worry about, but each desperate spasm it makes causes us all to jump backwards. After taking a group picture, I watch as Blok tosses the shark back into the sea and begins to bait another line.

The cook soon appears and elbows his way through the line of guys who are all fishing off the fantail. Grabbing some bait from a small white bucket behind him, he drops his line into the waters and settles into the escapist routine that only those who fish seem to understand. Of the other guys, only one has a proper rod and reel like the cook's. The rest are using a variety of makeshift tools: One guy uses a stick, another is jigging with just a bit of fishing wire spooled around a piece of plastic and weighted down with rusty nuts and bolts. As the sun begins to set across the harbour, the silhouetted sailors make small talk and stare intently at the water.

I spy Maciej Urbanski in the crowd. "These guys," he says, grinning, "you see how they fish? All the time, any chance they get, they fish. You know, there is not much else to do on a ship. So maybe this is more recreation than anything."

More guys walk toward us clutching mugs of tea, coming to hear either about the shark or toss their own lines into the water. Moments later, a second shark is caught, this one a small nurse shark with its mottled brown, cow-like colours. More photos follow, more peering into the mouth; then this one, too, is tossed back as the men glance at their watches, reel in their lines and return to work.

By late afternoon, permission has been received to heave anchor and head into the brackish estuary toward the final destination for this particular voyage. On this first trip back into U.S. territory since we left Maine over a week ago, the ship is preparing for the inevitable onslaught of bureaucracy and officialdom that awaits her in Jacksonville, Florida. In this post-9/11 era, there is an unspoken understanding that re-entering American waters from a foreign port brings increased scrutiny, even if that port is in friendly Canada.

The ship looks neater and more organized than when I first boarded her in Rhode Island. I note that a fresh Cypriot flag has been raised from our stern, replacing the slightly tattered one that had hung there before. And when I see Captain Wisniewski heading to the bridge to meet the pilot, I can't help but notice he is wearing a crisp white captain's shirt and dress pants. For once, my captain looks the role.

As we begin to enter the mouth of the St. Johns River, small pleasure boats and Sea-Doos dart about us. Farther into the river, the backyards of large homes pass on our port side. I can see screened-in gazebos and children's swing sets, propane barbecues, swimming pools and SUVs parked in driveways. I peer into the kitchens of these American dream homes, where meals are being eaten and televisions watched. Not a single person notices our passage or my presence on the open portside bridge wing.

My return to the embrace of North American society is troubling me, even though I've only been "gone" for a week. I'd switched on my cell phone the night before, for the first time in a week, and found I had service where we were anchored offshore. My phone was backlogged with voicemail messages, one of which informed me I needed to rearrange an upcoming interview with someone as quickly as possible. I'm going to have to quickly pack my bags and leave *Antwerpen* tomorrow afternoon, a few days earlier than anticipated.

As we creep upriver, I quietly wish we weren't moving so fast, even though we're barely making five knots. Up ahead of us is a fork in the river; to the left the St. Johns flows toward Jacksonville proper, past the container terminal and the industrial outskirts of the city. *Antwerpen* veers to starboard at the fork, into a small inlet. The sun is quickly setting ahead of us, dipping beneath a vista of nondescript warehouses, single-storey buildings and access roads that are hued in earthy brown tones so different from the sea's blues and greens.

The docking procedure here seems even slower than in other ports, and several times *Antwerpen* stops dead in the water while VHF radios crackle among the bridge, the tugs and the engine room. Off our starboard bow I see a large, oddly shaped vessel berthed opposite our destination. It's painted in that dull grey familiar to naval ships, but in the fading light I don't see any weapons on it, so I assume it must be some kind of supply vessel. Arc lights are scattered around the berthing area, casting shadows on some shipping containers to our starboard side and a few military vehicles off to port. There's a delay of some kind with the handlers on the pier, Captain Wisniewski tells me, and it will be another hour before tying up alongside, so I opt to head to my cabin and await the next morning.

Though my captain told me we were berthing at what is also a military facility, I am still unprepared for what awaits me when I walk on deck after breakfast. With my morning mug of coffee in hand, I stop dead in my tracks as I catch sight of one of the most impressive parking lots I've ever seen. Off our port side are hundreds upon hundreds of military vehicles lined up in neat formation, painted drab olive or desert yellow: transport trucks, gasoline tankers, water trucks, tow trucks and enough Humvees to give Arnold Schwarzenegger a heart attack.

Ahead of us an imposing array of M1A1/2 Abrams main battle tanks, amphibious assault vehicles and Bradley fighting vehicles are parked, their gun barrels pointed, thankfully, away from us. Between the tanks and the *Antwerpen* lies one of those giant loading cranes used in container ports around the world, only this one is emblazoned with USMC on its side, short for the United States Military Corps. And on the starboard side I see that there are thousands of container units stacked near warehouses. I am surrounded by the might of the American arsenal, albeit only a fraction of that nation's strength.

Antwerpen is discharging her cargo of gypsum at what is known as a prepositioning facility, one that just happens to be crucial to the most recent war in Iraq. The Marine Corps Blount Island Command uses this port as one of its key means of shipping equipment and *matériel* overseas. It's a vivid example of how commercial shipping has taught the military to most effectively transport its gear, utilizing containerization to speed the loading process.

The *Antwerpen*'s crew is already busy unloading the gypsum, heaping the white rocks into piles on the wharf beside mounds of coal that some other vessel has left behind. On the pier beneath me, a dark van pulls up at the base of the gangway and a group of uniformed men get out, dressed like police officers. They climb onto the main deck beside me and the first guy, a U.S. Customs official, nods my way and says with a gentle Floridian accent, "Dziendobry," which is Polish for "Hello." I stifle a laugh, since he's obviously mistaken me for a crewman.

As the Americans head inside, Rafal Winczo appears and tells me that I must appear at the captain's cabin in thirty minutes for customs and immigration clearance. When I make my way there, a line of deckhands stretches out the door of Captain Wisniewski's day room. I take my place at the end of the line and note a nervousness in the other men waiting to be interviewed. Perhaps it comes from growing up in a communist country. Or maybe it is just the sense that one person has control over their lives for a brief moment. Whatever the root cause, it is anathema to the freedom these sailors enjoy at sea.

By the time I am summoned into the cabin, the two American officials—including the one who mistook me for a Pole—look somewhat bemused as I explain what I'm doing aboard *Antwerpen*. Passengers on bulk carriers are a rarity and I fear my presence might create problems for the ship. But the Americans are friendly to me and actually appreciate that someone is writing about the world of merchant shipping. They stamp my passport and then gather their belongings, shake the captain's hand and head off.

After they leave, I ask Captain Wisniewski if I can have a few moments of his time. "Yes, yes, of course," he answers, beckoning me to take a seat while ordering up some coffee for the two of us. I tell him about the change in my plans and my need to disembark this afternoon. He looks at me for a long moment and then says, "Well, that will make both of us. It seems I am leaving the ship, too, tomorrow. My replacement is arriving today." This is a surprise, as I'd thought he wasn't due to hand over the vessel to another captain for another couple of weeks. But it turns out that his replacement is arriving early, later this afternoon in fact.

"This is a bit of a change for me," he muses as the coffee arrives. "I was not expecting to go so soon, but I received an email from head office last night that plans had changed. But this is what seafaring is like, yes? Always uncertain. And it is good—I will see my family soon. Still, it feels ... odd. Is that the right word?"

I realize that he is transitioning before me, from master of a sea-going vessel to Jacek Wisniewski, father and husband. He drums his fingers on his desk, which is devoid of the usual paperwork required to manage a floating enterprise like *Antwerpen*. His job is essentially done; he has successfully led the ship and her crew for the last four months, tramping up and down the Atlantic and Caribbean with a variety of cargoes for a variety of clients, maintaining schedules set by faceless individuals in far-flung offices. With the exception of a few reports to complete, Wisniewski has nothing to do until he leaves. He is grounded.

Wisniewski hands me my passport, which has been in his hands since I boarded his ship in Providence. Holding my international identity, I ask him if he'd show me something I've never actually seen: his master mariner's permit, the famous "ticket" that so many individuals aspire to. Laughing, he walks to his bedroom and returns with a stack of small cards. "I show you how many things I must carry to be a master," he says as he lays the cards on his desk. "I have a certificate for English proficiency, a certificate of basic safety training, personal safety training, advanced firefighting, medical care, GMDSS operator and, the last, the one you ask me about, the captain's licence."

His ticket looks like a driver's licence, with an unsmiling photo of Wisniewski peering from beneath the plastic lamination. It seems so anti-climactic, if that's the right way to describe it. I suppose I'd imagined some sort of fancy scroll, like the degrees handed to university graduates, instead of this simple card. I wonder how important this is to him and he pauses for a long time while looking at the permit and his photo on it.

"You know, for so many years I wanted to be a captain. It is little bit of the dream of the deck officer. I wondered how it would change me if I become a master, but I am not sure it has. Or maybe it is that I think you grow into being a captain, it is a gradual change. I mean, when I got this card, I was still chief officer on another vessel, so I could not be a captain immediately. But each voyage, each passing year, I feel a little more like a master. Just don't tell my crew that," he quickly laughs, before getting serious again and fingering the permit. "This … this is very important in my life. I keep it locked in the ship's safe in my cabin."

We sip our coffees for a few minutes and then I ask my captain if he's thought any more about the soul of a ship. This may be my last chance to ask him. Leaning back in his chair, he nods. "Oh, yes, I have thought about your question for some time. Does this ship—*Antwerpen*—have a soul? No, I do not think so. It has some … what is the word?" He reaches for a Polish–English dictionary on the bookshelf behind him and pages through it to find the term he's thinking of. "Ah, yes … it has some characteristics, if I pronounce that correctly. We have a sister ship to *Antwerpen,* the *Brussels,* and I have sailed with her. But she is not like this vessel; each one handles the sea in a different manner. But is that the soul that causes that? No, I think not. It is maybe the way the cargo is loaded or a piston on the engine is working. I do prefer *Antwerpen* to *Brussels,* but I think that is because this is my first vessel as captain."

How strong can the bond be between a mariner and his ship? I know that some of the deckhands feel that *Antwerpen* is merely their workplace and I also know that the modern shipping industry sees officers shuttled from vessel to vessel throughout the course of their professional careers. If *Antwerpen* has no soul to Wisniewski, what does she mean to him?

"I will tell you something," he answers me quietly. "This ship will always be a part of me. About a year ago, I had a collision, with *Antwerpen,* a collision on the Mississippi River. It was two o'clock in the night and I had the collision with barges on the river. Coming from up the river was a tug in tow, twelve barges pushed by a tug, and our pilot radioed the tug to say it was coming too much to our direction. So we stopped the engines, dropped the anchor, everything to avoid the collision with these barges and tug. But on our starboard were some empty barges, tied up to a pier, and we drifted to them and we get damage in forepeak, a hole in the forepeak area. It was not our fault—we avoided a collision with the moving barges—but, I tell you, it was a very bad feeling. Very bad. I could feel the impact; the ship shook. And I did my best, as a seaman I did my best, but still the ship was damaged. And I will always remember that and what happened to *Antwerpen.*"

The coast guard, it seems, investigated the accident and eventually Captain Wisniewski had to testify in a court in New Orleans, where the barge was deemed to be at primary fault. However, even though *Antwerpen* had a pilot aboard and was travelling in the correct channel, whereas the other vessel had veered out of its southbound traffic lane, the court's ruling still assigned a small amount of the blame to Wisniewski. One of the prime mandates of a captain is that he must do everything possible to avoid a collision. Luckily for Captain Wisniewski, the shipping company felt he had done as much as possible and he was given a second chance to return as master of *Antwerpen.*

As I finish my coffee, I see a more thoughtful and introspective man sitting opposite me, one who has declined any spiritual element to his vessel while revealing a bond born of injury to his first command. I doubt he would have revealed this side of himself if he were not about to head home tomorrow, nor would he have mentioned the accident to me at all. Any chance of continuing our conversation is cut short by the appearance of Chief Officer Bordon, who has some paperwork to be dealt with. Captain Wisniewski says he'll have a taxi ordered to take me to the airport in the afternoon, and then I take my leave.

Pulling out my hockey bag, I begin my methodical approach to packing. I'm used to doing this at short notice, but am still amazed at how much of my stuff has found its way into all the nooks and crannies of my cabin. It's a sign of how comfortable I've become during my time here on *Antwerpen,* and it creates another pang of regret at my early departure. While I roll up my T-shirts, fold my jeans, clean out the head (washroom) and organize my laptop, the sounds of the unloading of the cargo emanate from the bulkheads. As one of the buckets strikes the hull inside a cargo hold, the vessel shudders ever so slightly. The rush is on to empty *Antwerpen* of her temporary contents, myself included.

The mess hall is empty when I stop in for a last supper. Everyone, it seems, is busy with the discharging of the gypsum, so I eat my chicken cutlet in solitude, staring at the framed photos of *Antwerpen* in her younger days. When I finish, I pop my head into the galley to thank the cook for all his meals. He beams at the compliment and shakes my hand while saying, "Yes, but I think you are still too skinny for Polish girls. You come back and we fix all that, OK?" I assure him I will, if I can.

My flight is due to depart from Jacksonville Airport in midafternoon, so I still have about an hour before the taxi arrives. I stop by the captain's day room to say my goodbye. Wisniewski is sitting with his replacement and, after introducing us, my captain turns and grasps my hand warmly. In his quiet voice, he simply says, "Daniel, it has been a pleasure to have you aboard my ship. I do not think you will find another one like her on your journeys and hope you do not forget us."

I assure Wisniewski that I will never forget my time with *Antwerpen* and her crew and, in modest gratitude, present him with a bottle of twelve-year-old single malt Scotch for the crew's enjoyment. The captain is touched by this gesture and promises that it will be given to the crew on their next half-day off, when they have a little barbecue on the fantail and can relax and unwind.

I shake Captain Wisniewski's hand once more and wish him a safe journey home. He wishes me likewise and, then, as an afterthought, adds, "By the way, there is another hurricane coming this way. It should be here in about four days and this one could get bad. So maybe it is better you are leaving now, no?" He grins as he says this, knowing I'd much prefer to remain with *Antwerpen* than ride out a storm in a hotel room.

And that's it. I head below to get my gear, finding Rafal Winczo already waiting in my cabin. He helps me carry everything to the main deck and down the gangway. As I alight on the pier, I stumble and Rafal laughs after making sure I'm all right. Embarrassed, I think it interesting that I have no problem walking on a ship rolling in heavy seas, but dry land seems to pose a problem.

"Daniel, I must tell you it has been good to have you aboard. Everyone on *Antwerpen* knows about you and is glad there is someone interested in our lives. We live away from the world; no one really cares about us. Well, maybe not everyone, but do you know what I mean?"

I nod as he speaks with an honesty and warmth I've not seen before.

"But it is good that you get to go home. To see your son, your family. That is what we always wish after months here."

The taxi still hasn't arrived, so I decide to stretch my legs a bit and get them used to being ashore again. Beside me, the piles of gypsum resemble small Dolomite peaks that gain more height as the rocks crash onto the pier from the discharge boom, sending up clouds of dust. A trio of deckhands walks past me, smiling and waving, and then I see Chief Engineer Janusz Ostrowski getting off the ship. He wanders in my direction, his infectious smile lighting up his face and his handshake pumping up and down energetically.

The Chief tells me that he, too, has enjoyed having me aboard, and we walk together for a bit as he heads to a nearby trailer that serves as the port office to call home to his family in Poland. He must be missing them, I guess. "Yes, is true. But you see those guys," he points at the trio of deckhands who passed me earlier, "the one in middle is also missing family. He find out just today that his girlfriend have a baby. He is new father. He is very happy, of course, but will not see his child for some more months. He is a seaman."

I leave The Chief to find a few minutes alone with his wife on a long-distance line and make my way to *Antwerpen*. I sit on the pier just to stare at the ship. Unlike the Marine Corps tanks, the bulk carrier bears no signs of battle, even though the ship and her crew have also faced dangers. Well, that's not quite true, I realize. Her wartime experiences *are* visible in the streaks of rust that decorate her sides and the innumerable touch-ups of paint that have mottled her hull into a camouflage pattern meant to deter the sea. She's survived collisions, hurricanes, ice storms and heavy seas.

My taxi pulls up and the driver gets out to grab my bag. I take one last look at *Antwerpen* and remember my first impression of her back in Rhode Island—her nondescript nature—and realize how mistaken and superficial that was. She is an old ship, her equipment dusty and dirty, and she has definitely seen better days. After a quarter-century of dutiful service, she probably won't be around for that much longer.

But she does have character. I find a certain grace in the rake of her bow, the placement of her superstructure and the sweeping curve of her stern. Her gantry cranes swing and scoop, her conveyor belts run on their endless loops, and crewmen wander the deck with walkie-talkies in hand. She is alive.

7

GODS

Remember, Lord, my ship is small and thy sea is so wide.

—TRADITIONAL FISHERMAN'S PRAYER

"How can you traverse the oceans of the world and not be impressed? Of God in the raw. Us landlubbers just don't see it. Seafarers intuitively respond to questions of 'Who am I?' 'What am I about?' 'Who's greater than I?' and they understand those questions on a fundamental level, more so than we on land. They come up against the questions of faith in a real way that perhaps only comes to the rest of us at times of great crises."

The man who is providing me with these insightful gems has the intense look upon his face of a true believer. He uses his hands to repeatedly drive home his points—"God in the raw," "Who's greater than I?"—while speaking in a calm, tempered manner. He's not a mariner himself; he's a priest. Reverend Canon Ken Peters is helping me to understand just where God fits into the whole equation of seafaring today, beginning with a simple question: Do mariners have a strong spiritual sense?

Throughout my travels, one of the things I've shied away from is asking those involved with shipping about their belief in God. Any God. The reasons for this are simple: I feel that one's personal belief system is a matter of privacy; I care not whether one worships under the mantle of Christianity, Islam, Judaism, Hinduism, Buddhism or Animism. As well, no one I've met—neither the mariners nor others involved with commercial shipping—has ever openly espoused any theological dictums while with me; there hasn't been any proselytizing when I've been around.

But given that my search is for the soul of a ship, it became inevitable that I confront the religious aspect of this concept and try to understand where belief fits into the world of the merchant mariner. And figuring there's no better place to start than with a priest, I've made my way to St. Michael Paternoster Church in the City of London.

The church, which was designed by Sir Christopher Wren, is three hundred years old and sits a stone's throw from the river Thames. It is the headquarters of the Anglican Church's Mission to Seafarers, and within a windowless office Reverend Canon Ken Peters oversees things as the justice and welfare secretary, helping coordinate campaigns to improve the lot of mariners. Canon Peters is nothing like what I'd expected, not a stuffy sort of minister full of theological bravado. Instead, I find an outgoing and jovial bundle of energy with a lyrical Welsh accent, who sits beneath an icon of the Virgin Mary and infant Jesus as he outlines the work of the Mission.

"Our job, quite simply, is to address the spiritual needs of seafarers. We're not a proselytizing organization; our intent is not to convert people to Christianity. We are an active part of the shipping industry—we work in over three hundred ports around the world—and our chaplains don't just sit in their missions waiting for seafarers to come to them; they go out, visit the ships, sail with them, talk to them. I myself have journeyed to the North Sea, to Russia and to the Far East. So it's a global network, a real catholic church."

The Mission to Seafarers began 150 years ago, when Britannia ruled the waves and the red ensign of the British Merchant Marine could be seen fluttering in harbours around the world. Its original intent was to service the religious needs of British mariners, but it eventually evolved into its present form, with a more non-denominational reach.

As Canon Peters puts it, "Because shipping is a continually changing endeavour, the Church, which is notorious for a literal adherence to things, has changed immensely within the Mission. It makes us constantly re-evaluate how we do things. We now deal with all faiths and religions— Christian, Muslim, Hindu, Buddhist—and work alongside our friends in those communities. If, by the way we act aboard a ship, what we say and what we do, if we help encourage, say, a Muslim to be a better Muslim, then we've done our jobs. And a question we often get from seafarers of other faiths is, 'Why do you do this for us?' And our answer is simple: 'Because we love you.' Unequivocally. What other motivation is there for a ministry?"

To help the spiritual needs of seafarers doesn't just mean that the Mission's chaplains simply conduct prayer meetings or deliver Bibles, though they obviously do that. But quite often staff will find mariners desperate for word from home or a break from the shipboard routines, so they'll arrange soccer matches between crews, facilitate long-distance phone calls to family and, increasingly, access to email and the internet. The Mission has also become actively involved in helping seafarers who haven't been paid or are working in substandard conditions. The staff have become mediators within the shipping industry, having no direct ties to the owners or the trade unions. It's all about listening and responding. And learning.

"I have met seafarers who have humbled me simply by who they are," Canon Peters relates. "My life is a quest, I'm on a pilgrimage, I'm on a journey, whatever you want to call it, trying to understand the Almighty, trying to touch God and have God touch me. And some seafarers come out with such gems of poetical understanding without any formal training, without any intellectual quest; it's just natural."

Unfortunately, the opportunity to listen to mariners has been made more difficult in the last few years. Ever since the September 11 terrorist attacks and the increased security around ports and vessels, many merchant sailors have been unable to go ashore without pre-arranged documentation, especially in the United States. There have been cases of injured crewmen unable to visit a shore-based hospital because they lacked American visas. In one recent case, a Russian mariner was arrested and deported for walking twenty metres from his ship to make a phone call before immigration officials had checked his papers. More and more sailors are becoming prisoners of their vessels for months and months on end.

Loosening his clerical collar, Canon Peters explains a recurring problem that this situation has created. "One of the major challenges today is to persuade the ownership community that seafarers are not just a company asset or a commodity. They are the lifeblood; they are the ones that enable everyone else in the shipping industry to earn their living. The ship, more than perhaps anything else, embodies a globalism, irrespective of the trade that it is on. Seafarers are noble and dignified; they are not the potential terrorists. They are, in fact, the victims. Downtown Manhattan was evacuated on 9/11 by a flotilla of ships; they couldn't get off Manhattan without ships. But what was the first thing they [American officials] did? Penalize seafarers. Do you see airline crews not being admitted to countries because they haven't got a visa? No."

The sense of isolation that can come from being confined aboard a ship can also create some extreme reactions from mariners. Peters vividly remembers visiting a Malaysian ship years ago and noting that something did not "seem right" about it. As soon as he boarded the vessel, he was hustled up to the captain's cabin, where the Dutch master made a unique request.

"There had been a death on board the vessel and the crew, which was predominately Muslim, was unnerved by it. They refused to enter the crewman's cabin or the workspaces where he used to work. Through the captain, they asked me to perform an exorcism. So I went into the man's cabin and performed a Christian rite—Christian prayers, a sprinkling of holy water, burning of some incense grains—and the Muslim seafarers were satisfied. I'd laid to rest the 'ghost.' I was performing a holy ritual. In doing that, I had witness to God as the Creator, you can accept it as you wish, you can reject it as you wish. But for those mariners, the spirit of the ship was healed. You know, there are many things that we do not comprehend or understand. In Western science we are just beginning to explore the concept that water has memory. But seafarers are able to make that leap into a quantum understanding of Creation, they are not confined by the analogue process, they are able to think around subjects, outside the box, because they are just 'there'—vulnerable, detached, cut adrift from society. Let me tell you, I don't have the courage to be a seafarer."

WHEN ONE THINKS of the "courage to be a seafarer," the images that often come to mind are of a sailor being swept overboard in rough seas and his crewmates struggling to save his life. Or of a battered and beaten ship, whose crew is trying to keep her afloat in mountainous oceans, fighting its way through the waves to a safe haven. But a more practical representation of the courage required of a mariner is the ability to withstand months, even years, away from your home; to endure crappy weather; and to be isolated from the rest of society in a tiny cabin.

On one level, seafaring may not seem as physically taxing as, say, mining, heavy construction or working in a steel mill. But on another level, going to sea is one of the most arduous occupations you could choose. The hours are long, the days filled with endless routine, and the tolls—physical and mental—can quickly age you. As the Old Testament's Book of Lamentations, one of the most poetic parts of the Bible, says, "It is good for a man that he bear the yoke in his youth."

"To be a sailor … yeah, it's a young man's business, I think. But even then, man, it eats at you, no matter how strong you are." These are the words of a mariner, and a young one at that. Third Mate Prince Kashyap stands on the bridge of a container ship being buffeted by what he figures are four-metre waves and thirty-seven-knot winds, causing the vessel to roll about ten degrees from side to side. The vessel has an apt name—MV *Canmar Spirit*—and is en route to Montreal from Europe, a biweekly trip that is quickly turning sour as we head into "near-gale conditions," Force 7 on the Beaufort Scale.

"Oh, man, I hate this," he mutters as he stares at a weather fax that's just come in. "You know, this is just shitty." He places the fax on the navigation table and reaches for a set of calipers, tracing them across a chart of the eastern Atlantic. "This is going to last for a couple of days," he says as he looks up from his calculations. "Do you get seasick?"

Prince Kashyap is a thoughtful and outgoing guy who joined the *Canmar Spirit* two weeks earlier. He tells me that this is his first time aboard a container vessel and he's still getting used to things. He also clarifies his name, a constant source of embarrassment: It's the result of an English grandmother declaring of her newborn grandson that "he looks like a prince." The worst was when he was a cadet, six years ago, and served with a Pakistani captain whose name translated as "god of gods." Whenever the two were on the bridge together, the crew took to joking that there was the God with his Prince.

Born in Punjab, India, Kashyap's a good-looking young man with intense dark eyes, who would be beginning his climb up the strata of merchant officers were it not for the serious reservations about a life at sea that he has. To most people, he lives an enviable life: travelling the world, making a tax-free income better than most other Indians, part of an honorable profession with almost boundless possibilities for the future.

Yet when I ask him about his life as a mariner and what he wants to do, he is adamant about his plans.

"Let me tell you," he says, "as soon as this contract is over, I'm finished. No more of these months and months away from home, not for me. I'm going to go home, maybe go to Australia, work on my mate's and master's certification and then look for a job that isn't as hard, something on a coastal vessel, maybe, where I'm only away for a few days. I want something simpler."

Kashyap fell into seafaring by accident, not out of a love for the profession. With an engineering degree from the University of Bangalore, he was looking for a job that would help pay off his schooling debts and ended up working for a small shipping firm in India. From there, one thing led to another until, as he puts it, "I was spending seven, eight, nine months at sea. Brazil, Africa, Asia, North America. I've been everywhere. Bulkers, tankers, now container ships. But you see, it's a hard life. When I go home and pick up the telephone, all my friends are gone, moved away. I've lost touch with them all. I have no girlfriend, no wife. Naw ... this isn't what I want to do. I like it and I'm good at it, but I don't love it." He stares at the weather fax again and then turns to me. "I'm sorry if that doesn't sound very romantic, but I'm still in my 'getting acquainted phase.'"

There's a slight drizzle out the bridge windows as I glimpse land far off to the starboard side. It's the last of England on our quarter, where Penzance and Land's End are. Just to the left are the Isles of Scilly, separated from the mainland by the Seven Stones and with Bishop's Rocks on the other side. For centuries these outposts were the last sign of civilization seen by European mariners until they stumbled upon the New World, and the first to greet them on their bedraggled return. The seafaring writer Alan Villiers sailed these waters frequently in the 1920s and 1930s. In *The Last of the Wind Ships* he wrote:

The first week out is a bitter experience, with nothing much of romance about it. Somehow the voyage seems a ghastly business, then, and the sea ahead appears interminable ... it means something, when the land had slipped into the obscurity of the haze astern and will not emerge again from the haze ahead for four months or so—and perhaps never.

It's a sentiment that Prince Kashyap echoes to me. As the young man explains it, he goes through a number of distinct psychological phases when he's working.

"The first two months at sea are the hardest. You ask anyone, from the captain to the cadet, and they'll tell you the same thing. Because that's when you realize how cut off you are from everything. And that's the worst time for me. It's like a sort of depression stage, I can get so worked up that small things will bother me, really eat at me. But then you get the middle two months and things improve, you improve. And by the last two months you are at the top of your job. But then you have to go home, and the reverse situation happens there. I come home, pick up the phone to call my friends, and they're all gone. Moved to new jobs in other cities or whatever. So you go to the pub, play pool, watch TV ... and you're alone again. This is what I don't like about being a sailor."

Prince Kashyap is one of those individuals whom the sea has accepted, but who has not accepted the sea in return. Far more mature than his years, he yearns for something else in his life, as many young people do, while carrying out the duties and tasks he has been entrusted with. It is a universal emotional battle for seafarers, this balance between commitment and dreams. The desire for a better life, a better income and a future can often be at odds with the paper a mariner signs enjoining him to a vessel. For these sailors, the cage can be anything but gilded.

"For me, money is not the issue," Kashyap offers. "I want something more in my life. Because you will never get rich being a sailor, that's for sure. I make about [U.S.]$2000 a month as a mate, which is good for most people. But there's a human price to be paid, as well." He pauses and stares at the stacks of containers in front of the wheelhouse windows.

"And I hate bad weather, I really do. Not because I get ill, but because it's just another of those things that makes our lives a hell. I mean, our lives are already miserable. These ships," he gestures around the wheelhouse of the *Canmar Spirit*, "you know, when these container ships came along, it all turned to shit."

A CONTAINER SHIP differs from its ocean-going sisters in many respects. Containers are not as dirty as bulk carriers, not as smelly as tankers and not as boxy as car carriers. Other mariners sometimes poke fun at the fact that many container ship crews still wear a uniform, which is generally true, and at how clean the vessels are. But whatever advantages these carriers of pre-packaged commodities may offer in terms of appearance, they certainly lose in their monotonous schedules. Vessels like the *Canmar Spirit* are true "liners," sailing according to firmly pre-arranged timetables on fixed routes, not unlike passenger airplanes. One can look up the itinerary of a container ship, see its ports of call and confidently arrange for a thousand cases of fine Bordeaux to be delivered in a fortnight. Before there was a FedEx, there were container ships.

The MV *Canmar Spirit* is yet another Korean shipyard creation, the product of the Daewoo Shipyard in Okpo, a hundred kilometres south of Hyundai's Ulsan operations. She's a 4400 TEU container ship, a somewhat arcane definition meaning she can carry that many of the small containers known as 20-foot equivalent units, or TEUs, even though most containers used nowadays are 40 feet long. At 294 metres in length, the vessel is over 100 metres longer than the bulk carrier *Antwerpen* and the tanker *Emerald Star*, displacing 48,000dwt. Her hull, beneath a gleaming white superstructure seven storeys high, is painted a brilliant orange-red. *Canmar Spirit* has a crew of thirty, all of whom hail from India—a polyglot mix of Hindus, Sikhs, Muslims and Christians—but her home port is London and she flies the historic red ensign of the British Merchant Marine, a flag that has hung from mastheads for over three hundred years. In shipping terms, though, the *Canmar Spirit* is still an infant, and this voyage will mark the first anniversary of her entering commercial service on the cross-Atlantic route for which she was built.

The history of containerization is actually a half-century old now, though it really wasn't until the 1960s that the concept took off as standardized containers and uniform port handling facilities were developed. That means that today a steel box can be loaded in any number of terminals worldwide without any problems or discrepancies. Ships like the *Canmar Spirit* help move over seventy million containers annually; they are the silent servants that keep us clothed, furnish our homes, entertain our children and allow IKEA and Wal-Mart to spread to every corner of the globe.

The process of shipping that many containers would not be possible without the advances in information technology of the last few decades. When *Canmar Spirit* tied up at her berth in the immense Europa Terminal in Antwerp, a complex shore-based loading system began to swing into place. This container port on the Scheldt River is the fourth-largest harbour in the world, with 1700 berths taking up 130 kilometres of land along both sides of the waterway. Antwerp has been a gateway to Europe for centuries; for this reason Hitler ordered his rocket bombs, the famed V1 and V2 weapons, to be hurled at Antwerp in the waning years of the last world war with even more ferocity than was focused on London.

In the largest open-air storage facility that I've ever seen, thousands and thousands of containers are stacked far and wide. Piled two or three high, the containers are arranged in neat rows on the asphalt, their corrugated surfaces painted a mix of colours. How anyone can figure out which anonymous box goes where seems a mystery, but clues come in the form of mechanical creatures that inhabit this industrial wasteland.

Buzzing around the site are dozens of weird yellow contraptions that seem to have a life of their own—I try to count how many there are, but lose track at fifty. Riding on four wheels and rising higher than the stacks, these machines are the carriers that ferry the steel boxes from the holding area to the dockside, doing so by straddling the containers and picking them up by the corners. This is accomplished with astonishing efficiency, giving the place a futuristic feel, as though robots from a sci-fi movie have run amok. In truth, each carrier is operated by a human driver sitting several storeys above the ground, to whom a computer readout is relayed ordering him to pick up container XX and transport it to vessel YY.

Once those containers are deposited on the dock adjacent to the *Canmar Spirit,* one of three gantry cranes looming over the deck picks up the box and shuttles it to a pre-ordained position on the ship. It takes little more than ninety seconds for a good crane operator to pick up the container and deposit it aboard the vessel—again, an astonishingly fast operation. Bored by the monotony, some of the stevedores prepping the containers quayside make a game out of the procedure of placing small metal chocks in the corners of each box; they time themselves to see who is the fastest in a unique event I call the "forty-metre industrial dash."

Close to the industrial Olympians is a team of five customs agents, one of whom is holding a long, probing device that can check the interior environment of containers for trace residues of any explosive material, illegal drugs or stowaways, not unlike the way airport security scans luggage and such. It's a bit of a hit-and-miss proposition, and no technology exists that can look at each and every container shipped worldwide—not without slowing global trade to a trickle and affecting economies.

After a full day of loading, *Canmar Spirit* casts off her lines again and heads down the Scheldt River on a day named after the Roman god of merchants—Mercury (*mercredi,* French for "Wednesday," comes from the Latin *Mercurii dies,* or Mercury's day). Once she's transited the winding river to the Channel, she'll thence head south to Le Havre, France, where the process will be repeated until we are laden with several thousand boxes. (Most of the containers are stored in the hull; the boxes you see on the deck are the minority a vessel like this can carry. *Canmar Spirit* has seven holds forward and one aft of the superstructure.)

The pace of all this port activity is one of the reasons many mariners shy away from container vessels. Container ships spend as little time in port as possible and these facilities are inevitably located far from any real urban centres, so it's not like the crew gets much shore time to unwind. In Antwerp, the cab ride into town is something like U.S.$100; that's how far Europa Terminal is from the House of Rubens or the diamond shops. For many seafarers, these sorts of vessels are considered to be "gilded cages" and, unfortunately, the ships are here to stay.

THE MIGHT OF THE OCEAN remains as intangible as any theology for the vast majority of us who live on land. After twenty-four hours spent watching the *Canmar Spirit* pummelled by wind and waves, I decide that conditions have improved sufficiently for me to go on deck and experience the restless seas first-hand. As I step out onto the main deck, the wind immediately tugs at my foul weather gear, even though I'm on the leeward side of the ship. And as I peer over the handrail the full weight of that wind washes my face in salt water, stinging my eyes. The skies are overcast and the wind is still blowing at about thirty knots and the waves are three to four metres in height, so we're still bouncing around a bit here on the ocean. Imagine sticking your head out the window of a car speeding along a highway during a rain squall while the driver swerves erratically, and you'll have some idea of what it's like to walk on the deck of a cargo vessel as near-gale conditions abate in the North Atlantic.

Above the roar of the wind I can hear an odd mechanical grinding, like that of a dentist's drill, and follow it around to the back of the ship's house, where a deckhand is calmly grinding down aluminum pots from the kitchen. He's completely oblivious to the ship's motion and to me, so I leave him to his task and head forward.

On both sides of the ship there's a walkway beneath the containers that provides a somewhat sheltered means of getting about. Grasping the wire handhold on the interior side of the starboard walkway, I careen toward the bow, reminding myself of the old mariner's adage "One hand for the ship, one hand for yourself." About halfway forward, the containers provide a better windbreak and the going gets much easier. But now I can make out another sound: the creaking and moaning of thousands of steel containers lashed above me.

This sound is quite ominous, like something from a horror film, and causes the hairs on the back of my neck to stand up. The containers also bang against one another as the ship rolls from side to side, evoking visions of captive spirits encased in the boxes, desperate to escape but unable to do so. As I continue onward, the pleas of the fictional apparitions are swept away as the wind returns. I'm almost at the forecastle workspace and the crashing of the ship's bow into the fierce seas sends forth walls of whitewater that rise above me on the starboard side. The deck is awash and in constant motion, my raingear is slick and my grip on the handhold firmer. There is a definite sense of danger in the air up here as you stumble forward into the wind, your head down, spray enveloping you, the roar of the wind surrounding you. It's one of the most exhilarating sensations I've ever felt.

To watch these seas is to understand the respect sailors give them: They are vibrantly ferocious and malevolent. My hands are getting cold and sore from gripping whatever sturdy support I can find, and the ease with which a man could be swept overboard is readily apparent. Less so is what that man would be thinking as he struggled in these frigid waters and watched his ship sail on. This is unlike my encounters with hurricanes off the American coast, in that I realize there is no nearby coast guard station that can come to the rescue; we just passed the Mid-Atlantic Ridge about halfway between the continents; we're in the middle of nowhere. And since I know from checking the radar earlier that no other vessels are within a hundred miles of us, I become even more aware of our solitude.

I think back to what Canon Ken Peters said in London, about the idea that water has memory. It's not as far-fetched as it may sound. He was referring to recent research and the work of a physicist named Dr. Wolfgang Ludwig. As odd as it may sound, Ludwig theorizes that water may have memory properties similar to those of an elephant—that it can transfer information, once it has obtained it, to other systems such as living organisms. If you think of a stone dropped into a pond, the ripples that it creates may be considered a form of information transference, the dissemination of energy in small waves to other parts of the water.

Whether or not you agree with this concept, you cannot deny that the sea has a life of its own. It embodies a whole range of emotions—anger, pleasure, antipathy, remorse, sadness and joy. It bears all the hallmarks of an individual, with one body of water being distinct from another, and affecting different moods as its surroundings change. The Caribbean is in no way like the North Atlantic, nor is it the same in July as in November. The sea is moody, petulant and unforgiving of those who fail to heed its warning signs.

I think, too, of all who have come before on this northern route, their frail little craft assaulted by the same conditions that are mocking this giant container ship: Vikings in open longboats; Irish monks in leather-covered craft; nauseated emigrants crammed into sailing barks; merchant sailors in Liberty ships laden with explosives, praying a U-boat hasn't targeted them. One's faith in whatever God one believes in would surely be tested under such conditions, either reinforcing that belief or rendering it obsolete.

A HALF-HOUR LATER, I stagger into the wheelhouse thoroughly soaked and cold. Third Officer Prince Kashyap has the watch and greets me sardonically: "Now why on earth would you want to go out there in these conditions, man? Isn't it better to stay in here where it's nice and warm? And good thing you didn't drown," he jokes, while making some tea for us. "I'd be cursing you for all the paperwork."

As I slowly warm up, the mate tells me we're currently stuck between two weather systems, and having just made it through one near-gale, we're going to hit another one in fewer than twenty-four hours. It will be a real sou'wester, coming at us from the Grand Banks region. To make things worse, there's a high-pressure system bearing down from Baffin Island, so it looks as though we'll be getting it from two sides. A vessel like *Canmar Spirit* is built for these North Atlantic conditions, with an ice-strengthened hull, double bottom and some of the most advanced technology available to mariners. And a crew experienced in dealing with severe weather conditions.

"The worst condition I've ever seen was wind force nine," says Kashyap as he hands me my tea. "That's considered a strong gale. We were going from Madagascar to Cape Town in a 45,000dwt tanker, so something the size of this. There are extraordinary waves in that region, special topographic features. You have water walls and what you see is just water in front of you. Boom—it hits you! Ten-metre, thirteen-metre waves. It's scary. That was my first vessel as a cadet; I was jumping, puking, throwing up. You see a wall of water in front of you and then the water slams on the bow, pounding you, it's like being on a submarine. It went on for four days. You couldn't go out on deck, you just lie in your bunk, you work and you wait for it to end. Luckily we had a good captain, so we made it through OK."

The arrival of Captain A. S. Grewal, the ship's master, interrupts Third Officer Kashyap's tea break. We've only met once—briefly—as Grewal's also new to the vessel and has been busy getting acquainted with things. A skinny man casually dressed in a green polo shirt, Grewal has a wispy grey beard beneath expressive eyes and wears a kerchief on his head in deference to his Sikh religion. (Kashyap, who is also Sikh, is clean-shaven and without a turban or kerchief, preferring a more Western style of fashion.) Chain-smoking, the master huddles over the chart table with the third officer, checking on our course and the impending arrival of the weather systems.

Using a set of calipers and a pocket calculator, Captain Grewal sets to work pinpointing some waypoints on the chart, mumbling to himself. Our current position, N 49°12', W 36°18', has us less than a day away from the extremities of the sou'wester. The captain orders a slight change in our course to the north, so we'll hopefully avoid all but the outer edges of the storm. Otherwise, there's really not much we can do. "It's too late to head south of the system and turning back is not necessary. We'll just do what sailors always do: hope for the best." He turns to the third mate: "Inform the second mate that I want an update at 0500."

Kashyap quietly responds, "Aye, aye, sir." After Captain Grewal leaves, Kashyap turns to me with a sly smile on his face. "When the captain wants to be awakened at five o'clock for an update, you can be certain we're heading into rough seas."

MAYBE BECAUSE MANY of their tales seem too good to be true, it's often felt that mariners are exaggerating conditions at sea when they try to convince landlubbers of what they have seen. I mean, ten-metre waves in the Mozambique Channel? Could Kashyap have been embellishing, perhaps just a bit? Scientific reason has yet to prove the existence of the Bermuda Triangle, sea monsters, ghost ships or Atlantis. Landlocked brethren often discount the word of sailors—another reason mariners seem cautious about outsiders.

The tales told by North Atlantic seamen about massive walls of water, "rogue waves," which appear out of nowhere and can loom over a vessel, are a good example. Seafarers have described huge waves racing across the sea, rising to heights of twenty or thirty metres, as high or higher than the wheelhouse. For years scientists have dismissed the idea that ten-storey-tall waves could be anything but rare, putting them down to yet another nautical myth embellished by one too many drinks in port. Scientific projections of wave action always concluded that these freak ocean phenomena, though possible, should only occur about once every ten thousand years.

But a small team of European researchers began to look more seriously at this nautical myth, especially after analyzing data relating to the sinking of large vessels. They found that in the last two decades more than two hundred supertankers and container ships have sunk in extreme weather conditions. On average, two large ships sink every week somewhere on the globe, but the cause of their demise is rarely studied. Whereas a plane crash is examined in minute detail, the loss of a ship and its crew is often ascribed to "bad weather," an act of God.

As the researchers began to comb through mariners' reports, it became clear that not all of them could be fanciful flights of imagination. The captain of the luxury liner *Queen Elizabeth 2,* Ronald Warwick, reported encountering a rogue wave in the midst of a February 1995 hurricane in the North Atlantic. The wall of water, which he estimated at twenty-nine metres in height, seemed like the White Cliffs of Dover coming at him. In 2001, two other passenger liners, the *Bremen* and the *Caledonian Star,* had separate run-ins with rogue waves in the South Atlantic within a week of each other. Both ships' masters reported the waves to be about thirty metres high, large enough to wash over the bridge and smash the windows of the vessels. The *Bremen*'s damage was such that she was left powerless for two hours, drifting in the middle of the ocean with the crew frantically working to get her underway again.

In 2000 a comprehensive study called MaxWave was begun to collate all the data available and enhance it by using two European Space Agency satellites to map the Atlantic in search of rogue waves and the conditions that create them. From the MaxWave study, researchers found some disturbing data collected by oil rigs in the North Sea. Radar data from the Goma oilfield, in particular, showed 466 encounters with rogue waves during a 12-year period. The stable platforms provided objective measurements for researchers, such as when the Draupner rig used an onboard laser device to gauge a rogue wave of 26 metres in height on New Year's Day 1995. The same laser was able to measure the surrounding waves as being 12 metres high. This finally convinced the European scientists that they were looking at a much more common—and, hence, a much more dangerous—weather condition.

Keeping in mind that most vessels are built to withstand waves of no more than 15 metres in height, the revelation that 30-metre rogue waves are not, in fact, rogues is slightly disturbing to anyone stuck in the middle of the ocean. (By comparison, the December 26, 2004, tsunami that emanated from off Sumatra, killing well over 200,000, eventually reached heights of about 24 metres. Several merchant vessels in the area at the time survived, riding out the waves that only grew in strength as they came ashore.) Most mariners, though, remain taciturn when discussing such ocean conditions, which are just another part of their professional lives.

I STOP OFF to see if Captain Grewal is in his day office, but find, instead, a woman sitting on his sofa and holding a small red leather book in her hands. I realize that I've caught her as she was saying her prayers, but she quickly invites me to come sit with her, happy for some company. "Please come in, my name is Bhupinder. I am the captain's wife," she says, extending her hand in friendship. Gracious, in her late forties and with long brown hair, she is the first woman I've met aboard a commercial ship. The Grewals have been married twenty-five years now, and the entire time she's been a mariner's wife. It's fairly common among Indian crews for the wives of senior officers to travel aboard ship, sometimes even bringing their children. And it certainly changes the mood of a vessel.

"You know, we women have a calming effect on the men, I think," she says in her soft, almost delicate voice. "But there are certain unwritten rules that we must follow or things can get upset. I may be the captain's wife, but I cannot order the crew around or make demands on them. Sometimes I have heard of women taking advantage of this position, maybe interfering with things, and it creates a bad atmosphere. Very bad. For me, I just want to be near my husband."

Bhupinder Grewal grew up in the landlocked Indian state of Uttar Pradesh, which borders Nepal to the north, and had never seen the sea until she married and went to Bombay. This is the tenth vessel she's sailed on with her husband, and she won't go home until just before he completes the contract, in six months' time. With two grown children, she has fewer pressures on her than when the children were young.

"Those days, they were very difficult," she remembers. "He would be gone for nine months or more and I was all alone. A young woman in her twenties, the big city, no husband, that's when I realized what life was. And it was hard for him, too. When my husband lost his father, he could not come home, he was out at sea. He wasn't even there for the birth of our children—they were six months old, both of them, when he first saw them. I did everything for the children; he was not there. And I used to cry for days when he left; I cried like that for years. So, eventually, I said to him, 'I cannot do this. Can I come with you? With the kids?' And that's when I first started sailing."

Though generally overlooked in maritime history, women have been going to sea for almost as long as men have. In the nineteenth century, American whaling ships routinely left for two- or three-year voyages complete with the captain's wife and family. Other ships employed women as stewardesses and cooks, and female master mariners have worked commercially for over fifty years. Women mariners have even made their mark in the annals of piracy: Mary Read and Ann Bonny sailed the Caribbean in the eighteenth century, while Cheng I Sao commanded a ruthless Chinese pirate armada called the "Red Flag Fleet" in the early nineteenth century.

Bhupinder Grewal's remarkable life as a mariner's wife has taken her from rural India to Japan, Singapore, New Zealand, Australia, South America, Israel, America and even North Korea. (She and her husband, along with his crew, were "stranded" in North Korea for three months as a money dispute went on with the ship owners. About the only thing that she remembers is visiting Pyongyang, the capital, which she describes as "a ghost town.") But life aboard a cramped vessel does take some getting used to, she says. "You know, I just try to tune myself to the ship and its rhythms. I'm used to it now, and I don't mind being alone. I have my books, my tatting and, well, my husband. Frankly, I'm better off than him. My husband doesn't like brand-new ships; he says that new ships have more problems. And, besides," she quietly adds, "he doesn't really love the sea, not anymore. He may have as a young man, but not anymore."

It takes courage to be a sailor's wife, with the knowledge that you will only ever have a part-time husband for as long as he goes to sea. But that courage can also come in handy when at sea. "I remember one trip, when I was aboard with my daughter, who was one year old. We were part of a convoy of twenty-five ships heading through the Persian Gulf; this was during the Iran–Iraq War, back in 1985. We were headed for Bandar Khomeini, which is way up by the border with Iraq, and a report came in that the convoy might be targeted by missiles. So we all had to go to the fo'c'sle, everyone except the captain and the chief engineer. And we were scared, let me tell you. We just prayed and waited for maybe five hours. Luckily we got through OK, but the ship in front of us, an Iraqi missile hit it, went right through the hull. And they were lucky, too: the missile did not explode for some reason. So, sometimes it is not just the weather you have to worry about."

BHUPINDER GREWAL is absolutely correct that there are other threats besides the weather that mariners must deal with. And beyond war zones, the most dangerous threat by far is piracy. Virtually every mariner I've met can recount stories of run-ins with armed bandits throughout the globe. One night, Third Mate Kashyap calmly recounted, "Pirates? Oh yeah, I've seen them. Off South America, on a tanker. They'd climb aboard, get into the storage lockers up in the bow, steal ropes, whatever they could get their hands on. We just turn on the searchlights, try to scare them off, but never went face to face. No way, man."

The traditional image of pirates is the romanticized Hollywood version. But the reality, of course, is much, much more disturbing. The effects of piracy on the lives of seafarers have never been glamorous. Prostitution may be the world's oldest profession, but piracy isn't far behind, for its history goes back over three thousand years. Homer wrote about it in *The Odyssey*, Alexander the Great tried to eradicate it, and a young Julius Caesar was taken prisoner by pirates and held for ransom (he later exacted a brutal revenge on his captors). It is the dark spirit of seafaring.

Still, pirates have fascinated us for centuries and perhaps this interest stems from the cliché of the outlaw, or the underdog, who manages to fight back against the autocratic rulers persecuting the working class. Piracy has always been about economics, the poor seeking a living. The term "buccaneer," for instance, originates around 1630, when the Spanish drove French settlers from Hispaniola. Settling on the island of Tortuga, north of present-day Haiti, the impoverished refugees subsisted on *boucan,* the Carib name for a sort of barbecued dried meat, and eventually these *boucaniers* began preying on passing Spanish vessels.

Much has also been made of the quasi-democratic aspect of these Caribbean pirates, how they could "vote" for who would be captain or how they could receive monetary compensation for injuries (the loss of a limb, it was said, would earn a pirate eight hundred "pieces of eight," as Spanish coins were known at the time). Many mariners opted to become pirates because the working conditions on these bandit boats were marginally better than those on European vessels. This was still the era of press gangs, when groups of thugs wandered the waterfronts of Bristol, London, Halifax and dozens of other ports, kidnapping unsuspecting men into the Royal Navy. Anything must have seemed better than the harsh discipline and minuscule pay the navy was known for.

But there's often been a healthy dose of politics thrown in for good measure when it comes to piracy. For centuries, nations have turned a blind eye to criminal seafarers who preyed on their enemies' ships. Worse, countries would sometimes legally sanction the use of these brigands. As early as 1243, the English monarch Henry III was granting letters of marque to armed merchantmen, documents that allowed them to pillage the vessels of other nations (in return, these privateers, as they were known, agreed to turn over a percentage of the booty to the Admiralty, enriching the king's coffers). Sir Francis Drake, Walter Raleigh, Henry Morgan, Captain Kidd and John Paul Jones were all privateers at one point or another, attacking other seafarers in order to undermine maritime commerce.

The use of privateers was, in fact, a form of state-sanctioned terrorism, and it spread like a cancer as more and more mariners opted to join the ranks of those who sailed under the skull and crossbones. By the late seventeenth century, many of these seafarers had given up quasi-legal privateering for all-out piracy, and the great European powers realized that something had to be done to stem the threat to their cross-Atlantic trade routes. Any time governments opt to use terrorists as extra-judicial agents, the problem becomes how to put the genie back into the bottle. Almost as soon as piracy was eradicated in the Caribbean, navies were dealing with it elsewhere in the world: off the coasts of China, Africa, India, the Mediterranean, South America and Nova Scotia, in the English Channel, and pretty much anywhere a merchant vessel sailed alone and vulnerable.

Today, piracy remains an almost daily event. It's little known outside the world of mariners, another of the secrets they keep from us, but pirates attack bulk carriers in South America, oil tankers off Nigeria, container ships in the Bay of Bengal and tugboats near Vietnam. Piracy has evolved from what has been called "maritime mugging"—poor coastal villagers boarding ships to steal paint, ropes and other deck equipment—to a far more nefarious business. Organized crime syndicates and political groups have found that piracy is an easy way to make money and fund their campaigns. Al-Qaeda, Chechen rebels, Tamil Tigers, Bandah Aceh separatists and rogue military units are all getting in on the action, using sleek powerboats, sub-machine guns and high explosives against commercial ships. There are reports of ships and their cargoes disappearing entirely, the vessels reflagged and the goods sold off. As for the crews—well, they have sometimes disappeared as well.

In Kuala Lumpur, Malaysia, the International Maritime Bureau (IMB) maintains a Piracy Reporting Centre that has been tracking attacks and posts weekly updates on its website. The IMB estimates that in the last decade alone pirates have taken hostage more than 2500 seafarers, injured 378 and killed over 300, and most people think these statistics are far below the real figures. Mariners have a better chance of being attacked on the job than a commuter in the United States has of being car-jacked. In places like the Strait of Malacca, the narrow waterway separating Indonesia, Malaysia and Singapore, no vessel sails without constant look-outs posted and the crew on standby to repel boarders (usually using water hoses; very few merchant vessels carry firearms, and it is common practice to avoid a fight with pirates at all costs).

As the *CANMAR SPIRIT* begins to feel the effects of the approaching sou'wester, the seas worsen. In the officers' mess, the stewards have taken to soaking the tablecloths with water, so that dishes and cutlery won't slide about as the ship rolls from side to side. A young cadet sitting nearby, on his first transatlantic crossing, is visibly ill from the motion and I notice Bhupinder Grewal showing a motherly concern for him, suggesting some crackers instead of a hearty meal. After the young man leaves, she wanders into the kitchen and chats with the cook about preparing something simple for the cadet for lunch.

Late morning brings visibility that has reduced to, as Captain Grewal puts it, "Nothing. Zero." Standing on the bridge, he feverishly sucks on a cigarette while reading the latest weather updates. *Canmar Spirit* is making twenty-one knots through the heaving seas and fog, radars helping us along as our roll increases. We're still alone out here and have seen only one other vessel in the last two days, another container ship heading in the opposite direction. In the swells that surround us, our vessel has a tendency to ride up on the highest ones and then drive herself down onto the waters with a force that makes her entire hull reverberate.

For the next few days we'll be travelling through Captain Grewel's least favourite part of the Atlantic, a swath of sea that is prone to fog, storms and icebergs. The bergs are not a problem at this time of the year, he explains, but the winter months and June and July can be dangerous for mariners. In his experience, the only other waters that are worse for mariners are around the Aleutian Islands of Alaska. This area east of Newfoundland and south of Greenland brings the cold Arctic water of the Labrador Current together with the warmer Gulf Stream, so is prone to harsh conditions. Until we reach the Strait of Belle Isle off Newfoundland, the captain will be on edge, preoccupied with seeing that no containers get tossed overboard. Sometime tonight we'll be passing close to the resting place of the *Titanic,* a reminder of this region's dark history.

That evening, the ship begins to roll even more dramatically and I can hear the sound of dishes crashing from within the kitchen. The steward calmly suggests I store away anything that's out in the open in my cabin, so I head back there and begin methodically following his instructions. I've given up on using my laptop, so I pack it into a drawer and surround it with T-shirts as padding. I've also been reminded to make sure my life vest is in working order—a routine thing, I've been assured—so I pull it out from the closet and stare at the neon-red contraption for a long moment before putting it away.

A little after 2200, I make my way back up to the bridge, quietly opening the door to the wheelhouse and entering its darkened interior. As I do so, a voice calls out, "Hello Daniel," as Prince Kashyap greets me from his lair. Our speed has dropped a few knots as we battle the near-gale conditions coming at us, and we still have a few hundred nautical miles of rough seas to traverse before things should calm down. The *Canmar Spirit* has managed to make about 530 nautical miles each day of this trip, burning through 20,000 tonnes of fuel every twenty-four hours. On the darkened bridge there's just Kashyap and a deckhand quietly keeping an eye on a U.S.$30-million vessel, her $5-million cargo and thirty-one human souls.

I reel toward him as the container ship lists from one side to the other. According to the clinometer, the wheelhouse instrument that gauges these things, she's swinging through rolls of almost twenty degrees, sufficiently extreme to make you keep your hand on something solid. We're forty-two metres above the keel, so the effects of the ship's rolls are heightened up here in the wheelhouse. Out the windows, all that's visible is a loathsome sea intent on reminding us of our mortality; waves crash over the bow, splaying themselves on the steel containers forward. The ship lurches suddenly and I stumble before Kashyap grabs my arm.

"Hey man, welcome to God's world," he says while gesturing at the maelstrom surrounding us. "Isn't this something? And will you listen to that wind?" "That wind" is reaching speeds of fifty knots as shown by the ship's anemometer, howling at us and periodically washing the reinforced glass with spray. The ship itself is pitching as well as rolling; she'll crest a swell and point her bow down into the trough that follows. This causes *Canmar Spirit* to slide to the bottom of the trough whereupon the sea crashes over the fo'c'sle and we begin to rise to the top of the next wave. As her propeller cuts into the ocean, the ship shudders and shakes, the wheelhouse fixtures vibrating for a good thirty seconds until we once more crest the top and repeat the cycle again and again.

Visibility is poor in these seas; I can barely make out the mast that rises from just forward of Number One Hatch at the bow, 238 metres away, because of driving rain and breaking water. As the ship lurches once more on a starboard roll, Kashyap lets out a giddy, nervous laugh and his white teeth gleam in the darkened wheelhouse. For someone who said he hated bad weather, he sure seems to be enjoying himself.

"Naw, that's not it," he responds. "There is a certain awe that these conditions make me feel—you must feel it, too. And I have some fundamental tenets, one of which is to make the best of a bad thing. Trust me, I am not enjoying myself tonight, no one is. Do you think the chief officer can do his paperwork when it's like this? Can the crew go out and check on the containers? Are you crazy? Just look at these seas. And imagine what would happen if a ten-metre iceberg were to come in front of us right now with a rate of speed of forty knots. No lookout, no radar will see it—I wouldn't see it from here. Think about the impact. In this kind of severe weather you can't go outside and do any repairs. You just better pray and lower the lifeboats."

Of course none of us expects to die here in the Labrador Sea tonight. We're on a modern vessel equipped with state-of-the-art equipment and the long-range radar shows another half-dozen vessels in the area that could, presumably, come to our aid if needed. But the third officer discounts all that. "I honestly tell you that whatever knowledge I may have, there is one force—whether you believe it or you don't believe it— there is one force running the ship." He points to the heavens above. "You have to believe that force. It sounds ridiculous in the age of computers and satellites to be talking of supernatural things. But this is something that sailors believe. This is something that I believe."

There it is, an echo of what Reverend Canon Ken Peters told me in London, another thing that separates mariners from the rest of us. They may hide their faith under veils of bravado, but it lurks there somewhere below the surface. At times I've been able to glimpse it here aboard *Canmar Spirit:* Bhupinder Grewal's little book of prayers, a cross tattooed on the hand of a crewman from Goa, a small image of the Hindu god Ganesh taped to the main control console in the engine room.

In a moment of striking candour, Prince Kashyap stares out the starboard windows and says, "I'll tell you something about myself: I believe that if He's going to take care of me, I better respect Him. I may give six days to the Devil—cursing, thinking about women, stuff like that— but I will always give one day to God. One day a week I fast and try to think about things, OK?" It just so happens that the one day he gives to his God is today and I realize that I haven't seen him in the mess today at mealtimes.

For many mariners, the solitude of life at sea gives them the opportunity to do something akin to meditating on life. "Out here you think about a lot of things, about memories," Kashyap explains. "Yes, it's like meditating. You can't really talk with anyone else on the ship about personal things; there are the barriers of command and discipline here. But the hardships I've endured have made me a better person. Sailors understand things like what love is, what togetherness is, what is a relationship, how important is your mother and father and brothers and sisters. I dunno, we just think too much, I guess."

With that, Kashyap shrugs his shoulders and goes back to watching the North Atlantic's angry seas pummel his container ship. By the long-range radar, we see that somewhere out there in the ocean a dozen other vessels are now caught in the same battle against Mother Nature. Each must be experiencing the exact same conditions *Canmar Spirit* is, but we're all on our own out here. And if one of those ships were to flounder, there's not a damn thing we could do about it.

By DAWN, the hand of the Lord has stroked the intemperate seas and subdued their anger. We're now within the Strait of Belle Isle, which separates Newfoundland from Labrador, and the change from the night before is startling: The waters are smooth, the sky clear and sunny. It's such a dramatic change that it makes you wonder if last night's tempest was merely a dream. *Canmar Spirit* still has another day of sailing up the St. Lawrence River before arriving at her final destination of Montreal. For the crew, this is a time to relax a bit and welcome the embrace of my native land after the rocky crossing.

The container ship progresses through the Gulf of St. Lawrence, with the north shore of Quebec keeping us company on our starboard side. There are a couple of river pilots up in the wheelhouse, chatting in French to each other between giving course changes in English to the helmsman. Captain Grewal stands near the ship's wheel in his white dress uniform, listening to the pilot's orders. Off to one side, his wife, Bhupinder, sits quietly tatting away at a piece of lace while taking in the farms and small towns we pass. Meanwhile, Third Officer Prince Kashyap is looking haggard and tired as he checks a computer for any emails that may have arrived from the ship owners. All is once more peaceful in his realm.

One of the pilots says something to the captain, who grabs a pair of binoculars to scan the river ahead. There's an outbound container ship approaching us, which turns out to be a sister ship of the *Canmar Spirit*. Captain Grewal grabs the radio to "speak the ship," an old nautical term for gamming with her master. The two mariners relay weather information and make small talk; because of the weather we endured north of Newfoundland, the other captain has opted to enter the Atlantic via the more southerly Cabot Straits, in the hope he can miss the worst of the low-pressure zone still languishing somewhere out there.

Signing off, Captain Grewal wishes his colleague a safe journey and then turns to watch the other container ship pass on our port side. He can see her master waving from the vessel's bridge wing and returns the greeting before she slips astern of us. "She's a good ship, a good captain," he tells me as he watches the other ship fade over the horizon. It's a compliment he is able to make based on experience: In his quarter-century as a seafarer he's seen his fair share of good and bad vessels.

"Oh, yes, I can remember some bad ships, very bad ships. One in particular, I remember a trip on it and we had a death, a fire, injuries. There was just something about that ship. It didn't matter who the crew was, different crews had the same problems with it. That one was a man-killer, that's for sure. It was the ship that was the problem."

I note that he doesn't refer to the man-killer ship as "her" or "she," the usual feminine pronouns that sailors use for vessels. Instead, Captain Grewal has used the neutral "it" to describe the ship, as though it did not deserve to be familiarized. He kept it at bay, so to speak.

I ask him if he'd do it all again—go to sea—and surprisingly he says, "No way. Today there's too many regulations, too much pressure on the masters. A few years ago it wasn't so bad, but nowadays we have too much work to do. Besides," he adds, "in a few years it will all be Chinese mariners. You see, we Indians will be like the Britishers, a declining part of the merchant marine. I am now truly an 'old man' of the sea. My days are numbered. It will soon be time for me to go ashore." His wife pauses from her tatting and stares at Captain Grewal above her half-moon glasses as he says this. After a moment, she gives him a warm, welcoming smile and then returns to working the lace into an intricate pattern suitable for adorning a coffee table at home.

Thoughts of home are also evident in the number of cellular phones that have suddenly materialized among many of the crew. At first I can't figure out why until I spy a deckhand standing near the stern, busily tapping away at the number pad, and then I realize he's text-messaging someone. Being this close to land, we're within range of mobile phone service, and these simple messages are a cheap way to keep in touch with family and friends on the other side of the world.

That night, my last aboard the *Canmar Spirit*, the shoreline of the St. Lawrence begins to narrow its grip around the ship on both sides, holding us close in its welcoming arms. As in Jacksonville, it's possible to pick out living rooms with televisions glowing, people eating dinner in their kitchens and cars travelling on the coastal roads. Overhead, we're being treated to a dazzling display of the aurora borealis—the northern lights. They dance and soar high into the starry sky, and various officers and crew line the starboard side to watch this impromptu performance being put on for their benefit.

In two days' time the crew will be given a few hours of liberty in Montreal while the ship is tied up. For some this will mean the chance to catch a movie or hit a bar; for others it will mean making a beeline for the nearest electronics store to stock up on new DVD players or stereo systems (many of which will have been imported in container ships). Either way, it will be the only chance to briefly shed the trappings of a mariner's life and stroll in anonymity among those who know nothing of the sea.

Then, all too soon, it will be back to the ship and outbound for Europe again. The crew will do this again and again until their contracts are up, only to be replaced by another crew and then another, all of them waiting for the day when they're too old or infirm or are made redundant and are sent ashore one last time. In the meantime these seafarers will remain itinerant caregivers to the leviathan until she, too, loses her youthful energy and strength.

When the poet John Masefield wrote, "They mark our passage as a race of men; Earth will not see such ships as these again," he was referring to the end of an era, the era of the great sail ships of the nineteenth century. But those words could apply to the demise of any ocean vessel, even *Canmar Spirit,* for the day will eventually come when she will be too old to remain at sea. And as she makes her final voyage to the breaking yards, the memory of her will fade into the shadows of the sea.

8

UNDERTAKERS

It is easy to go down into Hell; night and day, the gates of
dark Death stand wide; but to climb back again, to retrace
one's steps to the upper air—there's the rub, the task.

—VIRGIL, *THE AENEID*

F ive months after my first visit to the shipbreaking yards of Alang, I've
come again to this final port of call, a place that many mariners
would prefer not to see owing to its role as the mortuary of sea-going
vessels. What had seemed so amazing on my first trip now appears somewhat more macabre after watching ships being designed, built and sailed

with such care and grace. For here is where these great sea-going leviathans, aged and infirm beyond their years, must face their destinies and await the arrival of the undertakers.

It's still early as I stand on the dirty beach of a shipbreaking yard with lethargic little waves kissing the shore. Dawn is just appearing on the eastern horizon of the Bay of Khambhat and I can tell it's going to be another sweltering day, hot even by the standards of India. In the last few weeks the thermometer has topped 40° Celsius here in Gujarat State. The monsoon rains that normally bring relief from the heat are nowhere to be seen, sitting somewhere out in the Indian Ocean like a pouting child, refusing to come ashore and increasing the misery on land. The effect of this unending heat on everyone—locals as well as foreigners—has been merciless, leading to a sluggishness that's hard to shake, a feeling not unlike sleep deprivation.

Riding at anchor in the bay are a half-dozen ships, their lights reflecting off the calm waters. They are awaiting the siren's song of the executioner to call them ashore, swinging gently at their watery berths as the offshore current tugs at them, digging the flukes of their anchors a little deeper into the muddy bottom. The skeleton crews aboard the vessels must be restless and fidgety as they lie in their bunks, waiting to finish this damnable business and get away. Until the tide comes later in the day, they will have little to do but pace the decks and make whatever final preparations are required to get their prisoners ready for the last voyage.

Everyone is waiting for the high tide that arrives in the afternoon. This is the first part of shipbreaking: getting the vessels ashore to the yards. The process is the same as in other breaking sites in places like Pakistan, Bangladesh and Turkey; it simply involves pointing a vessel toward the beach and driving her as fast as she can go onto land; the higher the tide, the farther ashore a ship can be beached. Then teams of workers can begin to cut the vessel apart with blowtorches. It's a labour-intensive endeavour, requiring only cheap manpower—and heaven knows, India has a lot of that.

Behind me, across a dusty road that serves as Alang's main street, lies a sprawling shantytown where many of the thirty thousand undertakers live. They have travelled to this place from throughout India in search of a better life, a cross-section of India's billion-plus population hailing from Uttar Pradesh in the north, Bihar in the east, Kerala in the south and Punjab in the northwest. Mostly Hindu, they are also Muslim, Sikh, Buddhist and Christian. They are teenagers, orphans, parents, widowers and the elderly. And almost everyone who works at Alang is male.

As I walk through the shantytown, it's easy to see that the huts the workers inhabit are cobbled together from bits and pieces scavenged off the ships: strips of wood, sheets of aluminum, old cabin doors and scraps of cloth curtains are the walls and roofs of the structures. Most are no bigger than a common garden shed, in which six or eight men will spend their evenings sleeping on hard platforms, the smell of sweat and the sound of snoring filling the rank air.

The men condemned to do the dirty work are still lying inside the tiny shacks. It is Monday, the start of the workweek here in Alang, and more than a few of the guys will soon be cursing the end of the brief weekend, that single day off that has passed so quickly. Sunday they slept in, bought vegetables in the market, made phone calls home, watched Bollywood films in the ramshackle cinema, played cricket in the clearing, visited the bootlegger, gambled and maybe went in search of prostitutes. But that was yesterday; today their destinies are in the hands of others.

By the time the sun finally appears low in the sky, the cooks have already awakened in the shantytown, stoking their fires and preparing breakfasts for everyone. They barely look up from the pots they are stirring as I wander past the open doorways and peer into the smoky, dark kitchens. Behind them, pigs wallow in the swill while stray dogs cast a wary eye at the omnipresent cattle that wander up and down the main street of Alang. There is still no wind up from the bay, so the smoke and smells linger over the huts where the workers are slowly rousing themselves.

Emerging from their plywood hovels, the men stretch and yawn and try to shake the sleep from their eyes before making their way to the cookhouses for food and tea. They stare at me, this foreigner in their midst, but also smile. They are the anonymous face of global shipping, men with darkened, muscular arms bearing the bruises and scars that all shipbreakers eventually acquire as marks of their trade. One of them speaks a few words of English and asks where I'm from. "Canada, nice?" he says, bobbing his head in the manner unique to Indians. When I ask where he works, the man quickly answers, "Alang. Alang shipbreaking. Big ship, Plot No. 5," while gesturing at a large vessel that sits beached in a yard across the street. She looms over us even from this distance, a half-demolished tanker with a dirty white superstructure and red-and-black hull, the hull cut open at the front to reveal a gaping maw that will swallow these workers up as surely as the whale swallowed Jonah.

The man heads off to join his fellow workers. They grab a plate of food, find a spot to sit, and eat using only their hands in the dusty courtyard that serves as a cafeteria. They still have lots of time before they need to be on the job, so some of the more devout take a moment after breakfast to perform *puja,* kneeling in front of one of the small Hindu shrines by their shacks, lighting incense and quietly praying to God to protect them. The smoke from the incense rises like their prayers, wafting over the shantytown until the gentle easterly breeze that has now appeared carries it inland, away from this industrial morgue.

SHIPBREAKING IS NOTHING NEW; as long as vessels have been built, those that didn't sink at sea were all eventually scrapped in one way or another. To some this is just a fact of life for a ship; to others it is the sad, igno-minious end to once-proud vessels. William Turner, the great English romantic artist, painted an evocative portrait of this subject in 1839. Entitled *The Fighting Temeraire, tugged to her Last Berth to be broken up,* it shows a veteran of Admiral Nelson's Battle of Trafalgar as she is towed upriver on her final voyage to a breaking yard. On viewing the completed work, William Makepeace Thackeray wrote, "The little demon of a steamer is belching out a volume ... of foul, lurid, red-hot, malignant smoke ... while behind it (a cold gray moon looking down on it), slow, sad, and majestic, follows the brave old ship, with death, as it were, written on her."

Shipbreaking used to be done mainly in Europe and North America, until labour costs drove the business to places like Japan and Korea (Ulsan's Hyundai yards were once busy with shipbreaking). But as the number of ships needing to be broken up increased, so too did the awareness of what many of those vessels harboured within their shells: toxic materials used in their construction thirty or forty years ago.

With an increase in various regulations, it eventually became unprofitable for First World shipbreakers to safely dispose of ships, and the industry moved, in the laissez-faire manner that seafaring so loves, to places more amenable. Realistically, with thousands and thousands of steel behemoths being declared obsolete or unsafe each year, there were only two options available: either let the ships rust away while tied up in some backwater or tear them apart and get rid of the things. The Indians decided to focus on the latter approach, becoming world leaders in the shipbreaking industry, along with China, Pakistan and Bangladesh. As well, they found that the high-grade marine steel used in the hulls of sea-going vessels could be turned into valuable material for the country's domestic construction industry. By some estimates, 15 percent of India's steel now comes from old ships.

The speed at which the shipbreaking industry has evolved here in the last two decades has meant that other nations are now eager to get in on the act. This was apparent when I met with members of the Gujarat Ship Breakers Association shortly after arriving. With the air conditioner turned far too cold by half, they solemnly filed into their boardroom to scrutinize me and explain their position. In particular, several of the ship-breakers—or ship recyclers, as they prefer to be called—were worried about their workers and what might happen should the industry decamp to China or Pakistan, or to newcomers like Vietnam and Turkey.

Alang, I'm told, has 173 different yards, of which over 100 are currently active scrapping vessels. In an average year, about 300 ships will arrive to be broken up, and Alang's yards have done away with over 4000 leviathans since the business started here in 1982. With 25,000 to 30,000 directly employed at the yards in Alang, and an equal number working in nearby "downstream enterprises" (such as rolling mills that use the steel from the ships), it is clear that scrapping merchant vessels is a multi-million-dollar endeavour the Indians want to protect.

Alang attracts so many workers because of the opportunity to make money, more than many could ever hope to imagine. They are part of the vast global migrations that have peopled gold rushes, oil fields, coal mines, steel mills and fishing fleets for generations. Invariably, these boomtowns sprout up around dirty, hazardous endeavours where the pay is higher because of the inherent dangers involved. Alang is no different.

The nut of the problem facing the business is that just about every vessel that arrives in Alang is a repository of hazardous waste in the form of asbestos, PCBs, lead, mercury, benzene, chromates and a variety of other man-made cocktails. When we were building these ships back in the 1960s and 1970s, environmental standards differed considerably from what they are today. These noxious elements have caused groups like Greenpeace and the International Labour Organization (ILO) to turn their attention to shipbreaking and the labourers employed in places like Alang. Their concern for the well-being of the workers centres on the effects of exposure to these hazards: A German researcher who studied the situation claims that one in four shipbreaking workers can expect to contract some form of cancer.

All this attention has made the businessmen who run Alang somewhat edgy about outsiders poking around their yards. They are not hiding— that would be a bit difficult when their enterprises take up ten kilometres of coastline populated by thousands of people—but they are a little tired of playing the villain.

One of the yard owners sitting in the boardroom addressed the situation by adopting the tone of a teacher to his pupils. Waving his finger at me, he lectured, "It is undeniable that there are some drawbacks, but the pollution created by mining, heavy industries or the manufacturing of steel, this is far greater than the pollution from ship recycling. If we did not do something about these ships, the pollution they would create in the sea would be a real disaster. Do you want that?"

He paused to allow me to make notes in my journal like a good student. When I'd finished, he calmly continued, "And, as for the workers, I will admit that things could be better. But in the last five years there have been very few accidents, almost zero. I can't say it's zero completely because there was an accident a few months ago, but it is all minor things." (The accident he referred to occurred three months earlier when the vessel *Amina* caught fire while beached in Alang. As reported in the local media, at least six workers died and more than a dozen others were injured in an explosion that might have been caused by a lit cigarette.)

The situation has improved somewhat, but there's still a long way to go before most shipbreaking yards approach First World industrial standards. The only solution, the businessmen say, is a massive infusion of capital into the entire process: money to strip hazardous waste from the vessels before they arrive in breaking yards, money to upgrade Alang's facilities and train its workers in proper techniques, and money to clean up the existing environmental mess that litters the shores here.

Will this happen? Well, not likely anytime soon, not when the West treats garbage disposal as callously as it currently does. The United States alone has hundreds of old ships quietly moored in waterways, which the government cannot figure out how to scrap. For instance, in the middle of the James River, north of Norfolk, Virginia, lies what is known as the "ghost fleet," over sixty aging ships that were decommissioned long ago but never disappeared. They are cargo vessels and military-support ships that once brought supplies to Second World War Europe, to Korea in the 1950s conflict and to Vietnam during the war there. Maintained by the U.S. Maritime Administration (known by its quasi-military acronym MARAD), the ships that make up this bizarre flotilla have deteriorated to the point where inspectors have stated that a hammer can penetrate some of the hulls. Yet within their combined hulls resides almost thirteen million gallons of oil and fuel; that's two million more gallons than the *Exxon Valdez* spewed into Prince William Sound. And just keeping the fleet afloat and upright requires seventy-five workers and more than U.S.$2 million a year.

The Indian shipbreakers would love to get their hands on the ghost fleet, but American federal law currently prohibits these ships from being sent to places like Alang. So as MARAD continues to think up an economical and safe solution to the ghost fleet, the businessmen in India will just have to make do with the thousands of other vessels waiting their turn in the breaking yards.

BACK IN THE SHANTYTOWNS, the undertakers are finishing up their breakfasts and preparing for the start of another workweek. Some can be seen brushing their teeth with twigs from a thorny bush, in lieu of a toothbrush, while others are already filing toward their respective work-sites as eight o'clock approaches. For the itinerant labourers, the tidal patterns unique to Alang are meaningless, except that they mark the coming of new carcasses; each full moon—like last night's—brings another harvest of steel to the Bay of Khambhat.

Slowly, imperceptibly, the still morning air of Alang begins to change. It is the ear that catches it first, the awakening of this boomtown: There is the gentle padding of rubber boots on the dusty tarmac as the first workers leave their hovels, the soft rustle of cyclists peddling along, the ringing of bells in the Hindu temples, the putt-putt of two-stroke engines in passing motor scooters. By 7:30 A.M. the small crowd of cyclists and pedestrians has evolved into a much larger group that soon numbers in the tens of thousands, everyone travelling along the asphalt thoroughfare in all directions.

An individual shipbreaker is easily lost among the scores of other workers making their way to work this Monday. Clutching battered hard hats, members of this army will stop at tea stalls to meet up with other labourers, all dressed in dirty cotton clothing with long scarves draped over their shoulders, chatting quietly in the way people do as they wait for the workday to begin while sipping sweet chai from small glasses.

They could be steel workers in Sault Ste. Marie, Ontario, or autoworkers in Detroit, Michigan, or coal miners in Donetsk, Ukraine, or shipbuilders in Ulsan, South Korea. They stream toward their gates like industrial workers have for hundreds of years. Some are eager, some are reluctant; some are happy, some appear to be drunk, others are definitely hungover; most are young, a few are very old. And, it is true, some will live and some will die. They are the basic commodities that supersede all else in the creation of wealth and the stimulation of economies, and few places are more aware of this value than modern-day India. Without manual labour, this subcontinent's great wealth of gold, diamonds, salt and spices, and even the intellectual resources that create websites, Bollywood films and nuclear missiles—none of these could be exploited without someone to do the dirty work.

Promptly at eight o'clock, sirens begin to wail up and down the site, signalling the start of the morning shift. Workers stream through the main gates of the various shipbreaking yards, handing their manager a piece of pink paper that is their timesheet and only piece of identification. A typical shipbreaking yard is fifty or one hundred metres wide, a couple of hundred metres long, and littered with bits and pieces of cut-up ships. The yard owner's office is found near the main gate, farthest from the shoreline, and the splendour of it or lack thereof reflects his prosperity. Some offices are merely shacks cobbled together from parts of vessels— perhaps an officer's wardroom reassembled on shore. Others are two-storey concrete structures with ornate verandas from which the senior managers can keep an eye on the workers.

As the sirens cease their warning cries, the labourers meander to appointed work areas in their plots. Some will begin to cut apart giant plates of steel from the hulls with blowtorches, rendering the plates into ever smaller sections that can eventually be loaded onto trucks by teams of men and delivered to the nearby rolling mills. Others will be detailed to supply the cutters with tanks of propane and oxygen to feed the blowtorches. Of the two hundred or so who work in an average yard, a quarter will enter a beached ship itself to cut through the bulkheads and hull and everything else that was so meticulously crafted in a shipbuilding yard twenty or thirty years ago. It is the work of these men inside the beast's entrails that feeds the rest of the breaking yard. Any slowdowns on their part can bring things to a halt in the plot, so the managers always seek a brisk pace.

WHILE THE DAY COMMENCES in the breaking yards, I fight my way past the lorries and other vehicles that choke the main street—the only street, actually—and head to the port authority's office. This three-storey structure is effectively Alang's city hall and I am to meet the de facto mayor, the most powerful man in this minor fiefdom. Whatever else might be said of Alang, one cannot accuse the authorities of squandering money on their own offices; the building is a crumbling edifice that smells strongly of urine as you enter it. There is no air conditioning, only ceiling fans that turn languidly in the morning heat. Outside a blue door on the second floor, I am asked to remove my shoes and wait until a bell rings from within, permitting entry to the sanctuary of Captain Y. P. Deulker.

Captain Deulker is a large man with a trim seaman's beard and a most quiet voice. His handshake is as limp as the air within his stark office, in which a neatly organized desk nestles beside a fax machine and a Hindu shrine. His designation of captain reflects his former career as a master mariner; his official title is port officer in charge of Alang, since this place is considered a maritime destination. The difference, of course, is that ships make a one-way voyage here; none ever leave Alang by sea, only by land. Beyond the administrative roles he performs, Captain Deulker oversees the most vital part of the shipbreaking process: He supervises the beachings that occur each high tide.

"The last few days have been quite busy," he says in a bored manner while signing papers an assistant keeps bringing him. "Because the water level is so good, well above eleven metres. There were thirteen beachings over the weekend and we still have another six vessels waiting for approval. You see, a vessel cannot be beached unless the banks have approved payment between the new owners—the breakers here—and the old ones. I have received approval to bring five of those ships in today, but if I do not get confirmation within twenty-four hours for the last one, it will have to wait another ten days for a high tide."

How a vessel ends up at Alang is couched in the secrecy of international banking and ship brokerages. In simple terms, when a ship owner decides to get rid of a vessel, he contacts one of a number of maritime brokers who work in places like London or Singapore. These middlemen then offer the ships to anyone interested, via websites and faxes. A shipbreaker puts in a bid—perhaps a million dollars for a large bulk carrier—and then waits to see if anyone tops the offer. It's not unlike buying a house, except this one is a rusting hulk laced with asbestos, PCBs, lead, mercury, benzene, chromates and a variety of other hazards.

Once more, the secretive nature of shipping has allowed those who wish to circumnavigate the rules to do so, and quite easily. A vessel can have its ownership transferred to an anonymous numbered company in any reclusive nation—perhaps Liberia or Mongolia—that will subsequently sell it to the breakers. Thus it is that respectable shipping firms can wash their hands of these deathtraps and announce, in all honesty, that they do not send their old vessels to Alang.

Captain Deulker's fax machine rings at the same moment an assistant enters the office. A whispered conversation and a glance at the incoming fax cause a smile to form across his face. "Another confirmation; that makes six ships to beach today, beginning after lunch." He consults a tide table for the area and says that the high water will reach 11.17 metres, more than enough to bring the hulls well up onto shore. "It takes about half an hour to do each ship, so I will beach four and a colleague will do the other two. A good day awaits us."

After being invited to watch one of the beachings, I'm hustled out of Deulker's office and past a dozen clerks preparing the paperwork and other details required to finalize the death certificates of the ships. They work without computers, entering information into old-fashioned ledger books and using sheets of carbon paper to make copies. It's all decidedly low-tech, but then so too is the actual shipbreaking.

Even while I stood inside Captain Deulker's office, the sounds of shipbreaking were noticeable, albeit muffled. But outside, the cacophony of Alang becomes overwhelming. The place resounds with a series of bangs, booms, crashes and thuds as giant pieces of steel are cleaved off the ships and then cut into ever smaller pieces. In essence, shipbreaking is about cutting large pieces of steel into medium-sized pieces, and then cutting the medium-sized sections into smaller ones. Of course this simplicity masks the skill needed to actually get at the steel plating. The shell of a ship is what is most valuable, for its steel is of the highest grade, but within this skeleton are the pipes, electrical wiring, engines, equipment, even the furniture, windows and toilets that must be removed.

As I look at the vista of Alang from street level, the superstructures of the ships form a steel curtain silhouetted against the sun, the portholes and windows staring back at me like unseeing eyes. Some of them have been cleaved open on their port and starboard sides, so that I can see clear into the bridge and other compartments. Others have had their bows cut open. They look like a youngster's model toys, half finished and waiting for the glue to set.

I'm joined by Pradip Acharya, an effervescent and organized Indian who is travelling with me as my translator and "fixer," arranging everything from interviews to meals and transportation. Meticulous to a T,

Acharya is my eyes and ears in shipbreaking, able to understand several of the languages and dialects spoken in Alang, including Hindi, Gujarati and Bengali. We're headed for a yard where a couple of vessels have recently arrived and work is underway scrapping them.

"The average worker here makes anywhere from 70 to 130 rupees a day, depending on the skill of their job," Acharya tells me. "In their home villages things are not so good. They might make about 30 rupees a day, maybe less. This is why they come to Alang." To put this in perspective, 30 rupees is the equivalent of just under 70 cents U.S., so an entry-level position at a breaking yard pays less than 18 cents an hour.

Passing through the gates of breaking yard Plot No. 7, I enter an utterly chaotic tableau. There are two small oil tankers beached in this yard, their size dwarfed by the ship in nearby Plot No. 5, where the men I'd seen eating breakfast would now be working. Here in Plot No. 7, groups of men are just beginning to clear out the crew's quarters on one of the smaller ships, tossing furniture over the side and lowering mattresses to the muddy ground. These items end up in one of a seemingly endless array of ships' chandlers that line the highway near Alang. For several kilometres along either side of the road, you can find beds, sofas, dining room sets, toilets, kitchen sinks, lighting fixtures, cutlery, books, flags, lifejackets, laundry equipment and lifeboats—all laid out in the open like some permanent flea market or estate sale.

Throughout the yard, men are hunched down and intently cutting away at pieces of steel. The standard tool of shipbreaking is a gas torch, which looks like a welder's tool and can burn through metal at an exceptional rate in the hands of an experienced worker called a "gas cutter." These torches use a mixture of propane gas and oxygen, which is cheap but highly explosive.

Down by the shoreline, sparks from a cutter's torch are spewing out the side of the second vessel. A labourer standing nearby tells us that they are about to remove an 80-tonne section of the hull. Small holes have been cut in the hull to provide ventilation and light, but it will still be cramped and hot inside the vessel. I'm told that some people say the mark of a good gas cutter is his ability to smell danger, to use his nose to detect the scent of explosive gases. But others say that no amount of skill can assure survival in the dark depths of a behemoth, that it's all about luck.

As the cutter working inside the hull completes a circuit to form a square, the flame from his torch dies off and there is a moment when I wonder what happens next, until I hear a screech and the steel gives way as the giant section of hull suddenly cleaves off and plummets to the ground. It can be an unnerving experience to watch 80 tonnes of steel fall and then to feel the ground shake beneath you, more so when it happens unexpectedly.

Walking down to where the two ships are lying, I feel the need to touch the vessels, to feel their aged hulls. Between the vessels, the offshore wind howls through the tunnel created in the narrow gap. Strands of seaweed lace one hull, billowing in the breeze, and the bottoms of both ships are encrusted with millions of barnacles, their edges razor-sharp. Some of the crustaceans are still alive, pulsing and undulating in their death throes. The hulls themselves are coarse, lifeless skeletons, cold to the touch.

On the shore near us, a tanker truck is being hooked up to a hose connecting it to one of the ships. The workers are about to start pumping out the remaining diesel oil in the bunkers that once powered the main engines, so it can be sold for use as fuel here in Gujarat. Some miscommunication between the truckers and the workers in the ship's engine room causes the fuel to begin flowing before the line has been secured. As a stream of black oil spews from the rubber hose onto the ground and down into the water lapping the shoreline, angry shouts and curses erupt from the truckers before the flow is shut off.

Behind the tanker truck, heaps of steel and mangled sections of bulkhead are scattered haphazardly about the plot. A crane swings wildly fewer than ten metres away, stopping near the piece of hull that has just fallen. It will soon move the hull farther up the shore so that cutters can do their work on it. Within this inferno I can make out the sound of someone singing, over by a group of cutters. Acharya explains, "That man is singing a Hindu song, like a Christian hymn. And over there, where that group is carrying a piece of steel, listen." I do, and hear a rhythmic chanting that would be familiar to anyone on a chain gang. "They do that so they can keep in step while carrying the load on their shoulders." As the men with the steel reach a stack of other plates, the chanting stops and then, at a command from their foreman, they deftly take a step to the side with military precision and drop the metal onto the heap.

Moments later a muffled "boom!" resonates from somewhere in the shipbreaking plot. Pradip Acharya hears it, too, and we turn to a cutter working close by to ask what has happened. The man barely pauses from his work, gesturing in an offhand way to my translator. "He says it is just a propane tank exploding. Nothing to worry about—it happens all the time." For a moment I wonder what the reaction would be if backyard barbecues exploded in suburban North America with the same regularity.

SEVERAL PLOTS AWAY, in No. 31, Asif Khan sighs as he stands in his empty yard. He's been waiting for a new vessel to arrive, but the paper-work is still not done so his yard sits idle. A few workers are doing some routine maintenance on a crane and others are heaping bits of junk into small piles. But the majority of his workers have been forced to find piecemeal jobs in other yards or have returned to their home villages for a few weeks. Since he's missed this full moon, he likely won't be able to reschedule a beaching for at least another ten days.

Asif Khan is the man most responsible for the existence of shipbreaking here in Alang. He sports a trim moustache beneath a prominent nose and speaks with a cultivated accent more English than Indian. Unlike most of the other businessmen here, he's a former mariner whose love of the seafarer's life was cut short by the demands of his family. Having forsaken a career that saw him rise to chief engineer, he returned to Bombay to join the family shipbreaking business in the early 1980s. At that time, most of the breaking work took place in what is India's largest city, but urban sprawl was creating problems.

"To do the breaking and everything requires a certain amount of industrial space," Khan tells me, "and Bombay is far too crowded, as you probably know. We knew about Alang because this area has some of the highest tides in the world, and that is important if you wish to put a merchant vessel onto a beach. So my brother and I came up here in 1982 and hacked our way through the thick bushes until we reached the beach at Alang, which was empty; we walked for five kilometres and encountered only one fisherman. And that day we walked out to the edge of the low tide mark and stuck a twelve-foot pole in the silt, then waited to see how high the water would rise. When it did, the stick disappeared under the water and we knew we had found a good place for shipbreaking."

Within a year of Khan's discovery, the first ship had been thrust up on the sandy shores of Alang and the industry was poised for growth. The tides he speaks about are quite phenomenal, rising above eleven metres when the moon is right. It is this hydrographic anomaly that has allowed Alang to become the number-one spot for vessels to end their seafaring lives. There's no need for a dry dock or wharf from which a ship can be disassembled; all you need to do here is run the vessel onto the shore and then begin cutting away with blowtorches. As you remove more and more of the ship, you attach cables to the hulk and winch it farther up onto the beach. This continues for as long as six months, depending on the size of the vessel, whereupon the process is repeated again and again. It's sort of like un-building the pyramids, a never-ending process that keeps the workers in Alang busy six days a week, year-round.

Khan also explains that there is a hierarchy here in Alang. At the bottom are general labourers, unskilled young men who do the grunt work of carrying steel plates or clearing away debris. Above them come the cutters, individuals who spend their days staring at a flame spouting from a torch while concentrating on cutting away at the steel. Next in line are the master cutters, the elite of the workforce. These are men with years of experience who do the major cutting of a vessel. Asif Khan tells me that he has nothing but the utmost respect for the master cutters, of which a yard may only have five or six. "The skill of those men is something to see. They are not trained in a school, yet they are like engineers. They can look at a ship, at its integral structure, and figure out how best to make the initial cuts. This is very important, because if they make a mistake, the entire hull could collapse."

Adding to the dangers of a structural collapse is the presence of gases that linger within the pipes lacing through a vessel. Naphtha and sulphur can build up in the pipelines, creating a potentially explosive situation without proper venting. It takes only one spark to ignite these highly combustible chemicals, so you could almost look on each vessel here as a potential Hindenburg, the German airship that exploded in 1937, killing thirty-six.

Asif Khan has a reputation here as a good employer, one who looks out for his workers and their well-being. Unfortunately, he can't provide for them without a ship on his beach, so his guys will have to place their trust in whoever else is employing them today. He sighs again before saying, "Maybe in a few weeks, then maybe we'll be busy again and I can have my men back."

To watch a master cutter in action is to see exactly what Asif Khan means about the skill level. In yet another shipbreaking plot, adjacent to the port authority, a large tanker lies about halfway through the scrapping process. Along with my translator, Pradip Acharya, I climb into her holds by scaling a rusting ladder coated with grease. The interior of this unnamed vessel is immense, rising over a hundred feet to the main deck above me. It feels like the inside of a great cathedral, with shafts of light streaming down from ventilation holes cut up high. There are rubber hoses leading from the beach up to a cross-bracing section about twenty feet up. They will provide the propane and oxygen for the cutters' torches.

Two men in hard hats climb into the hold, followed by a third worker, a young boy barely out of his teens. These are the master cutters and their assistant, and they are about to make the final cuts in the hull that will separate a section weighing in excess of 800 tonnes.

As I watch, the master cutters make their way up to the platform, climbing as nimbly as skyscraper steelworkers. They swaddle their heads with cotton scarves and take out small welder's glasses as they straddle the platform. One of them shouts to the assistant and he tosses a short section of rope to the man. It's a piece of braided ship's rope that is smouldering at one end; this is the match to light up the torch. The master cutter waves his hand across the unlit end of his torch, gauging the flow of gases against his palm until he's satisfied. Then he uses the rope to get a flame going and within seconds is focused on cutting through the hull.

The second master cutter takes up position on the other side of the hull and, following the same procedure as his colleague, works away on his section of steel. Sparks fly from the torches, cascading down in a dramatic light show. For the next hour, the master cutters will slowly and methodically burn through the hull until they have finished in this part of the ship.

Once they're done, the cutters lead me up to the main deck by climbing a set of ladders that sway. I try not to look down or think about falling and once I arrive on the main deck, notice that my legs are a little shaky. Up here the deck is littered with gas tanks, cutting torches, hoses and ropes, and about a dozen men are waiting for the master cutters to make their final incisions. Essentially, this 800-tonne section of hull is now held to the rest of the ship by two small sections of uncut steel.

Everyone but the two master cutters steps back to a safe vantage point and the men fire up their weapons once more. Two giant chains are attached to the front of the hull, linked to tractor engines down on the beach. Once the hull section is free, the tractors will pull the piece down, but they must wait for the cutters to finish, which only takes a few minutes.

There's a man with a walkie-talkie standing off to one side; after one of the master cutters nods at him, he speaks quickly into the radio and I can hear the tractor engines roar as their engines are revved up. At first nothing happens, but by staring at the cut line I can see the hull section beginning to move. Inch by inch the gap widens; when the gap is about a metre wide, the tractor engines shut down and everyone waits for gravity to take over.

I'm clutching a piece of handrail by the starboard side of the deck, staring at this piece of a ship that's about to become more scrap metal. For perhaps twenty seconds the hull pauses, as though saying goodbye to the ship, until it falls onto the shore, sending up a great plume of dust, dirt and grit as the deck beneath me shudders. There are smiles all around and the two master cutters walk to the very edge of the hull and peer down at what they've just wrought. They kneel to examine their cut marks more closely, running their fingers across the jagged metal with a sense of approval. Then a siren wails—it's lunchtime—so everyone takes one last look around before climbing back down through the holds and heading for shore.

By EARLY AFTERNOON, final preparations are underway for the beachings of the ships riding at anchor in the bay. Each yard that is to receive a corpse has been cleared of debris, and flags have been planted in the sand to help direct the vessels to their final destinations. In one yard, they are to receive a bulk carrier called *Sentosa*, 20,000 tonnes of raw material waiting to be "recycled." The yard owners have brought their families and friends to witness this event and they sit in a line on plastic lawn chairs, staring at the vessel. A few neatly dressed children scamper about while some workers watch from the sidelines, representatives of two very different castes of the new industrial age.

At a toot of a horn, the main gates are swung open and Captain Deulker arrives in his white Ambassador car festooned with a Gujarat Maritime Board pennant on the fender. Exiting the vehicle, Deulker appears in ceremonial dress whites, complete with a captain's hat, and swaggers over to shake hands with the important people. In one hand he carries a handheld radio, which he soon puts to use by calling the *Sentosa*.

"*Sentosa, Sentosa, Sentosa,* this is Alang port officer calling. Are you ready to proceed?"

"Alang, Alang, Alang, this is MV *Sentosa*," says the captain of the vessel with a heavy accent. "We are ready to go underway and wait for final course. Will there be a pilot coming aboard, over?"

Deulker chuckles as he keys his microphone. "No pilot, *Sentosa*, none needed." He then relays the course that the bulker is to make and watches as she weighs anchor and heads away from us, leaving a black plume of smoke from her funnel to be carried inland. While the ship does so, Captain Deulker accepts a cup of tea and fills me in on what's happening.

"I've ordered her to head out into the bay and then turn around toward us. This will give her more room to get up her speed. Then I just bring her into the plot." He will do this completely by experience, without any instruments. Deulker will eyeball the *Sentosa*'s bow, using the flags positioned on the shoreline and his own knowledge of the currents to thread the ship into the eye of the needle that is this ship-breaking yard. It is a skill few possess.

While we wait for the bulk carrier to get up steam, Captain Deulker reflects candidly on the beaching process. "When I started here a few years ago, one of my first beachings was a ship I knew well. It was the first vessel I had been a master on. I'd joined her in Vancouver, Canada. That ... was hard. Yes, it was. As she prepared to turn around—just like this ship is doing—I realized I couldn't do it. I could not bring a ship I had commanded ashore. I had to get someone else to do it." He lets slip a moment of emotion, but then catches himself. "It got easier after that. An executioner can't be getting emotional, can he?"

The *Sentosa* has made her turn and is now facing the shore. Deulker puts down his tea and becomes alert. "*Sentosa*, Alang. Captain, please make full maximum speed, repeat, full maximum speed."

"Alang, *Sentosa.* Full maximum speed, roger." And then a pause. "Alang ... it looks too small ... too small." The bulker's captain is worried about the size of the berth he's to make; he's also about to disregard a cardinal rule of seafaring: Don't go ashore.

Deulker tries to reassure the *Sentosa*'s master. "That's OK, Captain. Maintain present heading and speed. Everything will be fine."

I wander down to the shoreline to watch the approach of the ship, accompanied by a couple of workers who are here to see what tomorrow brings. The *Sentosa* creeps closer; though she's pushing her engines to the limit, she's still only making about fourteen knots, barely sixteen miles per hour. As her profile inches ever closer, I find myself alone at the edge of the water; the workers have retired to the sidelines.

By now the *Sentosa* is fewer than a thousand metres away and I can make out deckhands standing on her bow. There's a small shoal just off this shipbreaking plot, but Deulker orders the ship around it by using the water pressure beneath the hull to effect a sharp turn. He takes advantage of the Bernoulli effect, momentarily having the vessel hydroplane over the rocks. It is a masterful piece of seamanship and the *Sentosa*'s stern pivots at his command before correcting herself.

There is nothing but a few hundred metres of shallow water between the vessel and me. I can hear the sounds of water being pushed aside by her bow and the methodical cadence of her engines forcing her to her doom. The *Sentosa* now begins to loom over me and the urge to flee rises. I stand transfixed, however, unable to move as she bears down on land. She's now fewer than twenty metres away, going at full steam one last time. And then her hull finally makes contact—a soft whoosh as mud is displaced by steel, a wave breaking on the shoreline—and within ten seconds she comes to a complete halt, embedded in the sand eight metres away. *Sentosa*'s propeller continues spinning, trying to force her a few millimetres farther onto shore. Then her anchors are dropped, cascading down in a showcase flurry of sparks as metal scratches on metal until the flukes thud into the shallow water. After a couple more minutes, her engines are shut down, her propeller stops turning and the *Sentosa* is silent.

I glance at my watch:1357. The moment of her death. As of now, MV *Sentosa* is no longer legally considered a ship, her sea-going days over. She—it—is now just scrap metal.

As deckhands on the ship stare down at me from the forecastle and a few workers make their way closer to the hulk, I find myself without emotion for old *Sentosa.* Having observed her execution, I think I should feel something, but I don't. I never knew her when she was alive and vibrant, never sailed with her crew, never met her builders. Though I witnessed her final seafaring moments and can see her metres away, she is meaningless and anonymous.

With nothing more to observe, I walk back to see Captain Deulker shaking hands and sharing ice cream with the *Sentosa*'s new owners. There are smiles all around as the owners realize that they can begin cutting apart the vessel in a couple of days and recouping their invest- ment. With luck they'll make a profit from the ship, enough to pay for renovations to their palatial homes in Bhavnagar and Bombay. Off to one side, the workers who will flense this beached whale stare sullenly at the ship and the ice cream and the happy children, before heading back to their shantytown homes to rest up for tomorrow.

AN HOUR AFTER the *Sentosa*'s death, Pradip Acharya and I finish eating lunch in a small restaurant on the main street of Alang, a venue devoid of character but thankfully equipped with an air conditioner. Stepping outside, I am momentarily blinded by the intense sun as we stand staring at the expanse of Alang spread out before us. The restaurant's front door offers a slightly elevated perspective up and down the long line of shipbreaking plots that stretch over the horizon to the left and to the right. It is almost three o'clock in the afternoon and the plots on the other side of the road are scenes of activity as heavy cranes swing to and fro, and workers cut metal with torches and load trucks with steel plates. A slight haze hangs over most of the shipbreaking yards, pale blue smoke lingering from the cutters' torches until the offshore wind can disperse it.

But down to the left is a plume of smoke that is different. It's dark—black and menacing—not like the timid cigarette smoke surrounding it. And it is billowing energetically out of the superstructure of a large tanker—the tanker in Plot No. 5. Watching the angry cloud move skyward, I slowly understand that something ominous has occurred. My eyes follow the smoke down to the portholes beneath the bridge windows, trying to imagine what's caused it and where it's coming from.

Then I realize there is a slightly different tempo to the street in front of me, that something portentous has interrupted the normal sense of organized chaos. A Toyota minivan fights its way down the crowded thoroughfare from the direction of the burning ship, past where I'm standing and off to the right. As it passes in front, I can see that its back door is open to reveal someone lying prone inside. Moments later, a second and then a third van follow suit. Lying motionless inside the vans are human shapes covered in dirty white sheets, so you can't tell if they are dead or alive. But it doesn't matter, because that sinking feeling in your stomach makes you realize that both events—life and death—are occurring somewhere in Alang at this very moment.

Pradip Acharya heads off into the crowds to find out what's happened as I stare, stunned, at the smouldering tanker. On his return, Acharya takes me aside and speaks quietly to me, confirming my worst fears. Maybe it was the heat that did it. Maybe it was the darkness. Maybe it was the push to maintain a fast pace. Whatever it was, something has just gone terribly wrong in this place of death.

Apparently, at about 1430 an explosion occurred deep within the tanker in Plot No. 5. A cutter was working on the joint of a pipeline when a buildup of gases ignited from within it. In moments, a tongue of fire rocketed out of the joint and reached up about twenty feet, engulfing five workers. The ship's compartments resounded with a deep malevolence as the explosion echoed throughout the tanker. The screams of the ship-breakers followed soon after.

As the men inside the tanker scrambled to escape the lower decks, they struggled up unlit gangways through a cloud of dense smoke. The fire had burned their clothing and singed their skin; the explosion had knocked them against the steel bulkheads, fracturing their limbs. Collapsing on deck, they had no time to think about the others. Even so, it would not have mattered.

In less time than it takes to read this paragraph, six men died and five were severely injured. They were some of the men I had seen eating breakfast, brushing their teeth, laughing and praying. It would take a few days, but we eventually managed to discover some of the names of these formerly anonymous workers. Raju Yadav, Promod Bauri, Rannjit Khuswag, Anil Singh and Rangilal. These were the lucky ones, injured rather than killed by the explosion.

Raju Yadav had been in one of those minivans passing in front of me. His friend Bhubanessar had not. Emergency crews later extracted his body and the bodies of others who died, their remains charred by the intense heat and fire. The force of the explosion was such that two hatches on the tanker's main deck, each weighing about 130 tonnes, were torn from their hinges. A forensics team later concluded that the intensity was similar to the force of several hundred kilograms of exploding TNT.

The ship was called the *Inville,* a dry bulk/tanker that once weighed more than 130,000 tonnes and had arrived in Alang a few months earlier. I'd heard of bad ships, man-killers as some called them, but this was the first time I'd ever encountered one up close. *Inville*'s final voyage from Brazil to Alang had been fraught with problems, as though the ship knew where she was going to end up. Rounding the Cape of Good Hope and into the Indian Ocean, she almost beached herself south of Durban, pleading not to be scrapped. But after repairs were done in South Africa, the vessel plodded her way northward to the Bay of Khambhat, was grounded and then butchered, until she decided to extract a deadly tribute from the undertakers.

THOUGH WORK DOES NOT STOP completely at Alang, Plot No. 5 is closed while investigators scour the ship. Over the next few days it becomes clear that a foreigner's presence in the breaking yards is not welcome. A dark cloud has descended on Alang, as it always does after an accident. Though the owners prefer to gloss over such incidents, they happen far too frequently, not always ending in death but certainly in a lot of injuries. Steel falls, a worker falls, a tank explodes, a torch burns. If the ships that come here do have a soul, that soul cries out in silent pain as the workers desecrate it.

A few days after the *Inville* disaster, Pradip Acharya leads me to an oasis of green a kilometre outside the breaking site. Beneath a canopy of trees bearing fragrant champa flowers, peacock eggs lie on the ground while the parents screech from above and parrots and butterflies flit around. Near us, on one side, is an orchard of mango and papaya trees, while a farmer's field is next door. An old man tugs at a water buffalo in the field, trying to coax the animal to begin tilling.

It all seems so peaceful, save for the not-far-distant clank of falling metal and the drone of diesel engines. We're here to meet with a cutter who knows more about the *Inville* accident, a man who prefers to be known just as Patel. Patel has a trim moustache and sad eyes, and speaks in a voice so quiet that you must strain to hear it. He's snuck away from Alang on his lunch break, so we share a communal *thali,* or vegetarian meal, of rice, naan, paneer, daal and samosas. Patel grew up not far from here and remembers what Alang was like before the ship-breakers arrived.

"As a child, I thought this place was paradise," he says in his gentle manner while sitting cross-legged on the ground. "Families would come here, to picnic and swim and relax. It was our own private place. But I guess you cannot feed yourself with memories."

According to Patel, the fire on the *Inville* was much more serious than anyone is letting on. A friend of Patel's was among those killed in Plot No. 5, but when some workers went to see the body, all they found was a blackened shape. Someone recognized a piece of belt on the body, so Patel knows his friend died. He explains, "The only identification we carry when we go to work is our time card. So if someone dies, maybe if they are burned badly, who is to say that the foreman doesn't just rip up his card? No card, no worker. He never existed."

I ask Patel if the deaths on the *Inville* were inevitable. He pauses to think about this, staring away from me and toward the champa flowers. He rubs his eyes and stares at the grit on his hands. He picks up his hard hat, running his fingers over a crack in the plastic. He says nothing. Standing up, Patel gets ready to return to work, my question still unanswered.

Finally, he looks me in the eye and says in a weak voice, "No. The owners, the managers—they didn't want those guys to die. It just happened. As it always does. It is just the way ..." His words trail off and Patel stands there amid the lush greenery for a moment, shoulders sagging and fatigue etched across his face. Then he carefully puts on his hard hat and walks off, the mango and papaya trees swallowing him up as he returns to the shipbreaking yards.

EPILOGUE: Artisans

Full fathom five thy father lies;
Of his bones are coral made:
Those are pearls that were his eyes:
Nothing of him that doth fade,
But doth suffer a sea-change
Into something rich and strange.

—WILLIAM SHAKESPEARE, *THE TEMPEST*

The deaths of the shipbreakers in Alang did not, in fact, go completely unnoticed. The workers in several adjacent yards went out on strike for several days to pressure the owners about safety issues. Government investigators and police officers began combing the tanker *Inville* and questioning witnesses about the tragedy. And mainstream media in the country picked up the story for a few days and reported on the horrendous labour conditions at the yards.

In the end, though, life soon returned to normal in most of Alang. The disaster that officially killed at least six men was just another industrial accident, an unfortunate one, yes, but part of the cost of scrapping the world's merchant fleets. Like the ships they disembowel, the men who die in the breaking yards will be mourned by those who knew them, remembered by a few more and forgotten by most. To find the last vestiges of a vessel and all whose lives revolved around her requires looking beyond the breaking yards, to remote places like Sihor.

Sihor is a small village two hours west of Alang, and I've come here intending to visit one of the mills that utilize the steel from sea-going ships. These rolling mills, as they're known, use the pieces of hull and bulkheads as raw material to be made into things like rebars and I-beams for the construction industry. But there seems to be a problem of some sort at the mill in Sihor. The gates to the factory are locked and a suspicious security guard refuses to let us in, no matter what my Indian translator, Pradip Acharya, says. After a heated discussion with the guard, Pradip turns away from the man with a look of disgust on his face. "He says the mill is closed today and the owner has changed his mind about letting you see it. I do not know what is going on exactly, but the man," Pradip gestures at the guard who continues eyeing us from behind the metal gates, "he said there is a temporary slowdown of steel coming from Alang. So all the workers here were sent home yesterday."

It appears that no trucks have arrived from the shipbreaking yards laden with the metal plates needed. Perhaps the shipbreaking plot allied with this mill received one of the vessels that recently beached, one that has not yet been cut apart. Or perhaps the accident in Alang that killed the workers in Plot No. 5 has had some downstream effect on production. Who knows? The cagey security guard is certainly not going to tell us, so we go in search of other sights.

Once a capital in the Gohil Rajput dynasty, Sihor has long since faded from importance. A seventeenth-century palace, dilapidated and taken over for government offices, looks down on the village from a hilltop with a string of small streets emanating from the citadel. To walk up one of these narrow lanes is to travel back to a simpler time, before electricity, computers and electronics became so important to everyone. Yet it is these very things that the villagers of Sihor have embraced, but not in the way you'd normally think.

From the open doors and windows of various whitewashed shops lining the street comes the unmistakable sound of metal being hammered. In one shop, a man uses a mallet to methodically bang away at a large brass water jug; in another, a boy stacks shiny metal serving plates; a third shop reveals another craftsman working a brass urn into shape. We glimpse shy smiles beaming from within the darkened interiors, though none of the artisans stops his meticulous work.

From the doorway of another shop, four preteen boys in flip-flops and loose cotton pants watch my approach. They peek around the corner to gawk, hiding when I wave at them, but as I get closer the boys giggle and smile, beckoning me to come inside. Through a door protected by an image of a Hindu goddess, the youngsters lead the way to a small display case filled with gleaming brass pots, pans, bowls and cutlery. The owner appears, shoos the boys away and proceeds to lay the merchandise out in case a sale is pending.

To show the quality of his work, the merchant gestures toward the rear of the shop and, with the boys following like a pack of puppy dogs, I find myself in a tiny foundry where the utensils are created. It's not much bigger than a two-car garage, with a dirt floor, stone walls and a corrugated tin roof sheltering ten villagers hard at work. The focus of all this activity, also the source of Sihor's brass dishes, lies on the ground by the door: coils of electrical wiring from the ships in Alang.

The craftspeople here have become noted for their ability to recycle the wiring from vessels and turn it into household goods. An older woman in a dirty pink sari sits by a coil, stripping the plastic covering off with her weathered hands. She's getting at the copper that once carried electrical currents and can now be mixed with tin to make brass ingots. Her elaborate earrings and gleaming nose stone glitter inside the workshop. She tugs at her sari while taking sidelong glances at the foreigner in her midst. In the hot and dusty foundry she cuts and strips, cuts and strips, with all the experience of someone who does this far too often.

There's a small furnace at the rear of the foundry, tended by a rotund, balding man in a sweat-stained tank top who stokes the fire with hardwood that takes up an entire wall. Seemingly inured to the smelter's heat, he pokes and prods at it with a long pole, periodically stopping to take a sip of water from a jug on the floor as another bunch of wiring is placed within the oven to be melted down.

The smelted brass ingots come out the other end looking like pancakes. Once cooled, they can be pounded and shaped into all manner of saleable items. A young man picks up one of the ingots and places it on a metal lathe. As it turns, it begins slowly to take the form of a small bowl, shavings of brass spiralling off into a heap below. Another sari-clad woman gathers up the shavings so that nothing is wasted here. Within minutes, the bowl is finished and plopped onto a stack of others, and the process is repeated.

The beauty of the products made in the village is undeniable. Like the workers in the propeller shop in Ulsan, Korea, the residents of Sihor are more like artisans than mere labourers. Perhaps this is because their craftwork is so tactile and refined, and because it continues thousands of years of tradition. Regardless, there is joy in knowing that a part of a vessel will become not merely construction material or engine parts, but will grace someone's dinner table and be held in the hands of another human being. Maybe then, if you believe in karma, some of the spirit of a ship and those who knew her *can* be transferred, allowing the strength of her soul to live on in another.

As I WALK AWAY from the foundry in Sihor—a small, brass bowl tucked under my arm—my journey is finally complete. For two years I've been travelling the globe on this quest to learn more about commercial shipping and those involved with it, a seemingly simple proposition when I began. But the simple things in life are, of course, often the most difficult.

The journey has required crossing three oceans, nine seas and most of the planet's time zones; visiting twenty-five seaports and at least as many airports; and living on the road—or sea—for almost six months. I've met with hundreds of individuals involved with ships and observed countless thousands more. But even so, I've still managed only a glimpse into this ancient endeavour. The mysteries of seafaring come from its complexity;

it is the most disparate and far-reaching business yet devised by humans. It couples technology with ingenuity, bringing together two of our greatest assets as a society: the ability to create industrial titans such as ships, and the skill to sail them, which comes from mariners. There is no nation on Earth, no matter how landlocked, that is not touched by seafaring.

In the course of these travels, something that I've never really addressed has always lingered at the back of my mind. In fact, it only ever came up once with all the people I met around the world.

It was on the container ship MV *Canmar Spirit* near the end of her voyage from Europe to Canada. It was a beautiful morning and she was back in the embrace of dry land, with the coast of Quebec off our starboard side at the entrance to the St. Lawrence River. I was standing on the bridge chatting with Captain Grewal and Third Officer Prince Kashyap, when the captain's wife, Bhupinder, arrived. After a few moments of watching me, she walked over and fixed me with a quizzical look before asking a simple question: "So, Daniel, do you want to be a sailor now?"

It was a good question and I was stumped for an answer at the time. I can't even remember if I came up with a lucid response, but it certainly set me to thinking that day and well into that night. I thought about the crappy weather, the confined space on a ship, the separation from family and friends; I thought about the endless drudgery of work to be done, the social strictures and the physical toll ships take on individuals. I thought about all this and much, much more while staring at the night sky off the ship's starboard beam.

At a purely practical level, I am in my early forties, so it would be hard to envision changing careers this late in my life. But I suppose it is true that somewhere in my past I fostered a young man's dream of running away to sea, one that has been replaced by other dreams and desires and responsibilities. To a degree, this quest of mine into the world of commercial shipping has been a means of going back in time and looking at my own past.

I recall a mariner telling me about a visit to a certain northern port in which a local charity came aboard to distribute hats and gloves to the crew as protection against the winter elements. The sailor understood the gesture but was also somewhat offended by it, for it struck at his sense of independence and self-esteem. Those who make their lives from ships and the sea do not want our pity; they want our respect. They want us to realize the hardships they endure daily, the dangers that lurk around them and the loneliness that pervades their world. They want us to understand the pride that lies within each of them, from the lowliest deckhand to the mightiest master, from the poorest shipbreaker to the wealthiest ship owner.

So, if I could do it all over again, would I want to be a sailor? Absolutely. Because there is an honour in the profession of mariners, and I would feel privileged to be able to join the fraternity of those who go down to the seas in ships.

And what do I think about all this "soul" business? Well, I want to believe a ship has a soul, absolutely. Ships are just far too complex human creations not to have something in them. But having said that, I myself have never felt anything inherently spiritual about any vessel. What I have felt is the coming together of individuals and steel; I have felt a sense of soul from the crews, the builders, the shipbreakers and others. Without them, a ship is merely steel, wood and plastic—a shell.

There is, however, something else I've discovered on my journeys, and that is what I believe to be the source of this sense of soul. I think that those researchers looking at the qualities of memory in water are definitely on to something, for it seems to me that the sea embodies the memories of all of us, of life, of death, of history and of time. The sea caresses everything; the flow of being is remembered within its very molecules and atoms. I doubt science will ever be able to prove this and, in some ways, hope it never does. We don't need answers to everything; the intangible and the mysterious are an important part of existence, necessary requirements to prevent cynicism. And the sea remains the most mysterious part of our planet.

ACKNOWLEDGMENTS

To produce a work about an enterprise like commercial shipping has taken the assistance, confidence and support of hundreds of individuals spread throughout the globe, on land and at sea. This is the first time I've written a book, and to all those who helped me throughout the process I give my heartfelt thanks; to those I may have forgotten here, I give my deepest apologies.

The genesis of this work was a talented master mariner who befriended me in India, Captain Jose Thomas, who first suggested I consider looking at the life of a ship from birth to death and whom I thank—wherever he may be sailing. My time in India was also made all the more pleasant by my fixer and translator, Pradip Acharya, a hard-working and patient colleague.

Bob Abraham needs to be singled out for getting me on my first sea voyage, on the *Antwerpen,* and also for opening doors to South Korea and generally explaining the business of shipping to me. I thank Nancy Lucas and Steve O'Malley for hooking me up with Bob. The crews of the *Antwerpen, Canmar Spirit* and *Emerald Star* put up with my nosing around in their lives with wonderful aplomb. Stanley Pinto, the steward on the *Canmar Spirit,* was a godsend on that tumultuous crossing of the North Atlantic. I should also like to mention that the crew of *Canmar Spirit* was involved in a high-seas rescue a week after I disembarked in Canada, coming to the aid of a yacht taking on water in the northeast Atlantic. Well done.

While researching this book, I found a warm embrace from many Canadian Maritimers, including Heather Getson and Captain Matthew Mitchell at the Lunenburg Museum of the Atlantic Fisheries and Eric

Ruff at the Yarmouth County Museum, along with the staff of the Joint Rescue Coordination Centre and Captain Rick Gates of the Atlantic Pilotage Authority, both in Halifax. On my iPod, the music of the late Stan Rogers was a staple of my travels, reminding me of the majesty of the sea time and again.

In Ontario, I wish to thank all the individuals who provided me with background material on the shipbuilding process in Collingwood, and Sandy Mowat of CBC Radio who opened that door. William Andrews of New Wave Travel found the ways to get me where I needed to be, with humour and efficiency, as did Fred Cherney at The Cruise People. Lt. (N) Hamish Thom from HMCS *Regina* (out in British Columbia) gave insight into dealing with merchant ships in the Persian Gulf. And Dorothy Piner again proved her worth as an old family friend.

A considerable amount of background information and historical material for the book came from British sources, as befits a nation with such an illustrious maritime character. My many visits to the National Maritime Museum in Greenwich, possibly the greatest such museum around, were made all the more enjoyable by its staff and collections. NUMAST, the National Union of Marine, Aviation and Shipping Transport Officers, was an indispensable resource regarding piracy on the high seas. The ITF (International Transport Workers' Federation) provided information on flags of convenience and the welfare of seafarers.

Elsewhere in London I was the recipient of much care and advice from the officers and staff of The Honourable Company of Master Mariners aboard HQS *Wellington,* moored by the Victoria Embankment. Many thanks to Commander Ian Gregory, Priya Sohanpaul, Captain John Gray and Captain Simon Culshaw for guidance and camaraderie in the *Wellington*'s mess. At the Anglican Church's Mission to Seafarers, Peter Pickles helped in arranging my meeting with Canon Ken Peters. Michael Dowling and Sue Pringle gave me refuge and a place to crash while Dave Parry of the Royal National Lifeboat Institute shared tales of the sea over pints in Whitstable.

For those seeking more information on the state of shipping today, check out the Lloyd's Register, Clarkson Reports, BIMCO (the largest private shipping organization), the ILO (International Labour Organization), IMO (International Maritime Organization) and ICC (International Chamber of Commerce), all easily accessible on the web. So too is the European Space Agency's information about rogue waves.

Girish Lele facilitated my visits to watch the *Emerald Star* undergo sea trials in Korea and meet with International Andromeda's staff in Ulsan and in Monaco. From him, along with his gracious wife, Wibha, I learned much about commercial shipping and its impact on personal lives. While poking around the rarely visited Musée Naval de Monaco, I was treated warmly by an unknown older woman who worked there and embodied a grace and elegance that was admirable: Merci, madame.

A number of other authors provided support, both knowingly and unwittingly. John McPhee's *Looking for a Ship* is another good work, looking at merchant shipping back in the late 1980s, while Noel Mostert's *Supership,* written thirty years ago and sometimes hard to find, chronicles the rise of shipping in the last great boom period. David Bezmozgis provided me with confidence through his own work. And if there is one mariner whom I would have wished to sail with it is the late Alan Villiers, whose *National Geographic* articles I read and reread as a child at my family homestead in the bush of northern Ontario.

While the internet is a great tool for research, I still find the good old library an asset, and the Toronto Public Library system is one of the best around. To the librarians and staff at the Metro Reference Library, as well as numerous local branches, I say thank you.

For years I have received the support, care and love of a wonderful group of individuals without whom I could not have written this book. A deep and heartfelt thanks goes out to Alice Hopton, Sandra Lucas, Susan Meisner, Deborah Palloway, Shelley Saywell, Johanna Straub, Terry Macartney-Filgate, Lorna Novosel, Ken Furrow, Kwoi Gin, Lyn Ogilvy and Dave Steep.

My family has put up with my meandering lifestyle for far too long with good-natured humour, led by the most wonderful matriarch one could imagine, my mother, Arla Jean Sillers. And my son, Gavin, continues to be a source of inspiration and unfettered love.

Susan Folkins, my wonderful editor, guided me through this entire process with the greatest care and coaching, and I thank her warmly.

To Don Sedgwick, my agent at Transatlantic Literary Agency, I reserve special thanks for allowing me the opportunity to write this book. Along with Shaun Bradley, I found the best support system a budding author could imagine.

Finally, to all those who thought I couldn't do this, I hope the book proves you wrong. And to all those involved in commercial seafaring today, I give my thanks, respect and prayers that you are safe and sound as you go about your daily lives. This book is for you, for we are all bound to the sea.

BIBLIOGRAPHY

Baird, Donal. *Women at Sea in the Age of Sail*. Halifax: Nimbus Publishing, 2001.

Ballard, Dr. Robert D. *The Discovery of the Titanic*. Toronto: Madison Publishing Inc., 1987.

Byatt, Andrew, Alastair Fothergill and Martha Holmes. *The Blue Planet: A Natural History of the Oceans*. London: BBC Worldwide, 2001.

Carson, Rachel. *The Sea Around Us*. New York: Oxford University Press, 1951.

Chopin, Kate. *The Awakening*. Boston: Bedford Books of St. Martin's Press, 1993: 32.

Cockroft, David. "More than a loss of prestige." *Seafarers' Bulletin* (March 2003): 3.

Coggins, Jr., Andrew O. "Chapter III Literature Review," *Literature Review* (2005), <http://scholar.lib.vt.edu> (Accessed July 19, 2005).

Coleridge, Samuel Taylor. "The Rime of the Ancient Mariner," *The Complete Poetical Works of Samuel Taylor Coleridge*. London: Oxford University Press, 1968: 190.

Conrad, Joseph. *Heart of Darkness & Other Stories*. Ware: Wordsworth Editions, 1995: 28.

Conrad, Joseph. *Lord Jim*. Ware: Wordsworth Editions, 1993.

Conrad, Joseph. "The Mirror of the Sea," *Online Literature.com* (2005), <www.online-literature.com/conrad> (Accessed June 10, 2005).

Conrad, Joseph. *Three Sea Stories (Typhoon; Falk; The Shadow-Line)*. Ware: Wordsworth Editions, 1998.

Darwin, Charles. *The Voyage of the Beagle*. London: Penguin Books, 1989: 151.

Hesse, Hermann. *Siddhartha*. New York: Bantam Books, 1951: 142.

Hugo, Victor. *Les Misérables*. London: Penguin Books, 1980: 646.

Ingersoll, Robert. "Gold Speech," *The Complete Works of Ingersoll* (2005), <www.infidels.org> (Accessed July 19, 2005).

Ireland, Bernard. *History of Ships.* London: Hamlyn, 1999.

Langeweische, William. *The Outlaw Sea: A World of Freedom, Chaos and Crime.* New York: North Point Press, 2004.

Longfellow, Henry Wadsworth. "The Building of the Ship," *The Poetical Works of Longfellow.* Boston: Houghton Mifflin, 1975: 99.

Lundy, Derek. *The Way of a Ship: A Square Rigger in the Last Days of Sail.* Toronto: Knopf Canada, 2002.

McPhee, John. *Looking for a Ship.* New York: Farrar Straus & Giroux, 1990.

Melville, Hermann. *Moby-Dick.* Ware: Wordsworth Editions, 1993.

Montaige, Michel de. "Essays 1588," *French Quotes* (2005), <http://quotes.liberty-tree.ca> (Accessed July 19, 2005).

Mostert, Noel. *Supership.* NewYork: Warner Books, 1975.

Philbrick, Nathaniel. *In the Heart of the Sea: The Tragedy of the Whaleship Essex.* New York: Penguin Books, 2000.

Raban, Jonathan. "At Sea." *The Best of Outside.* New York: Vintage Books, 1997.

Raban, Jonathan. *The Oxford Book of the Sea.* New York: Oxford University Press, 1992.

Shakespeare, William. *The Complete Works of William Shakespeare.* New York: Avenel Books, 1975: 6.

Slocum, Joshua. *Sailing Alone Around the World.* Boston: IndyPublish.Com, n.d.: 1–5, 50.

Stevenson, Robert Louis. *In the South Seas.* London: The Hogarth Press, 1987.

Villiers, Alan. *The Last of the Wind Ships.* London: The Harvill Press, 2000: 102.

Virgil. "The Aeneid," *Masterworks of World Literature.* New York: Holt, Reinhart and Winston, 1955: 458.